The Shape of Evidence

Jacques-André Boiffard, *Gros orteil, sujet masculin, 30 ans* (*Big Toe, male subject, 30 years old*), published in the context of Georges Bataille, 'Le Gros orteil' ('The Big Toe'), *Documents*, no. 6, November 1929.

Zoe Leonard, *Untitled*, 1989, gelatin silver print, unique print, 25.4 × 20.3 cm.

Christopher Williams, *Untitled (Study in Yellow/Berlin) Dirk Schaper Studio, Berlin, June 21, 2007 (No.1)*, 2008, C-print, 50.8 × 40.6 cm.

Sophie Berrebi

vis-à-vis

Valiz

The Shape of Evidence

Contemporary Art and the Document

To Hubert Damisch, in friendship

Contents

7 Prologue Rummaging
17 Introduction Art Work, Document, Monument
47 One Anonymous Documents
95 Two (Dis)ordering the World
131 Three Industrial Images
179 Four Decolonising the Archive
213 Epilogue

221 Bibliography
237 Index
251 Acknowledgements
253 About the Author

‘On ne renonce jamais, c’est l’inconscient même, à s’approprier un pouvoir sur le document, sur sa détention, sa rétention ou son interprétation. Mais à qui revient en dernière instance l’autorité sur l’institution de l’archive ?’
— Jacques Derrida, *Mal d’archive,* prière d’insérer, 1995

Prologue

Rummaging

My parents are baby-boomers. Born in the mid-1940s, one on each side of the Mediterranean, they grew up in the post-war years and entered working life in the late 1960s. They have lived through the entire era of the Cold War, decolonisation, mass consumption, the unprecedented economic growth of the Western economies and the construction of the European Union. They were there in the 1980s, when the unending crises of deindustrialisation had their start and neo-liberalism took over. Of this past, longer ago than yesterday yet not fully historicised, I feel I know little. It's a period of time on the threshold between the historical and the contemporary; somewhat too abstract when taught in high-school history classes and too immediate when it was on the news.

A few objects and documents tenuously symbolise that past, and along with it, my parents and their

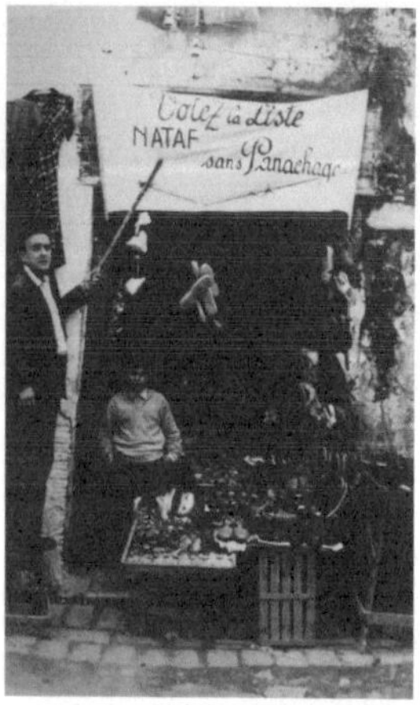

1 My father and grandfather, Tunis, undated photograph, photographer unknown.

2 Jean-Pierre Alllali, Annie Goldmann, Paul Sebag, Claude Sitbon, Jacques Taieb, Claude Tapia and Lucette Valensi (eds.), *Les Juifs de Tunisie: Textes et Images*. Paris, Éditions du Scribe, 1989, p. 85.

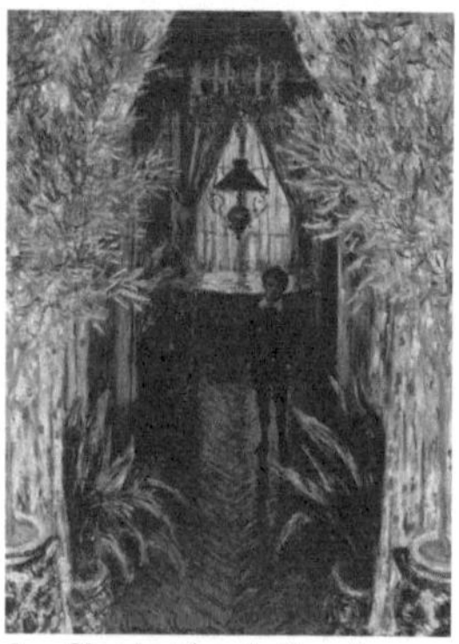

3 Claude Monet, *Un coin d'appartement*, 1875, oil on canvas, 81.5 × 60.5 cm, Paris, Musée d'Orsay.

parents. One of these is a photograph that shows my father around the age of ten standing in his father's market stall in Tunis.[1] Around him shoes are displayed, or rather piled up on boxes and crates, and dangle in clusters from the ceiling. In the foreground of the picture, his father points with a stick at an electoral banner painted on a cloth hanging above his stall. The election concerned was for representatives of the Jewish community in Tunis, sometime in the early 1950s. This is the only photograph I know of my father as a boy before he migrated to Paris in 1955. The picture is not a family snapshot; it was shown to me in a book on the Jews of Tunisia, where it illustrates a chapter on the politics of the Jewish community in colonial Tunisia.[2] Coming across it one day was a surprise for my family. A buried memory unexpectedly resurfaced, as history. My grandfather points at the banner whilst looking at the photographer; my father, receding in the shadow of the market stall, hands in his pockets, looks straight on with an inscrutable expression that reminds me of the little boy peering out of the plush Haussmannian interior of Claude Monet's *Un coin d'appartement* (*A Corner of the Apartment*), a picture that I associate with my own childhood in Paris.[3] Who took this photograph and why? Unknowingly to those depicted, it has been archived, rediscovered, and selected for reasons that had little to do with its protagonists. To the editors of the book in which it was reproduced, the image was nothing more than a historical document illustrating an electoral system and its grass-roots support. For me, however, this is a misreading of what is essentially a family picture.

From the maternal, French side of my family, I carefully preserve in a folder several handwritten notes addressed to my grandmother by Roland Barthes.[4] My grandmother had returned to her studies in the 1960s, after bringing up two children, and completed a PhD on the representation of academics on the screen, under the guidance of Roland Barthes.[5] Those short letters, in which Barthes agrees or differs with something she wrote, or summons her to supervision meetings, written on hotel stationary or slips of paper from the École Pratique des Hautes Études, keep falling out from between the pages of her annotated, original editions of his books that were also passed on to me.[6] I keep the books and the messages, although I find it somewhat hard to read Barthes while following in those family footsteps. Those little notes, which make me feel as though I were re-experiencing the devotion my grandmother had for her professor, bring Barthes uncomfortably close. They extend beyond their immediate subject, also reminding me of the Citroën DS that my grandparents owned and of the copies of *Paris Match* that lay about in their house, things

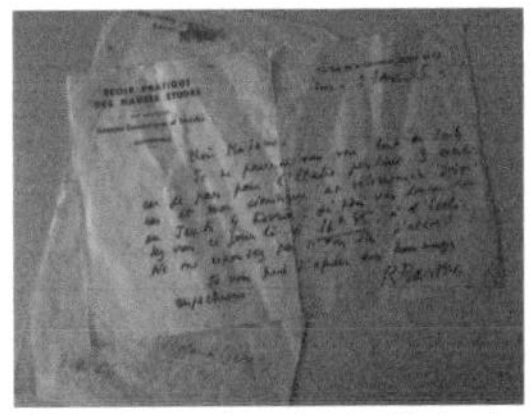

4 Autograph notes by Roland Barthes to Yveline Baticle, personal collection, the author.

5 My grandmother's dissertation was published as Yveline Baticle, *Le Professeur à l'écran*, Paris, Cerf, 1971.

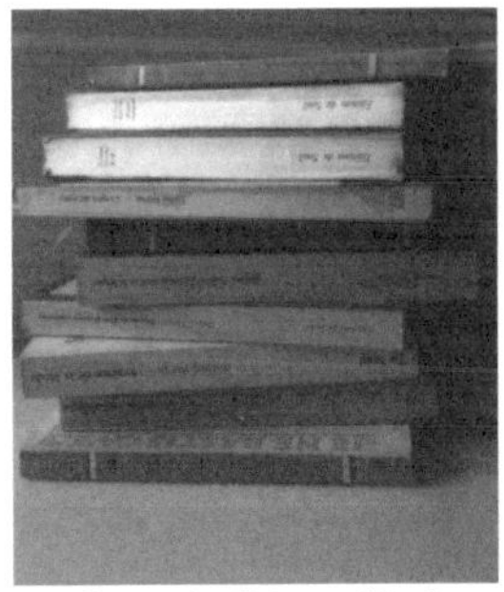

6 Original editions of books by Roland Barthes, personal collection, the author.

that Barthes subjected to analysis. What for him were 'mythologies' was for my grandparents everyday life.[7]

While Barthes feels too close, the photograph of my father in the market stall in Tunis, on the other hand, is too distant for me to integrate into a family narrative of migration and social emancipation. It belongs to a time and place I am irremediably removed from. Is the little boy in the photograph really my father? I do not even know his exact age. To appreciate the photograph and the handwritten messages, I need to go beyond their status as historical and personal documents. I must strip them of their context and dismantle the formal conventions that presided over their making. I have to find a way around Barthes' old-fashioned politeness, so different from the modern directness of his published prose; I must shut my eyes to the impersonal caption of the photograph, which says nothing of the people that appear in it. But is that even possible?

The Barthes of *La Chambre claire* (*Camera Lucida*) certainly thought it was. He believed in the photograph's univocal character that could not be challenged however long it were looked at:

> 'If the Photograph cannot be penetrated, it is because of its evidential power. In the image, as Sartre says, the object yields itself wholly, and

7 In his powerful film *Vita Nova* (2009), Vincent Meessen reflects upon the intertwining of life and work taking as subject matter Roland Barthes' family history and writings in the context of French colonialism. I am indebted to the artist for prompting me to delve into my own family history.

> our vision of it is *certain* – contrary to the text or to other perceptions which give me the object in a vague, arguable manner, and therefore incite me to suspicions as to what I think I am seeing. This certitude is sovereign because I have the leisure to observe the photograph with intensity; but also, however long I extend this observation, it teaches me nothing. It is precisely in this *arrest* of interpretation that the Photograph's certainty resides [...]'[8]

8 Roland Barthes, *Camera Lucida*, New York, Farrar, Strauss and Giroux, 1981, pp. 106–107.

The phrase 'arrest of interpretation' – for Barthes the mark of the evidentiary power of the photograph – describes well the stunning effect and persuasiveness of the document in general. The ability to *arrest interpretation* can be understood both in the sense of halting further questions and of capturing and captivating the attention of the viewer. In the family documents I have in front of me, this arresting power comes, for a great part, from specific formal elements: my grandfather in Tunis pointing at what the photographer wants us to identify as the subject of the image and, in Paris, the letterhead of the École Pratique des Hautes Études indicating the position of the author of the letter to my grandmother. Yet if I look beyond those elements, the evidence that the letter and the photograph present becomes muddled, unclear. Letter and photograph belong to different stories and contexts that can be identified and need to be pulled apart if we are to break through that arrest of interpretation. As John Tagg put it, responding to this passage of *Camera Lucida*:

> 'The very idea of what constitutes evidence has a history [...] which implies definite techniques and procedures, concrete institutions and specific social relations, that is, relations of power'.[9]

There is, in short, nothing evident about evidence. This is what Tagg sought to demonstrate in 1988, in *The Burden of Representation*. Delving into nineteenth and early twentieth-century collections of photographs assembled by prison administrators, the police, hospitals and city planning bodies in France, the United Kingdom and the United States, he explained how photography was constructed as judiciary, social, or medical evidence and appropriated by state institutions as a tool to exert power over individuals.

This book is about ways in which contemporary art critically addresses the question of the document as evidence. It is about a group of artists who, while not associated with the influx of documentary in contemporary art in the 1990s and 2000s, have placed the document at the centre of their practice. My aim in this book is threefold. It is first to analyse how, in their work, these artists appropriate, mimic

9 John Tagg, *The Burden of Representation: Essays on Photographies and Histories*, London, Macmillan, 1988, pp. 4–5.

or recreate visual and textual documents and how they present documents as products of sited conventions of knowledge production rather than self-evident and unambiguous entities. In works that play with the format of product photography or museum documentation, or that appropriate documents from colonial administrations and ethnographic films, these artists, I propose, make us aware of the ways in which authority is embedded in documents, by undermining or dismantling them. Because their practices show how this authority of the document is constructed historically, examining their work leads me to re-construct genealogies of the document, so that, interspersed throughout the book, I sketch out what could be a history of the document in modern and contemporary art, a history for which the introduction proposes a rationale of sorts. A third issue addressed in the book is the move from analogue to digital photography and film. It is not by accident that the artists discussed, all born between 1955 and 1970 in different parts of the world, often address issues relating to recent history. Jean-Luc Moulène (1955, Reims, France) photographs objects made by workers during industrial conflicts, while Zoe Leonard (1961, Liberty, USA) charts the globalisation of trade and the changing of old neighbourhoods in New York City. Christopher Williams (1956, Los Angeles, USA) produces a collection of photographs of objects that relate in different ways to the Cold War. Fiona Tan (1966, Pekan Baru, Indonesia) excavates ethnographic footage from colonial pasts, Sven Augustijnen (1970, Mechelen, Belgium) stalks ghosts of Belgian and Congolese history and Wendelien van Oldenborgh (1962, Rotterdam, the Netherlands) looks at the legacy of Dutch imperialism in present-day Brazil and the Netherlands. The periods of time these artists deal with are on the threshold between the historical and the contemporary, but they also mark a transition from the reign of the analogue to that of the digital. Their works all deal with periods of time when archives were collected and consulted as material things, perhaps the last moment in time in which archives exist in material form. What these artists make resembles documentary narratives, visual atlases, promotional images, and archives. But they work from within our digital age, take the digital in their stride, and thereby question the future of such documentaries, atlases, promotional images and archives in the context of their transformation into data: what happens to evidence when it becomes digital? When it becomes data? In looking back at recent history, their works present us a retrospective history of analogue to show us, perhaps, the disappearance of evidence.

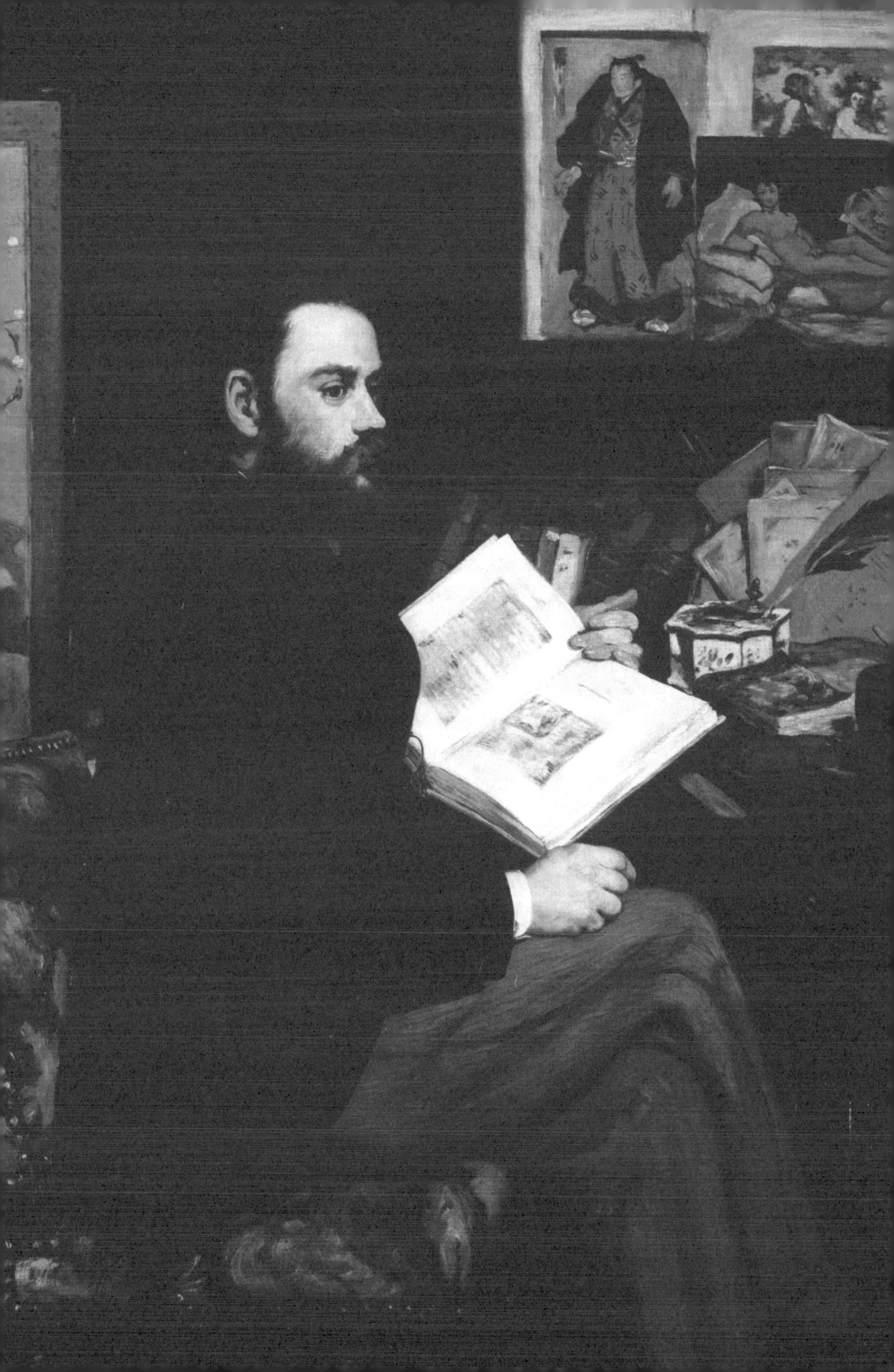

Introduction

Art Work, Document, Monument

'Documents for Artists'
— Sign outside Eugène Atget's photography studio, early twentieth century

'A document was a picture which had a job to perform.'
— Molly Nesbit, 1999[1]

'You see, a document has use, whereas art is really useless. Therefore art is never a document, though it certainly can adopt that style.'
— Walker Evans, 1971[2]

'What attracts me in photography is not so much a fine arts approach but rather photographs as documents. Not only journalism but the other roles that photography has played outside of the art context: aerial reconnaissance photography, science and medical photography, family snapshots. All the ways in which human beings have documented the world in an attempt to order it, in an attempt to consume it or rule it or hang on to it in some sense.'
— Zoe Leonard, 1993[3]

1 Molly Nesbit, 'Photography and History: Eugène Atget', in Michel Frizot (ed.), *A New History of Photography*, New York, Konemann, 1999, p. 401. Nesbit's important monographic study of Atget contains a section entitled 'The Document', from which the latter publication is partly derived. Molly Nesbit, *Atget's Seven Albums*, New Haven and London, Yale University Press, 1992, pp. 14–19.

2 Walker Evans, in Leslie Katz, 'An Interview with Walker Evans', 1971, printed in Vicky Goldberg (ed.), *Photography in Print*, Albuquerque, University of New Mexico Press, 1981, p. 364.

3 Zoe Leonard interviewed by Laura Cottingham, 'Zoe Leonard', *Journal of Contemporary Art*, vol. 6, no. 1, summer 1993, pp. 64–77.

Édouard Manet, *Portrait d'Émile Zola*, 1868, oil on canvas, 146.5 × 114 cm, Paris, Musée d'Orsay.

'Documents are usually condensations of power. They reek of authority, certification, and expertise and concentrate epistemological hierarchies.'
— Hito Steyerl, 2007[4]

'I. The art work is only incidentally a document.
No document is as such a work of art.
II. The art work is a masterpiece.
The document serves to instruct.
XI. The impact of an art work increases with repeated viewing.
A document overpowers only through surprise.'
— Walter Benjamin, 1926[5]

The citations compiled above as epigraphs are by artists, photographers, writers and art historians. Written at different epochs between the late nineteenth and the early twentyfirst centuries, each suggests a different understanding of what a document is. They go beyond the dictionary definition: a text, image or object used for purposes of identification, evidence, administration or education (from which the Latin root of the word, *docere* is derived). When Eugène Atget called his photographs 'documents for artists', he did not grant the term the same meaning that the surrealists and Walker Evans would later bestow upon the word. For Atget the term document defined a trade: pictures that 'circulated in the closed channels of painter's cartoons, decorator's folios and libraries' files.'[6] The surrealists

4 Hito Steyerl, 'Documentary Uncertainty', *A Prior Magazine*, 2007, pp. 303–308.

5 Walter Benjamin, 'Thirteen Theses against Snobs', Susan Sontag (ed.), *One-Way Street and Other Writings*, London, Verso, 1979, p. 66.

6 Molly Nesbit, 'Photography and History: Eugène Atget', p. 403.

who published some of his photographs in their journals would value precisely their anti-aesthetic quality.[7] This was also the case for Georges Bataille, who, in naming his journal *Documents* (1930–1931) used the term as a manifesto against *les Beaux-Arts*, while making a connection with ethnography and a host of other disciplines.[8] And when Walker Evans developed the idea of a 'documentary style' in the 1930s, the photographic document had become, as Molly Nesbit puts it, 'a supremely modern form, ripe for exploitation by modern artists.'[9] But what does this documentary style share with, for example, Mary Kelly's *Post-Partum Document* (1973–1979), with conceptual art and post-conceptual practices that employ photography, text and film to materialise ideas or to document processes?

The renewed interest in the document that can be observed in art practices emerging in the aftermath of the fall of the Berlin Wall and in a resurgence of discussions about decolonisation and the postcolonial is, again, sustained by different ideas. This time, in the 1990s, the document is burdened with a sense of emergency. Often endowing documents with a mystique of uniqueness and unquestionable truth, curators and critics speak of a 'need to document' the present political situation after the reunification of Europe; they propagate the necessity to rewrite or reclaim a recent history that has been

7 Concerning the taste of the surrealists for found photographs and banal documents, see Quentin Bajac, 'Le fantastique moderne', in Quentin Bajac and Clément Chéroux (eds.), *La Subversion des images: surréalisme, photographie, film*, Paris, Musée national d'art moderne, Centre Pompidou, 2009, pp. 120–128.

8 Denis Hollier, 'La Valeur d'usage de l'impossible', *Documents*, vol. 1, Paris, Jean-Michel Place, 1991, pp. VII–XXXIV.

9 Molly Nesbit, 'Photography and History: Eugene Atget', p. 401.

obliterated both by the economical globalisation and the political division between East and West, North and South.[10] Some art historians and curators concern themselves with the question of memory, history and alternatives to official narratives, taking not the document but the archive as a focal point.[11] Others attempt to define a documentary tradition in twentieth-century art that is in marked opposition to the media-saturated world of late-capitalism.[12] Elsewhere still, the critical study of the document and the archive has become a means to question the autonomy of art in neo-liberal society.

However different the concerns of these various practices, what they foreground is the intractable relation between the work of art and the document. To bring 'the real' into the realm of art opens up a vertiginous array of issues concerning the purpose and autonomy of art, issues that each generation of artists since the advent of modernism has reactivated for their own purpose.

The Art Work and the Document

In 1926, Walter Benjamin reflected on the relation between work of art and document in a short text entitled 'Thirteen Theses Against Snobs', published in 1928 in *Einbahnstraße* (*One-Way Street*), his

10 Vít Havránek, Sabine Schaschl-Cooper, Bettina Steinbrügge (eds.), *The Need to Document* (exhib. cat.), Zürich, JRP Ringier, 2005. See also Frits Gierstberg, Maartje van der Heuvel, Hans Scholten and Martijn Verhoeven (eds.), *Documentary Now: Contemporary Strategies in Photography, Film and the Visual Arts,* Rotterdam, NAi Publishers, 2005. See also Mark Nash, *Experiments with Truth* (2005), Philadelphia, The Fabric Workshop and Museum, 2008. Documenta X (1997) and Documenta 11 (2002) under the artistic direction of, respectively, Catherine David and Okwui Enwezor, both engaged extensively with documentary practices in the context of globalisation.

11 On the archive in the context of contemporary art see in particular: Benjamin H. D. Buchloh, 'Gerhard Richter's "Atlas": The Anomic Archive', *October*, vol. 88, spring, 1999, pp. 117–145; Hal Foster, 'An Archival Impulse', *October,* vol. 110, fall 2004, pp. 3–22.

12 This perspective is developed in particular in two issues of the journal *Communications,* co-edited by Jean-Francois Chevrier and Philipe Roussin: 'Le Parti pris du document. Littérature, photographie, cinéma et architecture au XXeme siècle', *Communications,* no. 71, 2001, and 'Des Faits et des gestes', *Communications,* no. 79, 2006.

book of 'aphorisms, jokes and dreams' as he announced it to his friend Gershom Sholem in the early stages of its conception.[13] Dividing the page in two columns, he listed on the left thirteen properties he ascribes to the work of art and on the right a corresponding number of qualities attributed to the document.[14] The work of art is presented first of all as the product of the artist, (Thesis I), as a masterpiece (Thesis II), as synthesising form and content to create meaning; it is synthetic, and as such an 'energy centre' that resists multiple viewing (Theses VI, X, XI). In the document by contrast, the formal element is negligible in contrast with the subject matter that is of prime importance (Theses V, VI, VIII, IX). Moreover, the document can 'overpower' but only by surprise: Benjamin states from the outset that it serves 'to instruct'.

This double list is preceded by a prologue in which Benjamin introduces the reader to a 'snob' who, in front of a child's drawing and a 'fetish,' declares: 'doesn't this make Picasso seem such a waste of time?' The theses that follow this statement read as arguments against the snob in which the work of art is favoured over the mere document. This is also the interpretation given by Rainer Rochlitz who sees in 'Thirteen Theses Against Snobs', along with two similar pieces, 'The Writer's Technique in Thirteen Theses' and 'The Critic's

13 Walter Benjamin, Letter to Gershom Sholem, 22 December 1924, cited by Susan Buck-Morss, *The Dialectics of Seeing: Walter Benjamin and the Arcades Project*, Cambridge, MA. and London, MIT Press, 1991, p. 16.

14 Walter Benjamin, 'Thirteen Theses Against Snobs', *One-Way Street and Other Writings*, London, Verso, 1979, pp. 65–66.

Technique in Thirteen Theses' the most theoretically engaged texts of *One-Way Street*. What is at stake in those essays, Rochlitz proposes, is how to balance the aesthetic challenge of the work of art with the efficiency of political action that is Benjamin's concern in these same years.[15]

The clear-cut distinction between work of art and document is not Benjamin's final word on the subject. In two essays dated a few years later, the author clearly attributes a subversive role to documents produced in avant-garde art and literature. In 'Krisis des Romans' ('The Crisis of the Novel') he notes that dada and surrealism would seize upon the document as a favoured form in their 'fanatical struggle with the work of art.'[16] And in 'Der Surrealismus. Die letzte Momentaufnahme der Europäischen Intelligenz' ('Surrealism or The Last Snapshot of the European Intelligentsia', 1929), he describes the surrealist productions as 'not literature but something else – demonstrations, watchwords, documents, bluffs, forgeries if you will, but at any rate not literature.'[17] In contrast with the 'Thirteen Theses', which reject the document when it is a child drawing or a fetish, in these two later essays Benjamin appears to side with the document when it is a format deemed necessary for the subversive mission avant-garde groups such as dada and surrealism assign to themselves. 'Thirteen Theses',

15 Rainer Rochlitz, *Le Désenchantement de l'art. La Philosophie de Walter Benjamin*, Paris, Gallimard, 1992, pp. 142–143.

16 Walter Benjamin, 'The Crisis of the Novel' (1931), reprinted in Michael W. Jennings (ed.), *Walter Benjamin, Selected Writings*, Cambridge and London, Belknap Press, 1999, pp. 299–304.

17 Walter Benjamin, 'Surrealism or the Last Snapshot of the European Intelligentsia' (1929), Susan Sontag (ed.), *One-Way Street and Other Writings*, London and New York, Verso, 1979, pp. 225–239.

'The Crisis of the Novel' and the essay on surrealism suggest a set of possible relations between art work and document that include masterpiece versus instruction, form versus content, an energy centre rather than a source of analysis, but also, subversion against tradition. Other distinctions will appear in Benjamin's writings in the years that follow, particularly when to these issues surrounding the work of art he introduces, in 1935, the question of technological reproduction in the essay 'Das Kunstwerk im Zeitalter seiner technischen Reproduzierbarkeit' ('The Work of Art in the Age of Mechanical Reproduction').

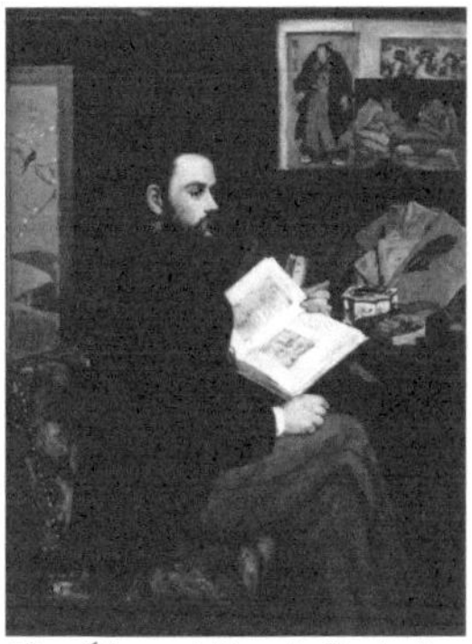

18 Édouard Manet, *Portrait d'Émile Zola*, 1868, oil on canvas, 146.5 × 114 cm, Paris, Musée d'Orsay.

19 The setting, made to evoke Zola's study, was put together in Manet's studio.

Some sixty years earlier, a multifold reflection on the relationship between work of art and document incorporating the question of technique could already be observed in Édouard Manet's *Portrait d'Émile Zola* (*Portrait of Émile Zola*, 1868).[18] Manet has depicted his friend Zola – at the time one of his strongest supporters – in what appears to be his study, sitting sideways at a desk scattered with papers, letters and pamphlets which burst from a letter rack.[19] Books are piled up and aligned against the wall; writing tools, a smoking pipe and a paper cutter complete the writer's paraphernalia. Zola is turned slightly to show his profile to the viewer, and looks out pensively, holding an open illustrated book resting on the desk. To his left is a fragment of a

20 George Heard Hamilton, *Manet and his Critics*, New York, W.W. Norton & Co, 1969, p. 98.

Japanese screen disappearing at the edge of the painting. To his right, a frame on the wall contains an assemblage of several prints: a Japanese woodblock print, a group of bacchantes, and a reproduction of Manet's own painting *Olympia* (1863). Those elements complete the overall image of an aesthete with progressive taste, an intellectual, then better known as a literary and art critic than as the novelist, polemist, engaged intellectual we know today.

Portrait of Émile Zola is often read as a testimony of the relationship between Manet and Zola. Scholars have tried to read the objects in the painting as items documenting this relationship: the greyish blue cover of a pamphlet bearing Manet's name that emerges from the letter rack on the desk is a reprint, published in 1868, of the 'biographical and critical study' Zola devoted to Manet, a text that followed up other articles on the artist. The reproduction of *Olympia* points to the important role played by Zola in defending the painting when it was ridiculed at the Salon of 1865. 'Never again would he write such direct and accurate criticism,' commented George Heard Hamilton, who points out that Zola's writing not only defended Manet against his detractors but also publicly recognized the painting as a masterpiece.[20] *Portrait of Émile Zola* thus appears to seal the close friendship between artist and critic. Some, noting the subtle shift in the gaze of Olympia, who looks downward here as opposed to staring straight out as she does in the real painting, have read this as a gentle encouragement to Zola to sustain his support of Manet.

However, in concentrating their reading on the dialogue between the painter and his friend, critics have seldom addressed more directly the three reproductions in the frame above the desk. What would it mean for Manet to reproduce in paint other techniques of visual representation? In a rare article on this subject, Theodore Reff has identified the Japanese woodblock print as the image of a wrestler by Utagawa Kuniaki II (*Ashū Ōnaruto Nadaemon (Sumō Wrestler Ōnaruto Nadaemon of Awa Province)*, 1860) and the larger image in the background, done in loose brushstrokes, as a lithograph after Vélazquez's 1628–1629 painting *Los Borrachos (The Drinkers)*. Taking into account the smooth texture and overall deeper dark tones with light grey highlights, Reff identifies the reproduction of *Olympia* as a photographic print.[21] The juxtaposition of a woodcut, a lithograph and a photograph in Manet's painting creates a variety of texture that shows the virtuosity of the artist venturing into the classical genres of trompe-l'œil and mise en abyme.[22] Yet for the contemporary viewer the interest of this specific juxtaposition lies elsewhere. The three prints represent three distinct means of mechanised

21 Theodore Reff, 'Manet's Portrait of Zola', *The Burlington Magazine*, issue 862, 1975, p. 39. Reff argues this whilst noting that the size of the reproduction does not correspond to any known contemporary photograph of *Olympia*.

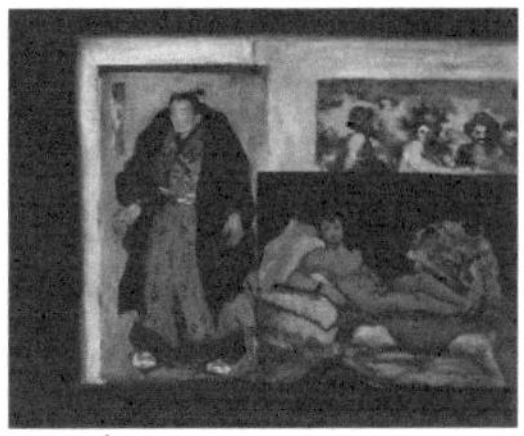

22 Édouard Manet, *Portrait d'Émile Zola*, 1868, Paris, Musée d'Orsay. Detail view.

reproduction. Indeed, they are the reproduction techniques singled out by Benjamin in the first pages of 'The Work of Art in the age of Mechanical Reproduction' where he sets up a historical background for his argument on the fading of aura and the demise of the unique work of art.[23] In this context, Benjamin presents woodblock printing, lithography and photography as the three most important steps in the development of the technical reproducibility of art. The woodcut, he explains, was the earliest form of reproduction of graphic art, while lithography – more so than etching – introduced in the early nineteenth century a swiftness of execution and production that made it possible to include images alongside text in newspaper publications. Shortly after, 'within a few decades of its invention', Benjamin writes, lithography 'was surpassed by photography.'[24]

Reading Manet's painting through Benjamin, we might say that those three pictures in the frame above Zola's desk write a short history of the mechanical reproduction of the work of art. Such speculation is an invitation to think about the entanglement of the work of art and the document in the age of Manet. Artists have always used prints as references and reproduced paintings within their own paintings, and by the late 1860s, almost thirty years after its invention, photography had become a

23 Some critics have pointed out the historical inaccuracy of Benjamin's account. See Jacquelyn Bass, 'Reconsidering Walter Benjamin. "The Age of Mechanical Reproduction" in Retrospect', in Gabriel P. Weisberg, Laurinda S. Dixon (eds.), *The Documented Image: Visions in Art History*, Syracuse, NY, Syracuse University Press, 1987, pp. 337–347.

24 Walter Benjamin, 'The Work of Art in the Age of Mechanical Reproduction', in Hannah Arendt (ed.), *Illuminations: Essays and Reflections*, New York, Schocken, 1969, p. 219.

habitual resource for painters. They used photographic documents as source in order to increase the accuracy of details and as models for likeness in portraits and nudes. But Manet's representation of a photographic reproduction of one of his own paintings invites us to delve further into the relationship between photographic documents and painting in the 1860s, seen in the light of Benjamin's essay.

One of the important consequences of the development of mechanical reproduction of art that Benjamin sets out to describe is that it conjures a different mode of addressing an audience. With the development of photography, the 'free-floating' contemplation of the art work (that subsided for a while in the earliest photographs) gradually disappeared. In its place, Benjamin argues, reproducible mediums (and photography in particular) call for a more inquisitive gaze: the viewer would search or scan a picture for the information it provides, information that is relayed and channelled by captions or 'signposts' – as he calls them – that offered, in illustrated magazines for instance, directives to the reader/viewer.

Manet's rendering of several reproductions and documents in his painting thus invites the viewer to switch from an overall contemplation to a probing gaze. Art historians have all too happily embraced this, seeking for information within the painting and

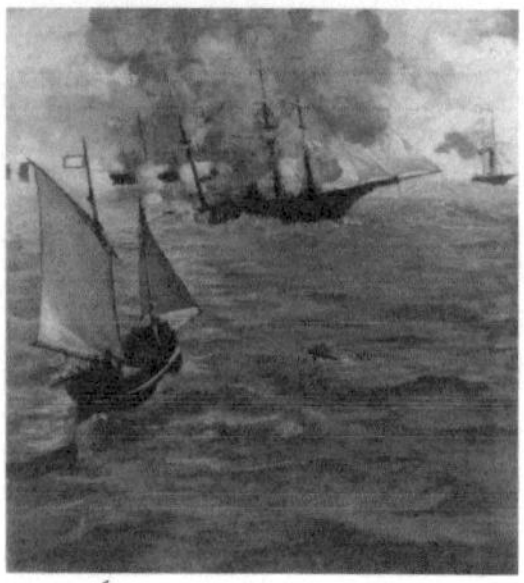

25 Édouard Manet, *Le Combat du* Kearsarge *et de* l'Alabama, 1864, oil on canvas, 137.8 × 128.9 cm, Philadelphia, Museum of Art.

duly identifying or 'captioning' the represented objects and documents. But where the painted photograph of *Olympia* is concerned, Manet has turned one of his own paintings into a document: the bold painting that once stirred the Salon has become a portable object in black and white, its aura dissolved through the reduced palette and size. Included in the *Portrait of Émile Zola* it becomes one of many documents that surround the writer at his desk.

What could Manet's meticulous reduction and transposition of *Olympia* into a painted photograph inside another painting signify? Should it just be read in the anecdotal terms of his relation with the public or his friendship with the portrayed writer? Or can we see it as a reflection on the fate of painting in the age of photographic reproduction, namely its obligation to circulate widely in a reduced and flattened version, a fate which André Malraux would later embrace in his *Musée Imaginaire* (*Museum without Walls*, 1947)?

If Manet's decision to reproduce *Olympia* in *Portrait of Émile Zola* entails a meditation on the defeat of painting as a material object, this would certainly not be the painter's last statement on the subject. Four years earlier, when he painted *Le Combat du Kearsarge et de l'Alabama* (*The Battle of the USS Kearsarge and the CSS Alabama*, 1864),[25] he was directly confronting press documents. The painting responded to a recent news item: the confrontation between a Federate and a Secessionist vessel off the French coast near Cherbourg. The engagement of the ships, concluded by the sinking of the CSS Alabama by the USS Kearsarge on June 30 1864, was an event that made the headlines in European newspapers and drew huge crowds to Cherbourg. Manet just missed the action but hastily painted his medium-sized version of the battle with the aid of lithographs depicting the event that had been promptly produced and widely circulated.[26] A mere two weeks after the incident, in July 1864, Manet's painting was on show in the window of Alfred Cadart's print gallery in Paris. Recent scholarship has suggested that the painter responded as much to the challenge of depicting history in the making as to that posed by one of his contemporaries, a lithographer and painter who within days of the event had produced and circulated his own, rather academic rendering of the subject in a lithograph. If that is so, the speed at which *The Battle of the USS Kearsarge and the CSS Alabama* was conceived and executed shows Manet taking on the kind of subject matter that would become the stock and trade of lithography and, in due time, of photography. He challenged the documentary exactness and rapid diffusion of the lithograph by proposing a painting that both responded to the latest news yet

26 David Degner, Juliet Wilson-Bareau, *Manet and the American Civil War: The Battle of USS Kearsarge and CSS Alabama*, New York, Metropolitan Museum of Art, 2003.

inscribed itself within a tradition of painting (seventeenth-century Dutch marine painting). Manet updated the traditional academic genre of history painting but escaped the academic rules to which the contemporary lithographer had submitted himself.

It may be this bold gesture that Manet sought to repeat in 1867, when, a few months before his *Portrait of Émile Zola* and again reacting to political contemporary events, he renewed his confrontation with the immediate representation of the news by painting the first of several works entitled *L'Exécution de Maximilien* (*The Execution of Maximilian*). The subject matter of this new project was the killing by firing squad, on 19 June 1867, of the short-lived emperor of Mexico who had been put in place four years earlier in a disastrous colonisation enterprise launched by Napoleon III which had provoked strong reactions in the press and the public. As news of the execution hit France in early July 1867, Manet set out on what turned into a considerably more long-winded enterprise than the *Kearsarge* painting. Although he seems to have determined the main lines of his composition early on, deciding to depict the moment of the firing squad shooting at Maximilian and two of his allies, it took him several months to realise the first of a series of three paintings, one oil sketch and a lithograph that occupied him over the following two years.

The available visual documentation of Maximilian's death depicted not the event itself, as in the case of the *Kearsage*, but the immediate aftermath. Photographs showed the firing squad posing at the execution site, a heap of blood-stained clothes on a bed and, eerily, individual views of the demised emperor's clothing, notably his frock coat and waistcoat, seemingly floating in mid-air on a neutral background. The most famous image of the series presented Maximilian's white starched shirt, displayed frontally, pinned to a door, creased and stained by bullet holes.[27] Most of these images were the work of French photographer François Aubert, who had accompanied Maximilian to Mexico as court photographer. His pictures were described at length in press articles in France; they even circulated as reproductions in the popular *carte de visite* format.[28]

If the reproduction of *Olympia* in *Portrait of Émile Zola* hinted at the fallibility of painting, and the *Kearsarge* showed its vigour, how did Manet negotiate the contribution of photography to the representation of the emperor's death? Juliet Wilson-Bareau argues that Manet's development of the subject matter across a series of works was the result of an attempt on his part to keep up with the pace of the news, as information progressively reached France and the rest of Europe.[29] Both written reports and images were gradually distilled through heavy

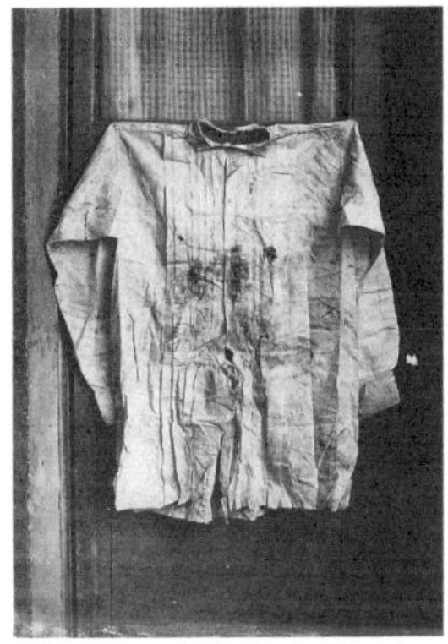

27 François Aubert, *Chemise que portait l'empereur durant son exécution* (*The Shirt of the Emperor, Worn during His Execution*), 1867, Albumen silver print from glass negative, 21.2 × 15.8 cm.

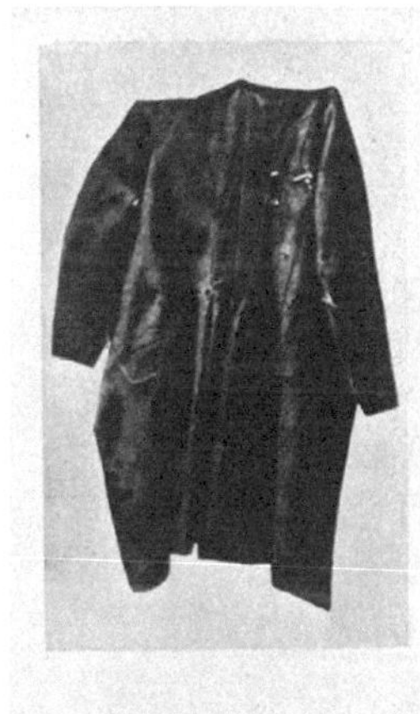

28 François Aubert, *Redingote que portait l'empereur Maximilien lorsqu'il a été fusillé le 19 juin 1867, (Frock Coat Worn by the Emperor Maximilian During his Execution on 19 June 1867)*, 1867, 10.3 × 6.2 cm. Paris, Musée de l'Armée.

29 Juliet Wilson-Bareau, *Manet: The Execution of Maximilian*, London, National Gallery Publications, 1992.

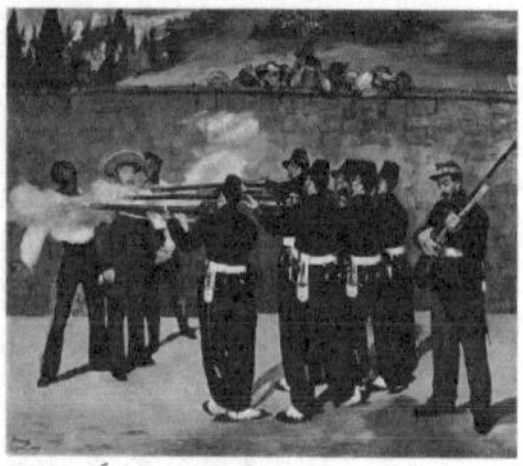

censorship. In the catalogue of New York's Museum of Modern Art's 2006 exhibition of the *Execution of Maximilian,* John Elderfield contests this interpretation. He argues instead that the visible reworking of the first painting and the subsequent images made by Manet show the artist carefully selecting from the available documentary evidence. Elderfield emphasises the sense of suspension and isolation between different parts of the third version painted by Manet and preserved in Mannheim.[30] He ultimately reads it quite boldly as an allegory of 'photography shooting painting', pointing out the stilled effect of the picture, the insistent pose of its protagonists, which would evoke the long poses in photography, and the painted smoke that brings to mind, for Elderfield, the complex flash system of early photography.[31]

When we compare the paintings to the photographic documents that have survived, a sense of competition certainly emerges, but not necessarily in the direction indicated by Elderfield. The photographs made by Aubert, and especially those that single out clothing items from the dead emperor, have the unequivocal quality of documentary evidence exhibited in court. Yet their power is also the mark of their limitations as documents, being able to present the material facts but nothing of the actual drama. Manet's paintings, especially the second fragmentary version kept in London and the third

30 Édouard Manet, *L'Exécution de Maximilien,* 1868–1869, oil on canvas, 252 × 305 cm, Mannheim, Städtische Kunsthalle.

31 John Elderfield, *Manet and the Execution of Maximilian,* New York, Museum of Modern Art, 2006, p. 153.

one in Mannheim, retained something of the aspect of the photographic documents historians believe the painter had access to.[32] Aside from the resemblance of Maximilian to well-known photographic portraits of the emperor, the uniforms of the firing squad are somewhat reminiscent of Aubert's photographs. Like those images, they seem to float on a neutral ground, similar in this to Manet's earlier painting *Le Fifre* (*The Fifer*, 1865–1866).[33] There, as in the later versions of the *Execution of Maximilian*, the outlines of the uniforms appear to follow the shape of the clothes rather than the body inside them. Absorbing different documents, selecting them for their informational content as well as for the particularities of visual conventions they displayed, Manet integrated the formal characteristics of documents into his painting, without following their logic. In other words, Manet's *Maximilian* poses the question of what a painting could do differently than photographs.

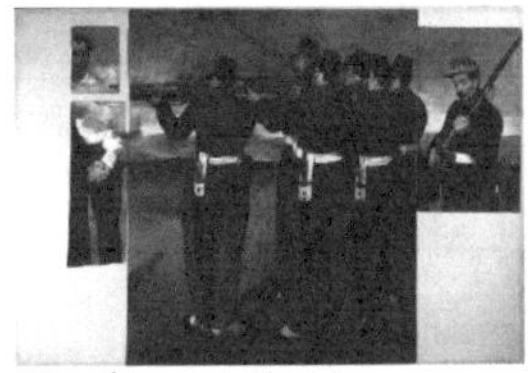

32 Édouard Manet, *L'Exécution de Maximilien*, about 1867–1868, oil on canvas, 193 × 284 cm, London, National Gallery.

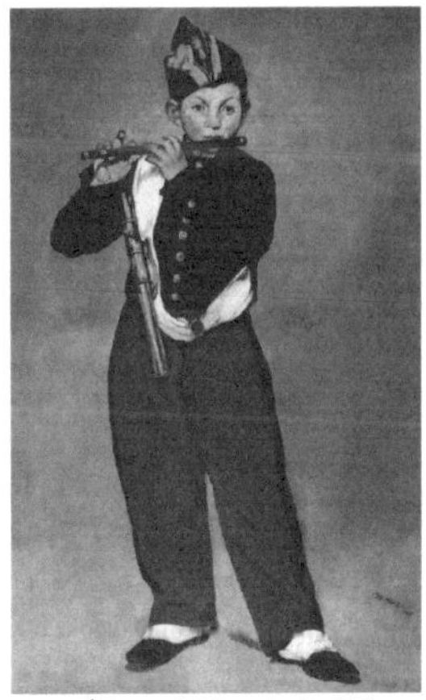

33 Édouard Manet, *Le Fifre*, 1866, oil on canvas, 160 × 97 cm, Paris, Musée d'Orsay.

The dialogue Manet developed between photography and painting may be identified more closely when we compare *Olympia* (1865) with early photographs of the female nude. The features of the painting that attracted the scorn of critics are precisely those that characterise photographic nudes from the 1850s: the 'dirty skin', the model's proportions, and graceless feet emerging from house

34 On the characteristics of early female nude photography see Eric Homberger, 'The Model's Unwashed Feet: French Photography in the 1850s', in Peter Collier and Robert Lethbridge (eds.), *Artistic Relations: Literature and the Visual Arts in Nineteenth Century France,* New Haven and London, Yale University Press, 1994, pp. 130–143.

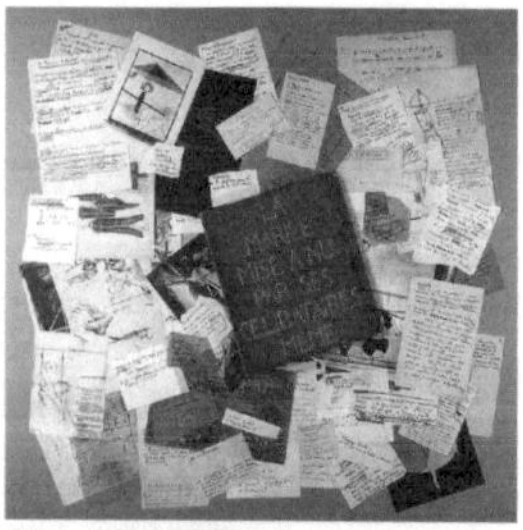

35 Marcel Duchamp, *La Mariée mise à nu par ses célibataires, meme (la boîte verte),* 1934, 33 × 28.3 × 2.5 cm, London, Tate Britain.

slippers.[34] Adopting a monumental format while making an explicit reference to an earlier work – Titian's *Venus d'Urbino* – Manet interwove, in *Olympia,* photography and painting. Where the *Portrait of Émile Zola* suggested, with its reproduction of *Olympia,* the possible fate of painting to circulate in reduced, colourless form, the painting *Olympia* staged a fascination, an emulation of modern art with the document in which the latter becomes a kind of hidden double, a secret sharer. This also what happens more extensively in the *Execution of Maximilian,* where Manet's repeated efforts to create a large-scale painting on the subject are conducted in negotiation with photographs of the event.

This idea of the document as a double of the work of art becomes explicit in the case of Marcel Duchamp, who decided in 1923 to leave his 'masterpiece' *La Mariée mise à nu par ses célibataires, même,* also called *Le grand verre (The Large Glass),* 'definitely unfinished', only to publish a decade later *La Boîte verte (The Green Box),* a collection of documents pertaining to the unfinished *masterpiece.*[35] *The Green Box,* whose full title is *La Mariée mise à nu par ses célibataires, même, (la boîte verte)* consists in a collection of ninety-four facsimile of sketches and notes. It bears an ambiguous status in relation to *The Large Glass*: it is both a document used by historians in their study of Duchamp's great unfinished masterpiece, and an art work in itself, a multiple, produced in a few luxury copies by the artist. The status of work and documentation appears, in this case, interchangeable: as one art historian puts it, it is only the convention of chronology that suggests *The Green Box* documents *The Large Glass* rather than the other way around.[36] In its unstable and double identity as work of art and document, *The Green Box* anticipated a host of practices that would develop later, in the 1960s around conceptualism, performance and land art. In a multiplicity of cases that include works produced in locations far away from any audience, events performed at a specific moment and works provided in the form of instructions to a third party, the work of art is presented to an audience through documentary means: photographs, films, notes, objects. The art work itself is elusive, sometimes impermanent. While this is sometimes presented as a side effect of these practices, the elusiveness of the art work and its reliance on documentary means can be understood in a different way: as a purpose in itself, a conscious and permanent deferral. 'The modern conception of an art whose content is no longer the image of the ideal, but the sensuous record of its pursuit', described Eric Gans in his reading of Balzac's *Le Chef d'oeuvre inconnu* (*The Unknown*

36 'If anything then, it is *The Large Glass* which could be seen as a supplement to *The Green Box*, the incomplete realization of a ruminating idea that could never satisfactorily articulate itself in purely visual terms.' Susi Bloch, 'Marcel Duchamp's *Green Box*', *Art Journal*, no. 34, (1), 1974, pp. 25–29.

Masterpiece).[37] In the case of Duchamp, *The Green Box* certainly represents such a sensuous record of the pursuit of the impossible masterpiece that is *The Large Glass,* and this impossibility looms large over Manet's repeated attempts at depicting the *Execution of Maximilian.* It is in this sense, then, that ultimately the document takes centre stage, as the consciously and permanently deferred promise of an ideal work of art.

37 Eric Gans, 'Balzac's Unknowable Masterpiece and the Limits of the Classical Esthetic', *MLN*, vol. 90, no. 4, 1975, p. 515.

Epistemology of the Document

In his account of a visit to Passaic published as an illustrated essay in *Artforum* in February 1967, Robert Smithson portrayed the suburban New Jersey town where he was born as a post-industrial wasteland.[38] He singled out a bridge over the Passaic River, a pumping derrick, water pipes sprouting out of a hillside, and a sand box in a playground as objects documenting the anarchic, industrial development of the area and its present state of desolation. Smithson supported his description with black-and-white snapshots of these objects, embedded in the pseudo-autobiographical account of a trip to his hometown. Perhaps surprisingly, the generic term he used to define the constructions he stumbled upon was not 'document' but instead *monument.*

38 Robert Smithson, 'The Monuments of Passaic', *Artforum*, February 1967. Reprinted as 'A Tour of the Monuments of Passaic, New Jersey', in Jack Flam (ed.), *Robert Smithson: The Collected Writings*, Los Angeles, University of California Press, 1996.

If documents refer to accidentally formed or deliberately constructed material traces of different sorts that are used for purpose of proof, education, or legal record, monuments, by contrast, are traditionally understood as intentional sites through which the past is memorialized. There is little doubt that a historian attempting to describe the process and elucidate the causes of the dilapidation of the Passaic landscape would define these constructions as involuntary documents rather than intentionally created monuments. Yet although Smithson uses the term consistently throughout his essay, his notion of monument is rather idiosyncratic, as is clear from a description of the fragmented landscape and scattered urbanism of Passaic, which, he writes, create 'monumental vacancies that define, without trying, the memory-traces of an abandoned set of futures'.[39] Smithson's purpose in calling those accidental documents 'monuments' of an already dilapidated future is to illustrate the notion of entropy, a discussion of which concludes his essay. Yet his deliberately awkward choice of words brings to mind Michel Foucault's coupling of document and monument in a passage of *L'Archéologie du savoir* (*The Archaeology of Knowledge*), published just two years later in 1969. As he reviews, in the introduction of his book, recent developments concerning research in the humanitics, Foucault points

39 Robert Smithson, 'A Tour of the Monuments of Passaic, New Jersey' (1967), in Jack Flam (ed.), *Robert Smithson: The Collected Writings*, p. 72.

out that for historians a central question has been a re-evaluation of the use and definition of the document, which 'is no longer for history an inert material through which it tries to reconstitute what men have done, or said, the events of which only the trace remains'. Instead history 'has altered its position in relation to the document: it has taken as its primary task, not the interpretation of the document, nor the attempt to decide whether it is telling the truth or what is its expressive value, but to work on it from within and to develop it: history now organises the document, divides it up, distributes it, orders it, arranges it in levels, establishes series.' A few lines further, he concludes: 'history in its traditional form, undertook to 'memorize' the *monuments* of the past, transform them into documents [...] In our time, history is that which transforms *documents* into *monuments*.'[40]

These last words read like an ironical nudge in the direction of the new school of quantitative history that employed emerging computing technologies to assemble and process vast quantities of data, one of the many signs that attest to the complex relations between Foucault and historians of his generation.[41] To understand Foucault's observation concerning the rethinking of the document in history, it is necessary to briefly look back at the 'critique of the document' led by historians grouped

40 Michel Foucault, *The Archaeology of Knowledge* (1969), New York, Vintage Books, 2010, pp. 6–7.

41 Jacques Le Goff recognized the importance of Foucault's *The Archeology of Knowledge* in conceptualizing the orientations of the nouvelle histoire. See Jacques Le Goff, 'Foucault et la "nouvelle histoire"', in Dominique Franche, Sabine Prokhoris, Yves Roussel (eds.) *Au risque de Foucault,* Paris: Centre Georges Pompidou and Centre Michel Foucault, 1997, pp. 132–137. More critical accounts of this relation between Foucault and historians of his generation are detailed in Jacques Revel, 'Le Moment historiographique', in Luce Giard (ed.), *Michel Foucault: Lire l'oeuvre,* Grenoble, Jérôme Millon, 1992, pp. 83–97, and François Dosse, *L'Histoire en Miettes: Des Annales à la nouvelle histoire,* Paris, La Découverte, 1987, and Christophe Prochasson, 'L'Histoire et Foucault', *Vingtième Siècle: Revue d'histoire,* no. 50, April-June 1996, pp. 123–124.

around the journal *Les Annales* founded in 1929 by Marc Bloch and Lucien Febvre, a journal that pioneered a rethinking of history and its methods, introducing within its field other disciplines such as geography and sociology.

The first step in this critique was the broadening of the definition of what constitutes a document. The sharpest description of this process is given by Marc Bloch in his posthumously published *Apologie pour l'histoire ou le metier d'historien* (*The Historian's Craft*).[42] In this seminal historiographical essay, Bloch argues that equal weight should be given to the written records (such as memoirs, minutes of official meetings and so on) willingly transmitted from the past into the present and to those involuntary material traces (such as archaeological findings or signs of daily activities) left by the past. Both types of documents require to be examined by the historian with a renewed scepticism, beyond the simple matter of truthfulness versus falseness. It is necessary, Bloch explains, to read between the lines of the written records and deconstruct their official discourse, but also to be aware that involuntary material traces can function as proof only if one knows what one is looking for: they 'only speak when one knows how to question them.'[43] This call for an active, critical consideration of the document was set up against the French positivist history of the

42 Marc Bloch, *The Historian's Craft*, London, Vintage Books 1964.

43 Marc Bloch, *The Historian's Craft*, p. 53.

mid to late nineteenth century and the 'submission and passivity to facts' demanded by the likes of Fustel de Coulanges.[44] Bloch and the Annales historians criticised the positivists' favouring of political history and their reliance upon official, state-produced archives (large collections of which had been assembled and made available to citizens during the French Revolution and the Napoleonic Empire).[45] Along with a critical approach and a widening of the idea of the document, historians of the Annales school advocated opening up history towards the social sciences, working for instance with demographers and geographers. In enabling historians to move beyond their disciplinary confines, the historiographical scrutiny of the production and interpretation of documents led to a broader reflection on methods of knowledge production.

In the 1970s, Michel de Certeau expanded the reflection on the document, in the context of what came to be called 'la nouvelle histoire' – which took up the legacy of the Annales[46] – by directing his attention from the documents used by historians to the activity of historians themselves. In a passage from *L'Écriture de l'histoire* (*The Writing of History*), written in the aftermath of May 1968 and with clear anti-authoritarian undertones, De Certeau points out the institutional quality of history as a discipline. A 'document' is never accidentally

44 Charles-Olivier Carbonell, 'L'Histoire dite « positiviste » en France', *Romantisme*, 1978, no.21–22, 'Les Positivismes', p. 183.

45 Charles-Olivier Carbonell, 'L'Histoire dite «positiviste» en France', p. 183.

46 De Certeau participated notably in the first volume of *Faire de l'histoire*; which coalesced the nouvelle histoire historians. Jacques Le Goff and Pierre Nora, *Faire de l'histoire: Nouveaux problèmes, nouvelles approches, nouveaux objets*, Paris, Gallimard, 1974.

'found', but in reality always knowingly constructed as such by the historian in her/his practice:

> 'In history everything begins with the gesture of *setting aside*, of putting together, of transforming certain classified objects into 'documents'. This new cultural distribution is the first task. In reality it consists in *producing* such documents by dint of copying, transcribing, or photographing these objects, simultaneously changing their locus and their status.'[47]

47 Michel de Certeau, *The Writing of History* (1975), New York, Columbia University Press, 1988, p. 72.

De Certeau's scrutiny of the historian's practice as a producer of documents sheds new light onto Smithson's *Monuments of Passaic*. For what De Certeau wishes to remind the historian of has been, in the field of art, an accepted idea since Duchamp's ready-mades: there are no such things as 'found objects', but only objects that are 'set aside', selected and re-contextualised: such is also the gesture made by Smithson when he photographs the bridge over the Passaic River, the pumping derrick and the water pipes on the hillside.

To call them monuments rather than documents, however, as Smithson does, is not a misnaming, but rather signals the authority under which he puts them. When Foucault explained that historians of the past transformed monument into documents, he pointed at their scepticism towards pre-established

48 Jacques Le Goff and Pierre Toubert, 'Une histoire totale du Moyen Age est-elle possible?', *Actes du 100e congrès national des sociétés savantes, Paris 1975, section de philolologie et d'histoire jusqu'à 1610, tendances, perspectives et méthodes de l'histoire médiévale*, Paris, Bibliothèque nationale, 1977, pp. 31–44. My translation.

truths emanating from 'monuments': state-assembled archives. Responding to Foucault's formula, and his quip that present-day historians turned documents into monuments – that is, re-created large collections of unquestionable data – 'new history' medievalists Jacques Le Goff and Pierre Toubert contracted the two terms to create something more of a working concept:

> 'The document is a monument. It is the result of the effort made by historical societies to impose, voluntarily or involuntarily, a certain image of themselves into the future. There is no truthful document. Every document is a lie. It is the task of the historian to deconstruct, to demolish this montage, to de-structure this construction, and to analyse the conditions of production of these documents-monuments'.[48]

If we follow Le Goff and Toubert, Smithson's use of the word monument only directs the attention of his reader towards the arbitrariness of his selection. The sites he selects are not 'monuments' of industrial waste in a classical sense of the term, but rather objects selected by the artist for the purpose of articulating a certain discourse.

My account in the following chapters is informed both by the discourse and methodology of historians, and by the conflation or interaction between the work of art and the document in recent art. I look at practices by artists who interrogate the way history has been constructed and presented. Of course, artists are not historians, but they function within the double logic – or double configuration – of *the art work as document* and *the document as monument,* which is the topic of my book.

The two aspects of reflection on knowledge production and the relation between art work and document come together in the practices of the artists that are discussed in the following chapters: Jean-Luc Moulène, for example, strategically uses the term document in the titles of his works as if to locate his practice beyond or beneath the making of art works, slipping into the role of an archivist, an ethnographer or a curator. And Christopher Williams, who works with long series of photographs collected under an umbrella title, uses the term 'Revision' in the title of each exhibition presenting series of his photographs, as if each instalment modified a corpus but also perpetually deferred the completion of his oeuvre.

In turn, these two issues – knowledge production and the relation between document and work of art – inform the methodology and the structure of the book, which is constructed around close readings of a small number of artists. These close readings stem from my desire to approach writing as a way of documenting my experience of the works such as I encountered them in galleries and museums, rather than working from reproductions and 'viewing copies' of DVDs. The works discussed in the pages that follow do not illustrate ideas or function as case studies but instead provide the source and starting point of the reflection that is developed in this book. Working closely along the grain of the art works the chapters that follow question and displace them, a method inspired by Hubert Damisch who, when asked how he worked with objects such as perspective and the cloud, replied: 'That's what I want to do, to succeed each time in displacing the objects slightly, and at that point they gain their function as theoretical objects'.[49] Further in the interview, Damisch provides a definition of the theoretical object that reprises earlier formulations by Louis Marin: 'an object that obliges you to do theory but also furnishes you with the means of doing it.'[50]

49 Yve-Alain Bois, Denis Hollier, Rosalind Krauss and Hubert Damisch, 'A Conversation with Hubert Damisch', *October*, vol. 85, Summer 1998, p. 8.

50 'A Conversation with Hubert Damisch p. 8.

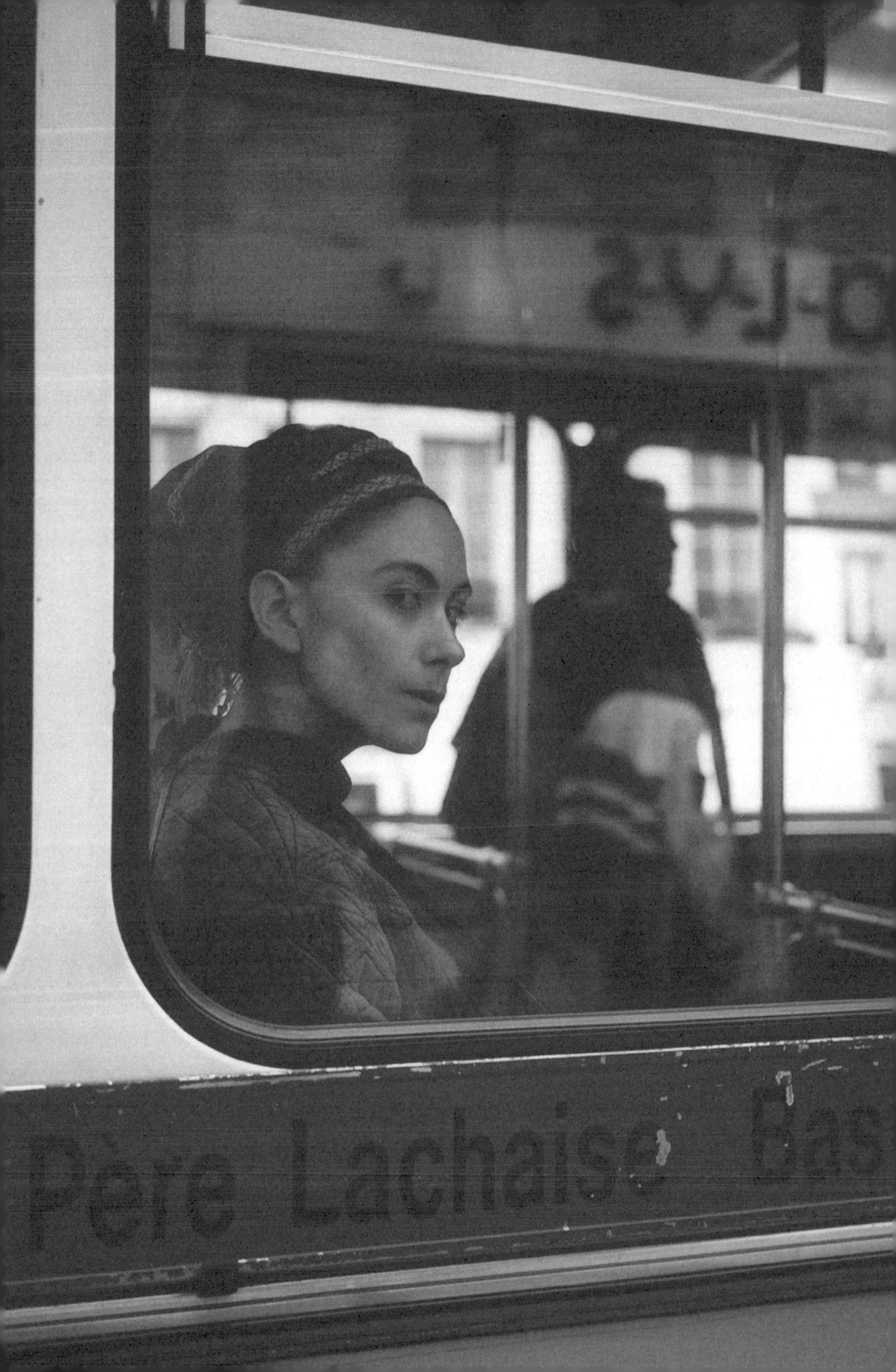
Père Lachaise

One

Anonymous Documents

Translated in English in 1977, Michel Foucault's landmark analysis of power and surveillance techniques in eighteenth and nineteenth century Europe, *Discipline and Punish* (1975) became an important source of inspiration for new studies in the history of photography that left aside artistic uses of the medium to delve into archives of state institutions such as prisons and hospitals to examine their use of photography. In key publications, Allan Sekula and John Tagg applied Foucault's study of the microphysics of power to argue that photography played a key role as producer of evidence within a network of technologies developed by modern states.[1] Around the same time that these texts were produced, a number of artists working in the aftermath of photo-conceptualism, developed photography-based work in which they examined the relationship between photography and power structures, and explored possibilities of resistance. Here I take up the work of Jean-Luc Moulène, an artist from a younger generation who manifests a continued interest in questions of labour, authority and anonymity. Through his photographic work and his use of the term document,

1 Allan Sekula, 'The Body and The Archive', *October*, vol. 39, winter 1986, pp. 3–64. John Tagg, *The Burden of Representation: Essays on Photographies and Histories*, London, Macmillan, 1988.

Jean-Luc Moulène, *Père Lachaise – Bastille*, Paris, 15 September 1998, Cibachrome print mounted on aluminium, 67 × 56 cm.

2 Jean-Luc Moulène, *Personne*, Bordeaux, Evento, 2009, 32 pages, colour, 46 × 31 cm.

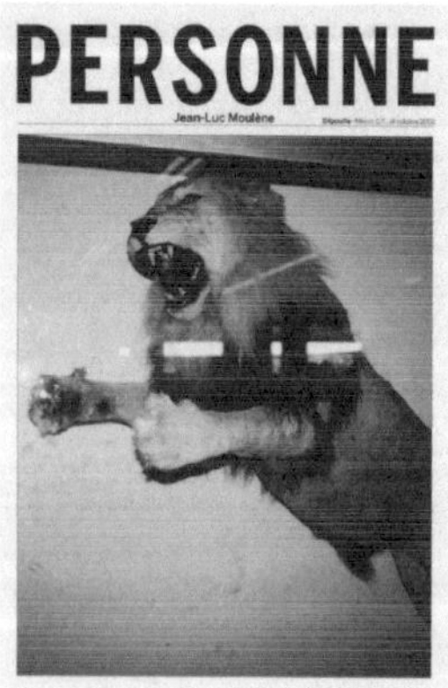

3 Jean-Luc Moulène, *Dépouille*, Mexico D.F., 14 October 2002, as printed on the cover of *Personne*.

Moulène addresses the subservience of photography to power structures; he proposes strategies of resistance via the deployment of alternative forms of authorship.

I am holding *Personne* in my hands. In French, personne is an ambiguous word: a noun identifying someone, and a pronoun that can indicate an unknown human presence, someone, just anyone, or an absence: nobody. More to the point, It is also the title of a work by Jean-Luc Moulène I am leafing through: an artist's book, or rather an artist's newspaper, a type of publication Moulène has long favoured. Berliner format, minimally designed, the newspaper contains thirty-two of his photographs printed full-page on thick white semi-glossy paper.[2] There is no text apart from the artist's name and the title printed in large block letters that stretch across the top of the cover page. Below the headline is a photograph of a taxidermically preserved lion that seemingly leaps out from a glass display case to confront the viewer with mock hostility (*Dépouille* (*Skin*), Mexico D.F., 14 October 2002).[3] The pictures that follow are similarly enigmatic. Shot, so it seems, in different places around the globe, they include street views, still-lifes, shop windows and unnamed people caught by the camera on the street or in public places. One of the most striking photos shows a young woman leaning against a partition wall in an airport hall (*Easy-Jet Girl*, Berlin, 7 July 2006).[4] Her posture visually transforms her into a caryatid supporting the wall, no more alive, despite her sun-kissed skin, than the plastic mannequin I come across a few pages later.

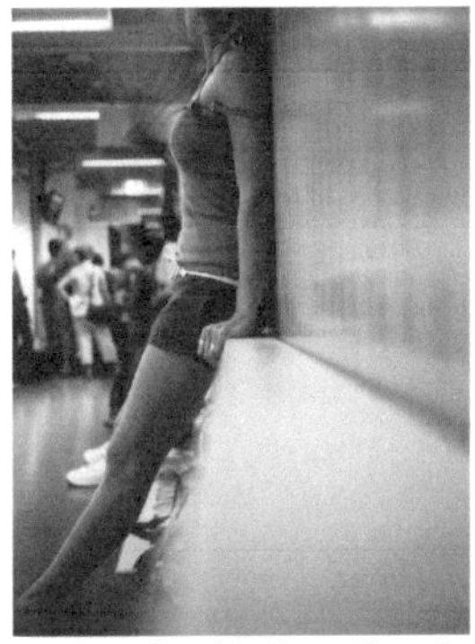

4 Jean-Luc Moulène, *Easy-Jet Girl*, Berlin, 7 July 2006, 42 × 28.5 cm, *Personne*, Evento, Bordeaux, 2009.

Scantily clothed, like a sci-fi game heroine, this mannequin stands in a department store alley, brandishing a bejewelled sceptre (*Princesse Surcouf*, Paris, 11 May 2006). On another page, several tailor's dummies dressed in creased white shirts are huddled together as if preparing to pose for a group portrait (*En chemise (Shirted)*, Paris, 4 July 2007). Although there is no explicit connection between the images, they all exude the same stifling atmosphere: men and women with averted gazes seem frozen, similar to the inanimate things they mingle with and to the stuffed lion on the cover: dead yet contorted into a life-like posture.

The only clue as to what these pictures may be about is in the title of the work, which comes back to me in the form of a banal remark: 'Il n' y a personne dans ces images': there is no one in these images. It is as if the air has been sucked out of them, as if they have all been photographed in the same way, the result of a camera scanning evenly the visual field and making no distinction between objects dead and alive.

5 François Arago, 'Report', 3 July 1839. Reprinted in Allan Trachtenberg (ed.), *Classic Essays on Photography*, New Haven, CT., Leete's Island Books, 1980, p. 19.

'Personne' as 'anyone' is the meaning I want to hold on to for now. Not only because the subject of these photographs seems to be a generic and global street life in which nobody and nothing in particular is identified, but more pointedly because the idea of *anyone* bears an important role in the history of photography. For photography was recognised early on as a deskilled technology of reproduction. Unlike etching or drawing, it could be practised by anyone.

The idea that anyone can use photographic equipment already came up in relation to one of the earliest forms of photography, the daguerreotype. In his famous speech at the French Chamber of Deputies in July 1839, given as he attempted to convince his fellow parliament members of the validity of the discovery of Louis Daguerre and Nicéphore Niepce, François Arago lauded the simplicity of the new procedure. Daguerreotype, he said, 'calls for no manipulations and can be performed by anyone. It presumes no knowledge of the art of drawing and demands no special dexterity. When a few simple prescribed rules are followed step by step, there is no one who cannot succeed as certainly and as well as can M. Daguerre himself.'[5] For Arago, presenting his report in order to secure a patent on the invention that would ensure lifelong revenues for Daguerre and Niepce, the simplicity of the technique was crucial. If the daguerreotype could be used by anyone with equal success, the resulting photographic documentation was sure to display a scientifically objective sameness. This versatility was augmented, Arago explained in his plea, by the suitability of the technique for a diversity of scientific applications, ranging widely from Egyptology to meteorology.

The number of such applications would eventually soar and Arago was certainly prescient in his argument concerning the sameness of photographic reproduction, which came to play an important role in the characterisation of scientific objectivity in the nineteenth century.[6] But the public use of photography was by no means restricted to the scientific realm. In the last decades of that century, following technical innovations such as dry plates and portable equipment that simplified its process, judiciary and medical institutions would increasingly employ photography to identify and record the populations that passed through them. In the 1880s Alphonse Bertillon developed for the French police a modern system for classifying and identifying repeating offenders thanks to physical characteristics, using photography.

This so-called 'Bertillonage' was but one of many uses of the medium that Sekula and Tagg identified in their writings. On the basis of Michel

6 Concerning the history of scientific objectivity and the role of photography within it see Lorraine and Peter Galison, *Objectivity*, New York, Zone Books, 2007.

7 John Tagg, *The Burden of Representation: Essays on Photographies and Histories*, p. 63.

Foucault's *Surveiller et punir* (*Discipline and Punish*, 1975), they drew a connection between the elaboration and strengthening of capitalist states in the late nineteenth century and the use of photography. Both authors reprised Foucault's analysis of the shift in the exertion of power from a spectacular and largely inefficient domination of the state over individuals in the pre-revolutionary era to the development of a network of institutions through which almost all population would be identified, taught, treated or punished. Hospitals, barracks, prisons and schools became tools through which countries such as Great Britain and France could distil what Foucault called a microphysics of power.

Working with different case studies, and in dialogue with Sekula's research, Tagg speaks of a 'rendezvous' between a 'novel form of the state and a new and developing technology of knowledge' that included photography. In the context of a positivist approach to knowledge, and within a network of procedures and techniques attached to different state institutions, photography 'functioned as a means of record and a source of evidence' capable of producing truth.[7]

For such a technology to function as evidence, a prerequisite was the visual sameness of photographic documents produced in different places and by different individuals. Evidence cannot stand to be obstructed by the idiosyncrasies of a photographer. Both Tagg and Sekula cite rules and manuals describing photography shoots: they involve specifics of light, framing, and preferred poses. Although detailed technical descriptions only appear in police manuals in the twentieth century, a certain photographic sameness and anonymity of authorship is visible in the portraits of inmates from medical, educational and coercive institutions from the late nineteenth and early twentieth centuries that both authors reproduce.

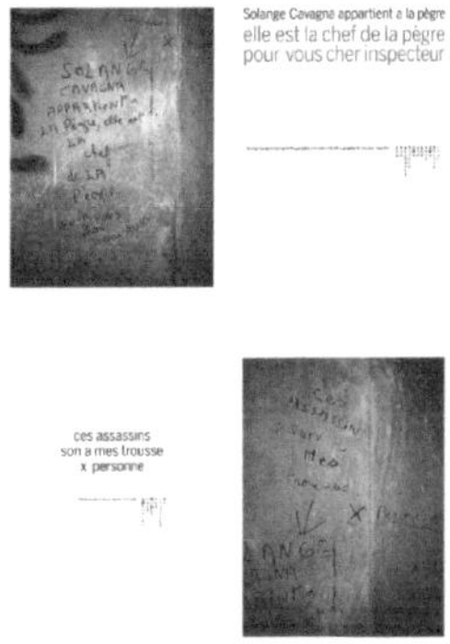

8 Jean-Luc Moulène, *Le Tunnel*, 2007, four-colour newspaper, 36 pages. 32 × 23.5 cm, 50,000 copies. Two double spreads.

In all cases the anonymity of the photographer is a necessity for the institution, and the archives comprised of such uniform documents are the extension of its invisible power. The document, in other words, can only bear authority if it is anonymous in its constitution.

Another form of anonymity can be encountered in slogans hastily painted or drawn on walls in urban public spaces. Such graffiti are the subject of a work by Jean-Luc Moulène from 2005, entitled *Le Tunnel* (*The Tunnel*). It consists of a series of photographs of anonymous messages scrawled on the wall of a covered passageway in Paris, juxtaposed with typographic transcriptions of the messages.[8] The photographs were recorded at several intervals between 1998 and 2001, and the photographs and transcriptions were published as a book in 2005 and as a printed supplement in newspaper format in 2007. The pictures of the graffiti evoke all at once ethnographic and sociological fieldwork, but also, in a more sinister way, police records serving to register the defacing of public property. The second part of the work renders such proximities more complex. The artist transcribed the messages, most of them violent menaces, in typographic characters. Rather than correcting the wild syntax and spelling of the messages, the typographic text is contaminated by the slang. In its text and photo structure, documenting a limited urban space, *The Tunnel* is reminiscent of Martha Rosler's *The Bowery in Two Inadequate Descriptive Systems* (1974–75).[9] Rosler's photo and text piece consists of black and white photographs of storefronts littered with empty bottles and cigarette butts, alternating with blank cards – unprinted photo paper – that carry typed words describing the vagrant population of the Bowery that is absent from the photographs. The piece addresses what Rosler perceived as the incompetence of words and images to represent the poverty of the Bowery. It clearly shows her objections to the strand of reformist documentary photography she calls 'victim photography'.[10]

But here, rather than feeding on the inability of photography and text to do justice to a social reality, Jean-Luc Moulène stages what Alexandre Costanzo

9 Martha Rosler, *The Bowery in Two Inadequate Descriptive Systems*, 1974, 45 black and white photographs mounted on 24 black panels, each print 20.3 × 25.4 cm, details.

10 See Martha Rosler's essay 'In, Around, and Afterthoughts (On Documentary Photography)', *Decoys and Disruptions: Selected Writings 1975–2001*, Cambridge MA. and London, MIT Press, 2004, pp. 151–206.

and Daniel Costanzo call the 'power of the anonymous'.[11] The authority of language is demoted as the straight photographs let the unruly, violent language permeate and ultimately overcome the strictures of language. The credit line suggests as much. It reads: 'Le tunnel est anonyme. [...] Les documents du tunnel, sis boulevard de Bercy à Paris, pris en 1996, puis les 8 septembre 1998, 31 mai 1999, 4 mai 2000 et le 3 mars 2001 sont de Jean-Luc Moulène.' ('The tunnel is anonymous. [...] The documents of the tunnel, located boulevard de Bercy in Paris, taken in 1996, then on 8 September 1998, 31 May 2000 and on 3 March 2001 are by Jean-Luc Moulène.') That the tunnel would remain anonymous is the proof of the failure of photography to act here as a police auxiliary. The identity of the perpetrators remains unknown, and anonymity is displaced from state authority to the street.

11 Alexandre Costanzo & Daniel Costanzo, 'La Puissance de l'anonyme', *(Des)générations*, issue 14, September 2011.

What remains then in question is the role of the artist. What does it mean for an artist to be the author of documents, as the credit line of *The Tunnel* states? John Tagg formulates the problem in the *Burden of Representation*. Surveying the decades following the invention of photography, he argues that the photography industry was 'divided between the domain of artistic property, whose privilege, resting on copyright protection, was a function of its lack of power, and the scientific-technical domain, whose power was a function of its renunciation of privilege'.[12] In other words, he posits a clear-cut separation between the renunciation of power by individual authors and anonymous photography used as an instrument to exert power.

In authoring the 'documents' of *The Tunnel*, Jean-Luc Moulène messes up the neat opposition conceived by John Tagg. The artist manifests an interest in analysing the manifestations of authority in photography and developing a practice that questions these manifestations by developing a dialectical relation between authorship and anonymity.

This has been Moulène's recurring interest. In a book published in 2007 alongside a monographic exhibition of his work at Culturgest in Lisbon, reproductions of the artist's drawings, objects and photographs are combined with documents from American and French archives showing prison inmates and arrested alleged prostitutes posing with name plates, a series of photographs that had given rise to legal battles, and a series of nineteenth-century pornographic photographs in which women's sexes are visible while their faces are concealed.[13] The artist's own pictures are in dialogue with these found images. In the series *Les Filles d'Amsterdam* (*The Prostitutes of Amsterdam*), Dutch sex workers pose naked with their legs apart and their face towards the camera, combining in a disturbing way

12 John Tagg, *The Burden of Representation*, p. 63.

13 Jean-Luc Moulène, *Opus 1995–2007 / Documents 1999–2007* (exhib. cat.), Lisbon, Culturgest, 2007.

the poses of the faceless porn photographs and police identity portraits, thus subverting both conventions. In *Après la Loi (After the Law)*, Jean-Luc Moulène asked a woman to pose in a photo booth to make a portrait that followed the then newly passed legislation concerning identity photographs.[14] This kind of work takes after that of Michel Journiac, one of the principal figures of the French body art scene in the 1970s, for whom Moulène at one time worked as an assistant.[15] Producing objects, installations and performances, Journiac used photography not only to document live performances but as an integral part of his work. He developed a specific vocabulary indicating the status of each category of photographic work. Next to the term *actions photographiques* used for performances that were specifically done to be recorded on camera, he frequently used the phrase *constat d'action* (certified report of an action). This terminology endowed the data collected from a performance with the official value of a certificate or an affidavit. In *Hommage à Freud – constat critique d'une mythologie travestie* (*Homage to Freud, Critical Report on a Travestied Mythology*, 1972), Journiac took up the format of identity photos. Dressing up successively as his mother and father and pairing the resulting images with portraits of his mother and father, the artist disrupted the exactitude of identity photographs commonly used in official

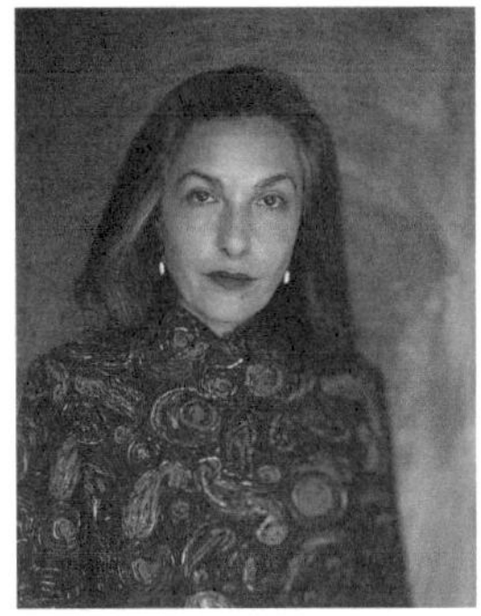

14 Jean-Luc Moulène, *Après la Loi, 16 avril 1990, 'Photomaton'*, Cibachrome print, mounted on aluminium, framed, 49 × 41 cm.

15 Moulène recollects his relation with Michel Journiac in 'Histoire de l'image de Darek: témoignage de Jean-Luc Moulène', in Vincent Labaume (ed.), *Michel Journiac* (exhib. cat.), Paris and Strasbourg, École nationale supérieure des beaux-arts, Les Musées de Strasbourg, 2004, p. 166.

documents thanks to the inexact likenesses in each of the pairs, which in turn suggested complex issues of family relations.[16] There is a clear continuity between a work such as *Homage to Freud* and Moulène's own *After the Law* or *Personne,* but in these images as in his vocabulary of *constats d'action* Journiac appears less to question the formal construction of photographic evidence than to upturn it, to turn the coercive power of the police inside out, by appropriating it for his own work. Moulène's practice certainly finds its roots in the identity politics of Journiac, yet his interest goes further. He addresses the way visual conventions of documentary evidence are developed in photography and imposed as generic and innocuous. Looking back at his formative years in an interview with Briony Fer, Moulène underlined the importance but also the limitations of photography in the context of performance art: 'all [the artists] were using photography as evidence. That's where I took up the work.'[17]

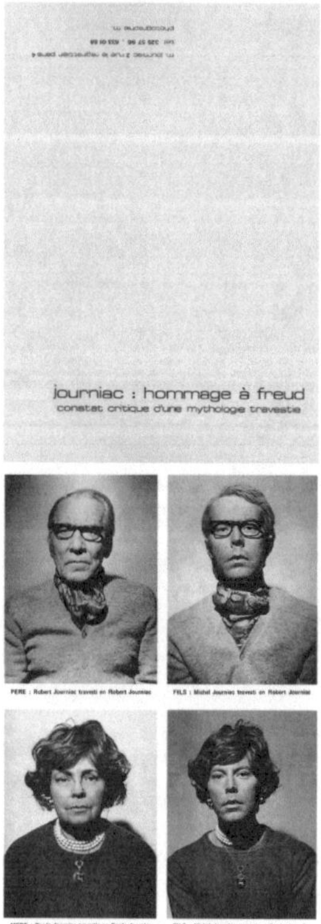

16 Michel Journiac, *Hommage à Freud: constat critique d'une mythologie travestie* (1972), posted image, recto verso, 29.7 × 21 cm.

17 'Each Any: Interview with Jean-Luc Moulène, Paris, October 2008', in Jean-Pierre Criqui (ed.), *Jean-Luc Moulène* (exhib. cat.), Nîmes and Cologne, Éditions du Carré d'Art and Verlag der Buchhandlung Walther König, 2008, p. 135.

Impersonal Diaries

Bus 69 has come to a halt on the rue Saint-Antoine, near the Bastille, on its route between the Eiffel Tower's Champ de Mars and Père Lachaise cemetery. People have stepped in and out. The bus is about to resume its journey and steers away from the curb. At that instant the photographer catches the glance of a girl sitting on the bus, staring out into the street. He takes a picture. Immediately afterward she will respond furiously to his action, cursing, perhaps even banging onto the Triplex glass of the window-pane. There is no sign of this, however, in the image we are looking at. At most we discern a probing or puzzled look on the young woman's face at the moment she turned slightly and noticed the photographer from the corner of her eye. At first view, Moulène's *Père Lachaise – Bastille (Paris, 15 septembre 1998)* looks like an example of street photography.[18] It presents the photographer as an image seeker, out to capture fragments of life on the streets of a large city. This kind of photography results from a split-second decision that its author makes, noticing something out of the ordinary, perhaps just out of curiosity. 'To see what something would look like once it has been photographed': that is how Garry Winogrand tersely put it, in an often-quoted formula that did much to assign an indelible mark of carefree subjectivity to this particular kind of street photography.[19] But surely, this is what *Père Lachaise – Bastille* is about: 'lightning-fast shots' and similarly brief and anonymous urban encounters.[20] It is a modernist trope, in other words, replicated in countless texts and films, perhaps traceable as far back as

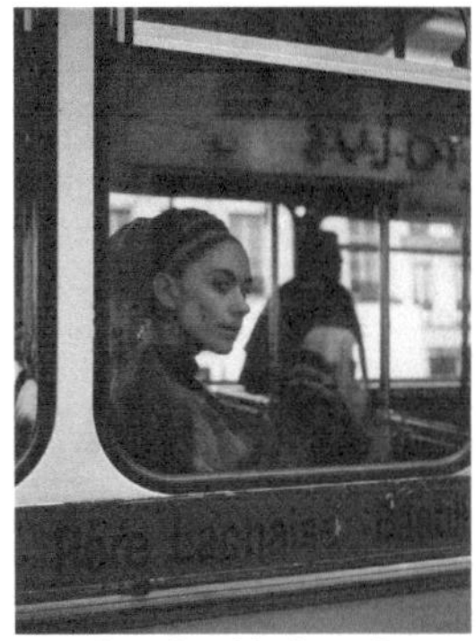

18 Jean-Luc Moulène, *Père Lachaise – Bastille,* Paris, 15 September 1998, Cibachrome print mounted on aluminium, 67 × 56 cm.

19 For a review and discussion of this much-quoted formula, see Barbaralee Diamonstein, 'An Interview with Garry Winogrand', in Barbaralee Diamonstein, *Visions and Images: American Photographers on Photography, Interviews with Photographers,* Rizzoli, New York, 1981. For a critical evaluation of the carefreeness of street photography, see Martha Rosler, 'Lee Friedlander, An Exemplary Modern Photographer', in Martha Rosler, *Decoys and Disruptions: Selected Writings 1975–2001,* Cambridge, MA, MIT Press, 2001, pp. 113–32.

20 Diamonstein, op. cit.

21 'The street about me roared with a deafening sound.
[...]
A lightning flash... then night! Fleeting beauty
By whose glance I was suddenly reborn.'
Charles Baudelaire, *Les Fleurs du Mal* (1861). English version: William Aggeler, *The Flowers of Evil,* Fresno, CA, Academy Library Guild, 1954.

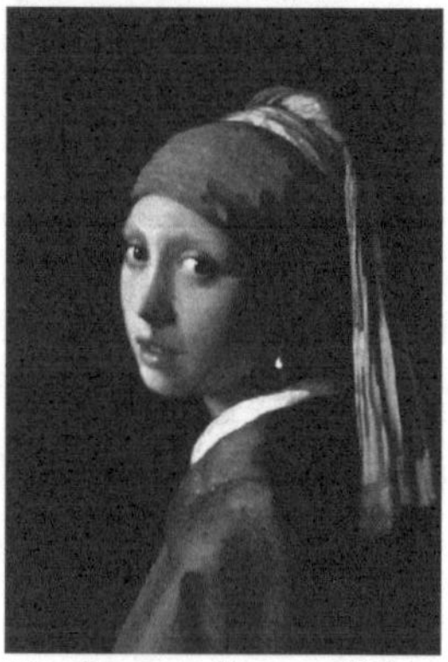

22 Johannes Vermeer, *Meisje met de parel,* around 1665, oil on canvas, 46.5 × 40 cm, The Hague, Mauritshuis.

23 'Will I see you no more before eternity?
Elsewhere, far, far from here! too late! never perhaps!
For I know not where you fled, you know not where I go,
O you whom I would have loved, O you who knew it!'

Charles Baudelaire's poem 'À une passante' ('To a Passerby'):

> La Rue assourdissante autour de moi hurlait
> [...]
> Un éclair... puis la nuit! – Fugitive beauté
> Dont le regard m'a fait soudainement renaître.[21]

For the poet, this brief sighting is to be followed by loss. For the photographer, it is accompanied by a second moment, one of recognition, as the woman's face, turning inquisitively towards him, briefly yet unmistakably brings to mind Vermeer's *Meisje met de parel* (*Girl with a Pearl Earring*) of about 1665.[22] Framed by the bus window, the three-quarter profile head with its anachronistic turban-like hairdo vividly becomes a delayed mirror image of the painting. At the end of Baudelaire's poem, the disappearance of the woman is evoked in a flurry of abandoned possibilities. The insolvability of the situation is signified by the clatter of tenses:

> Ne te verrai-je plus que dans l'éternité?
> Ailleurs, bien loin d'ici! trop tard! jamais
>   peut-être!
> Car j'ignore où tu fuis, tu ne sais où je vais,
> Ô toi que j'eusse aimée, ô toi qui le savais![23]

In the photograph, by contrast, a comparable clash of temporalities is a sign that the picture lives on.

Walter Benjamin pointed out this quality of the photographic image in his 'Short History of Photography', noting that 'the real has seared the image' and inviting the viewer to 'find in a photograph that inconspicuous spot where in the immediacy of that long-forgotten moment the future subsists so eloquently that we, looking back, may rediscover it'.[24] The juxtaposition of tenses, so similar to the combination of present, past and pluperfect subjunctive in Baudelaire's poem, allows Benjamin to introduce at this moment the position of the viewer. It is the viewer who, finding that 'inconspicuous spot' in the image, will rediscover that 'long-forgotten moment' in which the future can be discerned. But what exactly is this moment? Is it the sudden exchange of glances or is it the moment when the similarity with the Vermeer painting becomes evident? Is it a matter of encounter or of recognition? And if it is the latter, when did it occur? Was it at the moment the artist took the photograph or later, when he selected it to be part of his corpus of works, to be published in a book and shown in an exhibition? Or perhaps even later, when it appears in the eye of the beholder? Moulène's *Père Lachaise – Bastille* gives no preference to either of these possibilities; it sways between them all. The impression of transience, conveyed so effectively in the diagonal lines of the picture, the sideways glance and even the

24 Walter Benjamin, 'A Small History of Photography', in Susan Sontag (ed.), *One-Way Street and Other Writings*, London, Verso, 1979, p. 243.

25 Roland Barthes, *Camera Lucida* (1980), London, Vintage Classics, 1993.

literal inclusion of a vehicle, is simultaneously halted, replaced by a mental image of a masterpiece of seventeenth-century painting that superimposes itself onto the photograph. Here photography takes centre stage. In associating within a single image the apparently irreconcilable forms of subjective snapshot and visual icon, *Père Lachaise – Bastille* functions as what Moulène has called a 'theoretical act': it becomes a paradigm of photography conceived as simultaneous discovery and recognition, where the first term signals the personal moment of the encounter, the second the more distant, impersonal moment of identification of the picture as the Vermeer. This impersonality, the fact that the identification is collective rather than individual and idiosyncratic, is what distinguishes this approach to the photograph from, for instance, Roland Barthes' 'punctum', which identifies a personal reaction to a detail identified in an image that touches or disturbs the viewer and gives it a particular meaning.[25]

The dual quality of a photograph like *Père Lachaise – Bastille* is in reality already signalled in the contradictory title of the series to which it belongs: *Journal impersonnel* (*Impersonal Diary*). This consists of an open-ended sequence of pictures made since the 1990s, all precisely dated and located. Their variety of subject matter is bound together by the idea of a diary: a day-to-day record of things and people observed on the streets of various cities, in rural settings, both indoors and outdoors. Yet the idea of a diary, usually confined to the private and the personal – even if it implicitly acknowledges the possibility of being made public[26] – is here qualified by the adjective 'impersonal'. This puts us in mind of a paradigm of photography conceived as discovery and recognition. Practiced in this way, photography stages an encounter between the impersonal and familiar on the one hand, and the private on the other. The two terms of the encounter are thus encapsulated in the phrase 'impersonal diary'.[27] In Moulène's work, the 'Impersonal diary' becomes a kind of document, governed by the dialectic of private and public, known and unknown, which is brought about by the photographic paradigm of discovery and recognition. Perusing the series in different publications on the artist, the movement of discovery and recognition can be seen to recur from one image to the other. In *Cathédrale* (*Cathedral*, Cologne, 16 March 2002) Moulène has approached the building from the right side of the square, raising his camera as he approaches it; he captures the façade in a slight oblique tilting of the camera that admits a slim inverted triangle of sky in the top right. Again, however, as in *Père Lachaise – Bastille*, the impression of a furtive gesture contrasts with the fact that the close-up, the particular framing

26 See Arlette Farge, *Le goût de l'archive*, Paris, Seuil, 1989, p. 6.

27 In the classification of Moulène's works in a 2007 exhibition catalogue, the words 'Impersonal Diary' follow the term 'Document'. Jean-Luc Moulène, *Opus 1995–2007 / documents 1999–2007* (exhib. cat.), Lisbon, Culturgest, 2007.

and even the various shades of grey-blue that cover in small strokes the façade, bring a painting to mind, in this case Claude Monet's serialised depictions of the cathedral of Rouen, repeatedly painted between 1892 and 1894 so as to reflect different weather conditions. Elsewhere in *Impersonal Diary*, a photograph entitled *Chef* (*Chief*, Paris, 11 April 1998) shows a man in shirt and tie fixing an empty supermarket shelf.[28] Is it the shop manager who has taken over this menial task, removing his jacket to get down and dirty in a display of macho authority only betrayed by the feminine *contrapposto* that echoes countless mannerist and baroque depictions of Venus?[29] Such images and others function on a principle of transposition, transformation and displacement from one image to another. For the viewer, these visual strategies turn otherwise silent, complex images into an inter-subjective experience – or perhaps the illusion of such an experience – between artist and viewer, for which 'Impersonal diary' serves as catchword.

The idea of the impersonal may also have other connections. It recalls for example Claes Oldenburg's reply to a journalist who questioned him about his habit, in his early practice, of quoting or referencing the work of other artists, such as Jean Dubuffet: 'It's true that every artist has a discipline of impersonality to enable him to become an artist

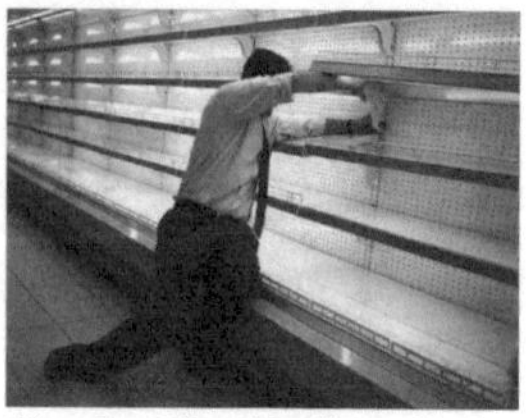

28 Jean-Luc Moulène, *Chef*, Paris, 11 April 1998, Chromogenic print mounted on aluminium, 160 × 210 cm.

29 I am thinking here specifically of Bronzino's *Allegory with Venus and Cupid*, of about 1545. On *contrapposto* in another of Moulène's photographs, *Môme-Bastille (Paris, 1990)*, see Vincent Labaume, 'Neutral Love', in Moulène, *Opus 1995–2007 / documents 1999–2007* (exhib. cat.), Lisbon, Culturgest, 2007, p. 139.

in the first place.'[30] For Oldenburg, impersonality, reflected in forms of citation, is a technique of self-education, not unlike the traditional educational process of copying the old masters. Moulène's impersonal diary, however, suggests a reversal of Oldenburg's 'discipline of impersonality': it is no longer an educational process but rather the result of an internalised visual culture that re-emerges in order to be shared via the 'impersonal' records that form his 'diary'.

Surrealist and surrealism-related images are frequently encountered in *Impersonal Diary. Viande/Os* (*Meat/Bone,* Barneville, 16 February 2001) displaces the still lives that Wols photographed in the 1930s, which combined, in heterogeneous and partly abstract compositions, rough cuts of raw meat with everyday objects. Wols enhanced the visual strangeness of these textures by removing the food from its habitual culinary contexts – 'they are neither hunting trophies nor steaks', writes art historian Christine Mehring describing them.[31] Moulène's photograph, by contrast, shows a neatly cut frozen steak that suggests an entirely different, if still sinister relation to food production and consumption.

A picture of the Seine, as dirty and muddy as a roadside gutter, *La Seine à Paris* (*The Seine in Paris,* 3 October 2010), reverses the effect achieved by André Kertész in a 1929 close-up view of a gutter

30 Quoted in Bruce Glaser, 'Oldenburg, Liechtenstein, Warhol: A Discussion', *Artforum,* 4, no. 6, February 1966, pp. 20–24. On Oldenburg's referencing of Jean Dubuffet see my article 'Paris Circus New York Junk: Jean Dubuffet and Claes Oldenburg, 1959–1962', *Art History,* 29, no. 1, 2006, pp. 79–107.

31 Christine Mehring, *Wols Photographs* (exhib. cat.), Cambridge MA., Busch-Reisinger Museum, Harvard University Art Museums, 1999, p. 23.

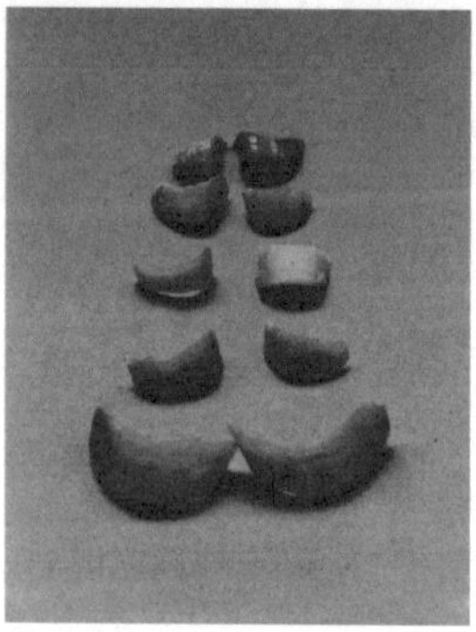

32 Jean-Luc Moulène, *Ongles*, Paris, 5 November 1999, Cibachrome print, Diasec, mounted on aluminium, 64.5 × 52.5 cm.

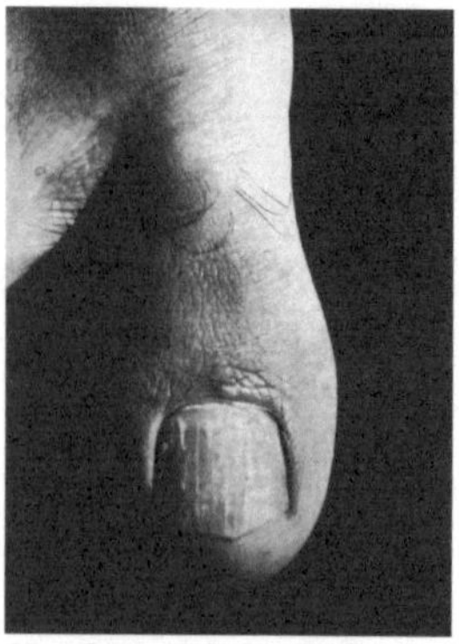

33 Jacques-André Boiffard, *Gros orteil, sujet masculin, 30 ans* (*Big Toe, male subject, 30 years old*), published in the context of Georges Bataille, 'Le Gros orteil' ('The Big Toe'), *Documents*, no. 6, November 1929. Reprinted in *Documents*, re-edition, Paris, Jean-Michel Place, 1991, p. 299.

that is surreptitiously transformed into a river: *Sans titre (Caniveau)*, (*Untitled (Gutter)*, 1929). Moulène's *Ongles* (*Nails*, Paris, 5 November 1999) presents a row of cut fingernails on a medium blue paper background.[32] The nail shreds are aligned not in a row, but turned around and stacked vertically in a column from small to large. The unusual disposition creates a strange anthropomorphism in which they become ribs forming a thorax. The displacement here is double: from nails to chest and from Moulène's image to Jacques-André Boiffard's photographs of toes commissioned by Georges Bataille and published in the journal *Documents* in 1929. Emerging from a dense black ground and isolated from the other toes, Boiffard's *Gros orteil* (*Big Toe*) confronted the reader in full page, 'face to face', creating a disturbing sense of anthropomorphism that Moulène displaces, triggering a similar sense of unease.[33] In *Donostia/San Sebastian* (2000), a tub of meat being dragged with a butcher's hook along a sidewalk reveals heads of animals in the left foreground that counterbalance the cut-off heads of the figures in the right foreground. Again, something of the anthropomorphism of surrealism is at work here. The photograph is reminiscent of Eli Lotar's famous views of the slaughterhouse of La Villette, in the north of Paris, published in 1930 in *Documents* to accompany the entry 'Abattoir' ('Slaughterhouse') in

Georges Bataille's 'dictionary' section of the journal.[34] Moulène's photograph is at odds with the dimension of sacrifice and ritual with which Eli Lotar's images became imbued thanks to Bataille's text. It provides a glimpse of the rationalised channels of food production and distribution. Yet something disturbing remains, triggered by the visual pun of heads lost and found. Although Moulène has an extensive knowledge of the history of art, the history of photography and surrealist photography in particular, his photographs rarely cite or re-enact existing images directly. Instead, they rework and displace some of the mechanisms that recur in surrealist compositions.

Moulène's interest in surrealism did not come out of the blue. That a number of his images from *Impersonal Diary* can be related to photographs that appeared in surrealist or affiliated journals testifies to his particular affinity with this format as a medium for the circulation of photographs. His own offprint newspapers, such as *Personne*, *Le Monde*, *Le Louvre* (2005) and *Le Tunnel*, take up the legacy of surrealist journals such as *La Révolution surréaliste* and *Documents*. Moulène's use of production processes, layout and printers similar or at times identical to those used to produce mainstream newspapers echoes the allusions to the non-artistic press in the surrealist journals.[35] As Dawn Ades pointed out

34 Eli Lotar, '*Aux abattoirs de la Villette*', three photographs published in the context of Georges Bataille, 'Abattoir', *Documents*, no. 6, November 1929, Reprinted in *Documents*, re-edition, Paris, Jean-Michel Place, 1991, pp. 328, 330.

35 For most of these publications, Moulène worked closely with the graphic designer Marc Touitou, who was responsible, among other projects, for renewing the layout of the French centre-left newspaper *Le Monde* in 2005–06.

in 1978, the layout of *La Révolution surréaliste* was a pastiche of the popular scientific magazine *La Nature*.[36] But what appears more striking when leafing through *La Nature*[37] is the similitude between some of the photographs and captions that appeared in its pages and the photographs in the surrealist journals. [38] These journals were the most important context of publication for a certain type of banal, documentary-like photographs, photographs that in the past decades have come to be recognised as an essential part of the canon of surrealism.[39] The purpose of *La Nature* was to report to a wide audience, scientific discoveries and their technical applications; it covered a diverse range of topics, from innovative American milking machines to the art of ship decoration.[40] Its reports on experimentations and new technologies are accompanied by a large number of photographs and technical diagrams. Some of these images, by their incongruity and their cryptic relation to the caption that accompanies them, seem very close to photographs that made their way into the pages of *La Révolution surréaliste* (1924–1929) and later in *Documents* (1929–1930).[41] The diversity of areas addressed in *Documents*, which included numismatics, archaeology and anthropology, seems at times to mirror *La nature's* curious juxtaposition of subjects within individual issues.[42] It exemplified the strong 'anti-aesthetic' stance taken by its main editor,

36 Dawn Ades, exhibition and catalogue *Dada and Surrealism Reviewed*, London, Hayward Gallery, South Bank Centre, 1978.

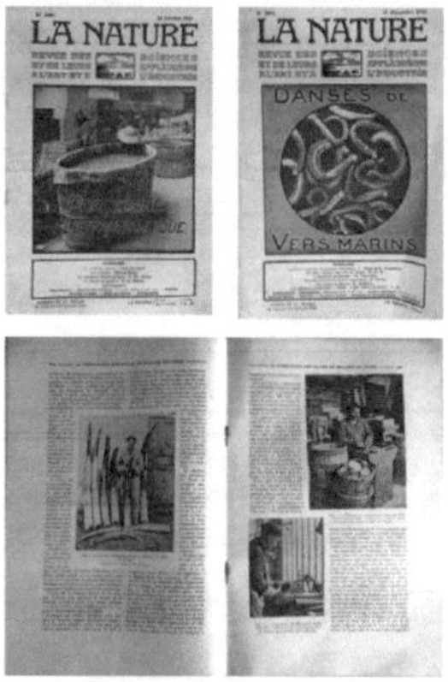

37 Cover pages and double spread of *La Nature*.

38 The complete collection of *La Nature*, published between 1873 and 1962, has been digitalized by the Conservatoire national des arts et métiers (Cnam) and can be consulted at <cnum.cnam.fr/fSER/4KY28.html>. Last retrieved 16 March 16, 2012.

39 The use of visual material in *Documents* is extensively analysed by Georges Didi-Huberman in *La Ressemblance informe*, Paris, Macula, 2006. An informative source and survey of the material is found in Dawn Ades and Simon Baker's *Undercover Surrealism: Georges Bataille and Documents* (exhib. cat.), London, Hayward Gallery, 2006. Ian Walker's *City Gorged with Dreams: Surrealism and Documentary Photography in Interwar Paris*, Manchester, Manchester University Press, 2002, is the only study devoted as a whole to the corpus of documentary-like photography published in and around surrealism.

40 *La Nature*, issue 2570, July 1923, and issue 2792, September 1928.

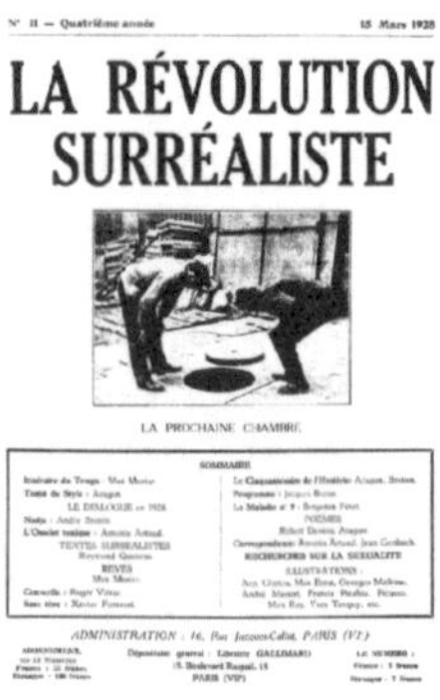

41 *La Révolution surréaliste*, cover page issue 11, 15 March 1928.

42 Concerning the general positioning of *Documents* and its intellectual project, see Denis Hollier's seminal introduction to the reprint of the journal: 'La Valeur d'usage de l'impossible', in *Documents*, Paris, Jean-Michel Place, 1989.

Georges Bataille. As for *La Révolution surréaliste,* art historians have noted that the cover of the first issue carried group portraits of the surrealists in postures similar to those of scientists solemnly conducting experiments that appeared in *La Nature.* Throughout its five years of existence, the surrealist journal continuously appropriated and reworked scientific documentation, press photography, police portraits and other types of photographic documents used for scientific, judiciary and press.[43] But in adopting the visual language of scientific positivism and its conventional rules of composition, surrealist photography displaced these images. Some were parodies, others, like Boiffard's disturbing photographs for *Documents,* exceeded their documentary function. Others still had the quality of found images lacking a logical connection to the context in which they were presented.

In reprising or displacing surrealist images that themselves stemmed from a critical reading of established genres and photographic conventions, Jean-Luc Moulène, perhaps paradoxically, endows surrealist photographs with a documentary legitimacy. His repeated indirect references to surrealism create a corpus of images identifiable for their particular subject matters, compositions and camera angles. In short, they make up an identifiable visual style that contrasts with the more established styles of

43 On the mock scientific group portraits in *La révolution surréaliste,* notably the one on the cover of the first issue in December 1924, see David Bate, *Photography and Surrealism: Sexuality, Colonialism and Social Dissent,* London, I.B. Tauris, 2004, chapter 1.

44 Olivier Lugon, *Le Style documentaire d'August Sander à Walker Evans 1920–1945*, Paris, Macula, 2001.

documentary photography from which surrealism has traditionally been excluded.[44] In the images of *Impersonal Diary*, Moulène identifies and continues a photographic tradition that includes images by Boiffard, Lotar, Wols and others as a visual alternative to other canonical traditions of photography, represented by such figures as Walker Evans and August Sander and their enduring legacy in contemporary art. Moulène's photographs engage with the histories of photography not to decode the meaning of these histories or their individual meaning but to understand the function of images rather than their meaning. In doing so he behaves like Bataille, who ascribed to his *Dictionnaire critique* the task of defining the function rather than the meaning of words.

Objets de grève

Objets de grève (*Strike Objects*) is a series of photographs of objects produced by factory workers during social conflicts. Its genesis dates back to the late 1980s when the artist purchased a copy of the Paris edition of the *International Herald Tribune* published on 7 June 1987, an issue in which all the illustrations had been blanked out as a result of a strike led by the photo-engravers. In the following years, Moulène set out to research and collect other such idiosyncratic items produced by workers taking hold of production facilities in order to promote their cause or financially support themselves during strikes. The objects that he found, such as cigarette packs, clothing items and train tickets, emanate from a wide range of manufacturing industries. A recurrent tactic used by workers is to replace the standard information printed on these objects by resistance slogans: a frying pan from the Tefal manufacturer is inscribed with the words 'liberté – justice – emploi – solidarité' on its base; a Lip watch is engraved with the words 'Conflit Lip 17.4.73 – 29.1.1974 – Vente sauvage' ('The Lip conflict of 17 April 1973 to 29 January 1974 – open sale'); and a pack of Gauloise cigarettes reads 'Dégustation / vente interdite / 20 cigarettes fabriquées par les travailleurs en lutte' (Pantinoises) ('Tasting sample / sale prohibited / 20 cigarettes manufactured by workers involved in a conflict').[45] Many items, like the Gauloise cigarette packs manufactured in red instead of the trademark blue, and a Nina Ricci dress with a blood-coloured hem, are altered in colour, adopting the shade of the most prominent French workers' unions, Confédération Générale du Travail (CGT) and Force Ouvrière (FO).[46] Mainly produced during the 1970s and 1980s at the peak of the crisis of the manufacturing industries in France, these objects are one-offs, fabricated in small series that disrupt the normal

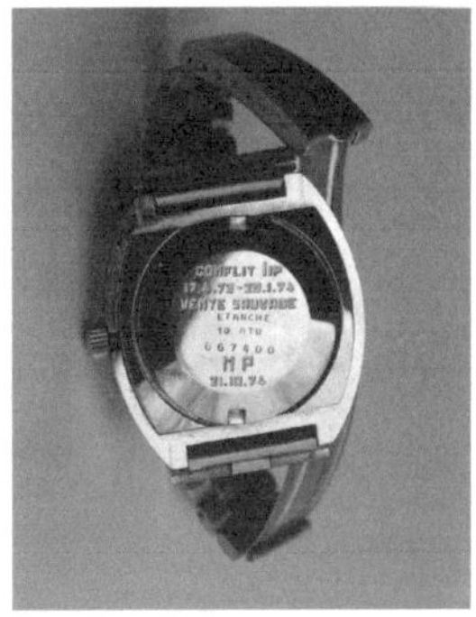

45 Jean-Luc Moulène, *39 objets de grève presentés par Jean-Luc Moulène/Lip, Souvenir 1er conflit* (Lip, Souvenir of 1st Conflict), Paris, 1999–2000. Cibachrome print, Diasec, mounted on Forex, 47 × 36 cm.

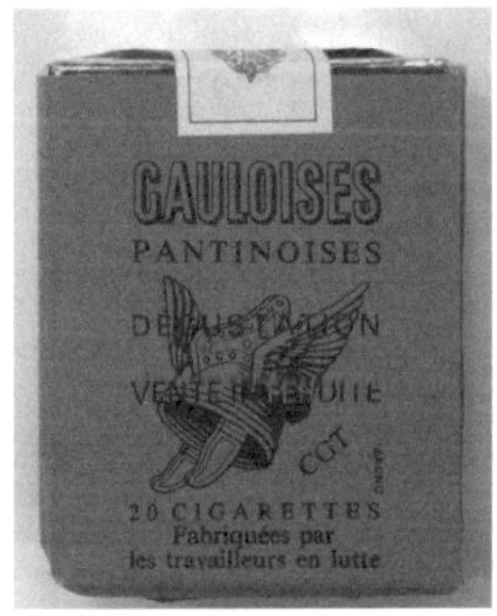

46 Jean-Luc Moulène, *39 objets de grève presentés par Jean-Luc Moulène/La Pantinoise*, Paris, 1999–2000, Cibachrome print, Diasec, mounted on Forex, 47 × 36 cm.

47 'Vingt-quatre objets de grève présentés par Jean-Luc Moulène', La Galerie, Noisy-le-Sec, 20 May – 13 July 1999.

process of commercial production. Workers replace the usual mass circulation network of these objects (or in the case of Nina Ricci a characteristically restricted circuit) by a local one. They alter the standard rules of commercial exchange – in some cases, the products are distributed freely – thereby creating a micro-economy that counters the large-scale capitalist exchange system. Little known beyond the local areas where the strikes took place and the objects have circulated, these productions were given visibility by the artist. As a first result of his research he presented in 1999 a series of twenty-four photographs entitled *Vingt-quatre objets de grève présentés par Jean-Luc Moulène.*[47] The collection grew to forty-one in 2001. Two series of images – *Seize objets de grève présentés par Jean-Luc Moulène* and *Vingt-quatre objets de grève présentés par Jean-Luc Moulène* – were acquired in 2003 by the Musée National d'Art Moderne – Centre Georges Pompidou. The same year, the artist donated the objects he had collected to the Archives nationales du monde du travail in Roubaix, where they can be consulted as the 'Fonds Jean-Luc Moulène' (reference 2003 025 004). In appearance, this division between what constitutes the work and what its source is, is exempt of ambiguities of authorship. There is no question here of appropriation or even of turning an archive into a work of art; the objects belong to an official archive and the art works have entered a museum institution.[48]

Yet the titles chosen each time by the artist, as well as the photographs themselves, shake these certainties. The phrase 'Presented by' contained in the title evokes protocols in medicine and the social sciences in which cases are 'presented' by scientists to their peers in order to construct them as objects of study. Such a presentation speaks of scientific impartiality; the use of the phrase by Moulène suggests that he approached his subject with a comparable goal of detachment and neutrality. The Michel Foucault of *Moi, Pierre Rivière, ayant égorgé ma mère, ma sœur et mon frère* (*I Pierre Rivière having slaughtered my mother, my sister, and my brother: A Case of Parricide in the Nineteenth Century*) comes to mind here. In his preface to the presentation of this famous case of nineteenth-century parricide, Foucault carefully placed himself at a remove: 'Nous avons décidé de ne pas l'interpréter', he explained, justifying the verbatim reproduction of the extraordinary autobiographical account of the murderer with the wish to let the document speak for itself, outside the narrowing boundaries of scholarly categories: 'Nous lui aurions alors imposé ce rapport de force dont nous voulions montrer l'effet de réduction' ('We would in that case have imposed certain power relations the reductive quality of which we wanted to

48 Detailed captions by Viviane de Tapia, explaining the specific context of each object, now accompany the presentation and publication of the series.

show').[49] Moulène similarly endows photography with the mission of *presenting* objects rather than *interpreting* them. His title emphasises the evidential quality of the photographs, their status as two-dimensional visual records. The documentary quality of the artist's photographs was underscored when the photographs were used, in 2003, as illustrations for an anthropological study of the strike-related objects within the context of twentieth-century labour history. Analysing them as manifestations of the self-representation of workers on strike and pointing out their archival value within the industrial heritage, the author of the article carefully described the objects rather than the photographs that represented them.[50]

The suggestion that the photographs are less important than the objects they depict gets stronger when we translate the phrase 'presenté par' as 'offered to' and consider the archive as its aim. In that case, the photographs of the objects become the traces of items deposited and later donated to the Archives nationales du monde du travail. Yet, as in *Personne*, this semantic ambiguity is paradoxical. In depositing or donating the 'Objets de grève' to these archives, the artist renders them socially, politically and historically visible in a context that had previously ignored them. He initiates historical and scholarly recognition of specific idiosyncratic productions.

49 See Michel Foucault, *Moi, Pierre Rivière, ayant égorgé ma mère, ma sœur et mon frère*, Paris, Gallimard, 1973, p. 19.

50 Jean-Charles Leyris, 'Objets de greve, un patrimoine militant', *In situ*, issue 8, 2003. Available online at <www.insitu.culture.fr/article.xsp?numero=8&id_article=leyris-0/>. Last retrieved 1 May 2012. The author does mention the multiple identities of the photographs as documents and works of art, but he does not go on to conduct an anthropological study of the photographs themselves.

At the same time, however, he effectively removes them from circulation, letting the photographs remain as the sole visible trace of the objects. It is the photographs rather than the objects that circulate; that are used as illustrations in a scholarly article; that are reprinted in books and presented in exhibitions.

The strong visual quality of the photographs accentuates their prominent position in this process. Moulène tightly framed each object and photographed it individually against a neutral background in natural light. In exhibition displays these images, printed on glossy paper and mounted on aluminium, appear to hover at a slight distance from the wall. Rather than being presented as visual documentation on viewing tables or hanging on walls with detailed captions, the photographs are turned into objects themselves. Their object-like quality upsets the idea of documentation. As a consequence, the material items that have been collected and archived become the documentary source of the art work. This reversal is implicit in the title and clarifies it: the *Strike Objects* 'presented by Moulène' are not the objects themselves but the work of art bearing this title. Even the phrase 'objets de grève' is not a generally used term but one thought up by the artist.

Thierry de Duve considers acts of this kind – labelling and offering particular objects – to be a means by which artists present themselves to the

51 Thierry de Duve, *Voici, 100 ans d'art contemporain* (exhib. cat.), Brussels, Musée royal des beaux-arts and Ludion, 2000, pp. 13–55.

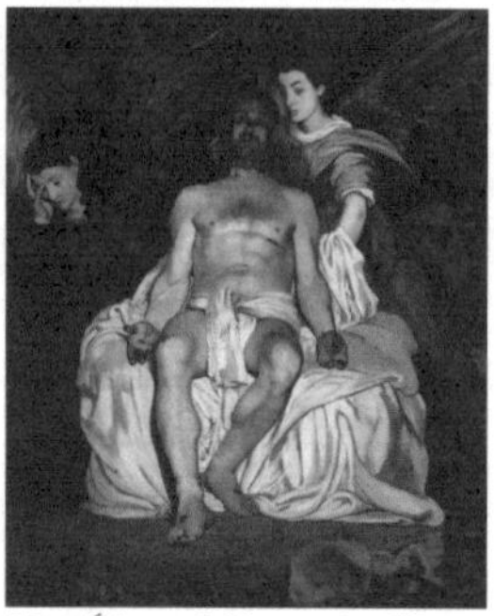

52 Édouard Manet, *Le Christ mort et les anges*, 1864, oil on canvas, 179.4 × 149.9 cm.

53 De Duve, *Voici, 100 ans d'art contemporain* p. 242, note 14.

54 The Confederation générale du travail, created in 1895, is one of the largest workers' unions in France.

public.[51] The history of such gestures begins, for him, with Manet's *Le Christ mort et les anges (The Dead Christ with Angels*, 1864), an arresting depiction of Christ at the moment of his resurrection, rising frontally with the support of two angels to face the viewer.[52] In 'presenting' the *Strike Objects* Moulène perhaps follows De Duve's genealogy, presenting himself as an artist to the public. In upturning the relationship between the photographs and the objects he does more, however, than claim attention for his own position. Firstly, he presents the *Strike Objects* to us as viewers; in creating these art works he provides a context for their reception, a context that includes its viewers, none other than 'we', 'us'. Secondly, in reversing the relationship between the photographs and the objects they reproduce, he underscores the instability of photography as a fine art medium and its dependence on specific contexts of reception. De Duve observes that 'we', like the pronoun 'personne', refers to anyone; it is a generic form of address.[53] 'We' are the museum viewers who discovered the *Strike Objects* at the Pompidou Centre after their acquisition in 2003, and for whom they were no doubt primarily an art work by Jean-Luc Moulène. But 'we' are also the union members who viewed those photographs as documents of historical objects when they were shown at the annual congress of the CGT in March 2003.[54]

Consistent with the confusion surrounding the objects and their photographic reproduction, like the objects themselves, 'we' are both at the same time.

'These Statues are Mute'

A pensive-looking execration figure from Ancient Egypt, a seventeenth-century ceramic Magdalene in ecstasy, a demure Aphrodite and the Babylonian Pazuzu raising his hand as if to say 'Beware!' or perhaps just to greet me are, along with twenty other precious objects are the protagonists of *Le Monde, Le Louvre,* a work by Moulène exhibited in the Louvre museum in November 2005.[55] It consists of twenty-four photographs, a newspaper supplement printed and distributed with the French newspaper *Le Monde* and a video, entitled *+ d'ordre, – d'ordre, Le Louvre (More Order, Less Order).*

Moving away from the history of labour examined in *Strike Objects* and the graffiti of *The Tunnel, Le Monde, le Louvre* examines a different kind of object: precious statuettes of divinities from different periods and places, all preserved in the collection of the Louvre. Here, the subject is a different kind of authoritative discourse: that of the museum and its rituals of conservation, its rules of classification and presentation.[56] Awoken from their slumber in the

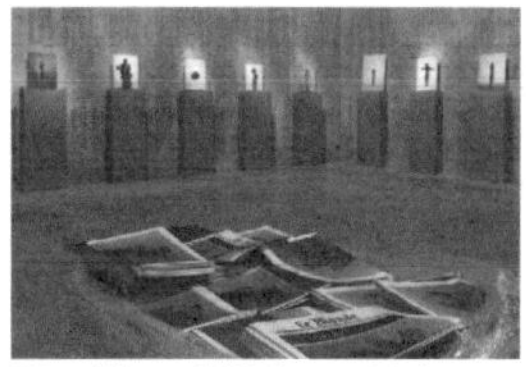

55 The exhibition, which resulted from a commission to the artist by the Louvre, ran from 1 December 2005 to 10 February 2006 in the Salle d'actualité du Louvre médiéval, aile Sully. Exhibition view.

56 On this 'spatialisation' of art history in the museum and in particular the way it can be recapitulated by walking through the museum, see Philip Fisher, *Making and Effacing Art: Modern American Art in a Culture of Museums,* Oxford and New York, Oxford University Press, 1991, p. 9.

museum's storage or removed from their glass display cases, the 24 small sculptures – mostly, but not exclusively, representing human figures – have been photographed individually, in natural light, against bare, neutrally coloured backgrounds, ranging from greyish-blue to light ochre.

These statuettes, which unquestionably belong to the French cultural heritage and reflect the history and policy of its foremost museum, have been grouped together by the artist. Usually overshadowed by larger masterpieces in museum displays or juxtaposed with others in vitrines, here for once they take centre stage. The artist's arbitrary selection of 24 objects – a gesture that likens him to a curator – moreover cuts through the collections of the museum and does away with its rigid divisions into departments and periods. It proposes an alternative narrative throughout the museum holdings. I can walk from a dancing Greek youth to a medieval Christ, compare a carved alabaster Babylonian goddess with a pre-dynastic Egyptian woman made of crocodile bone. The intervention of the artist upsets the hierarchy of the museum, its codes and rituals.

This space is given physical and psychological expression through another work in the November 2005 exhibition in the Louvre: the newspaper supplement entitled *Le Monde, Le Louvre* containing the same series of photographs.[57] The newspaper was available in the exhibition of November 2005, piled high on wooden palettes for visitors to take home; it was also distributed with the regular Île-de-France edition of *Le Monde* dated 30 November 2005. Circulated at 50,000 copies, *Le Monde, Le Louvre* brought to light the geopolitical background of Moulène's selection of objects.[58] The juxtaposed names of two pre-eminent French institutions present side-by-side two conceptions of the world. The world according to the Louvre begins with France in its middle and radiates outwards, expanding historically through cultural affinities, colonial histories and war. The world of *Le Monde* analyses and informs its readers about the world today seen from a centre-left perspective. Moving across these geopolitical mappings, Moulène's tour of the world in 24 images brings together different cults and civilisations, from France to Greece and from Egypt to Syria, and juxtaposes contrasting perspectives of ancient history and current affairs. In distributing his newspaper object so widely, the artist moreover addresses the extra-diegetic space of the museum conceived as an institution in which each object has a particular place and role within an organised narrative.

Le Louvre displaces the habitual role of photography within its walls. In the traditional order of this museum, photography belongs to the curatorial files;

57 Moulène has explained in an interview that the print version is the original format he had in mind when he made the photographs. Diserens, 'Entretien avec Jean-Luc Moulène', *Le Monde, Le Louvre*, Paris, 30 November 2005, p. IV.

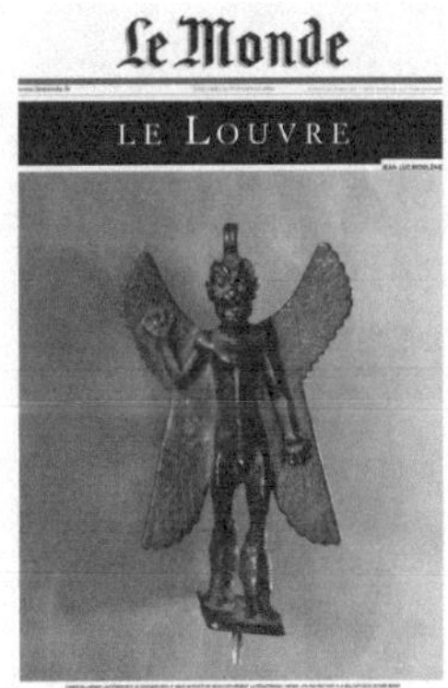
Le Monde
LE LOUVRE

58 Jean-Luc Moulène, *Le Monde, Le Louvre*, front page, 2005, four-colour printed newspaper, 47 × 32 cm, 50,000 copies.

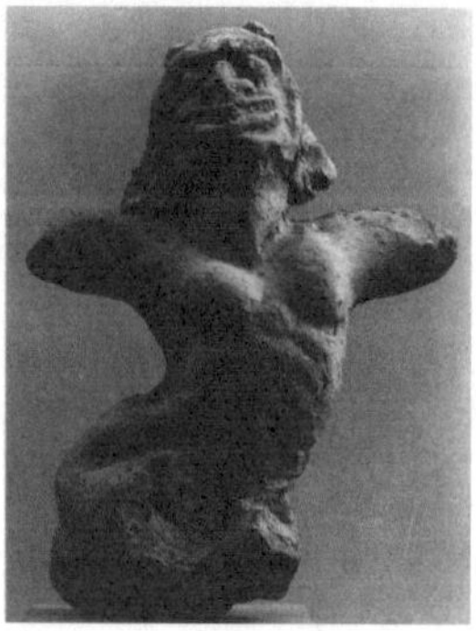

59 *Figure of a 'grotesque': a fit of hysteria or tetanus?* Roman Imperial era, terracotta figurine, height, 10.8 cm. The artist discusses this object in Corinne Diserens, 'Entretien avec Jean-Luc Moulène', *Le Monde, Le Louvre*, Paris, 30 November 2005, p. IV.

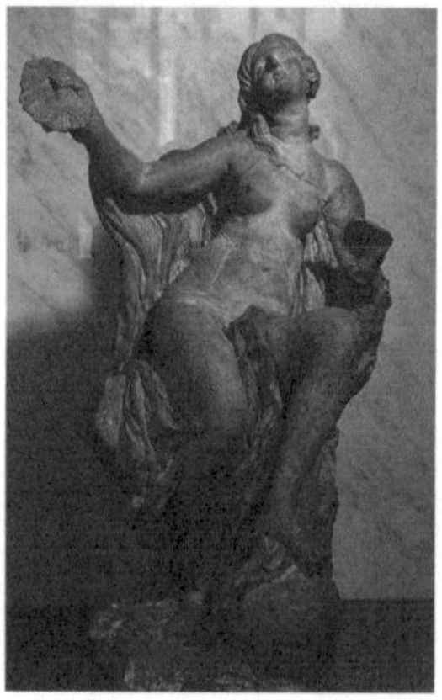

60 Gianlorenzo Bernini, *La verità*, c. 1645, terracotta, 53 × 36 × 36 cm.

the galleries are reserved for works of art. Photographs of the works in the collection, accompanied by written catalogue entries, are to be found in Atlas, the digital database of the museum. In photographing statuettes from the Louvre collections, Moulène not only displaces photography from the digital archive to the galleries; he also produces new images that expose the way in which the order of the museum is inscribed within its archival photographs.

The visual documentation in the Atlas database of *Sainte Madeleine en extase* (*Saint Magdalen in Ecstasy*) reveals how closely the archival image matches the sculpture's title. By presenting the statuette from the side, the black and white photographic document included in Atlas reproduction highlights the tension of her body directed towards the sky. Similarly, a terracotta figurine from Smyrna is tilted upwards and shot in low-angled illumination that accentuates its distorted smirk as well as the figure's twisted torso, quite fittingly for an object interpreted as representing a fit of hysteria or tetanus.[59] Bernini's model for his allegorical monument *La Verità svelata dal Tempo* (*Truth Unveiled by Time*, 1645–1652), is shot from below to bring out its main sculptural lines and against a background of white veined marble in anticipation of the planned monumental version now in the Galleria Borghese.[60]

Moulène's photographs create visual and conceptual opposites to these archival images. Aiming his camera at their eyes as if to capture their gaze, he shows another side of the same objects. Instead of staring adoringly towards the heavens, Mary Magdalene looks back towards us viewers, as does the Smyrna figurine, which now beams against a luminous blue ground.[61] Bernini's *bozzetto* of *Truth* is no longer majestic. She is a voluptuous figure with a radiant face emerging from the ample pleats of a gown that seems to hide truths rather than reveal them.[62] Whereas the pictures included in Atlas optimise the outlines of the sculptures, often opting for profile or three-quarters views that avert the faces, Moulène's reverse shots modify these conventions. Facing front, the objects become more compact and less legible and identifiable in terms of period or style. The contrast between the different images reveals how closely the archival photographs match the curatorial information provided in the titles of the works; this is the case whatever the period at which the archival photographs were taken.[63] If the museum assigns a particular place and role to a work, its documentary reproductions tend to reflect that placement. If Moulène's reverse shots challenge the visual conventions and illustrative nature of archival documentation, what role does his *Louvre* attribute to photography in the museum?

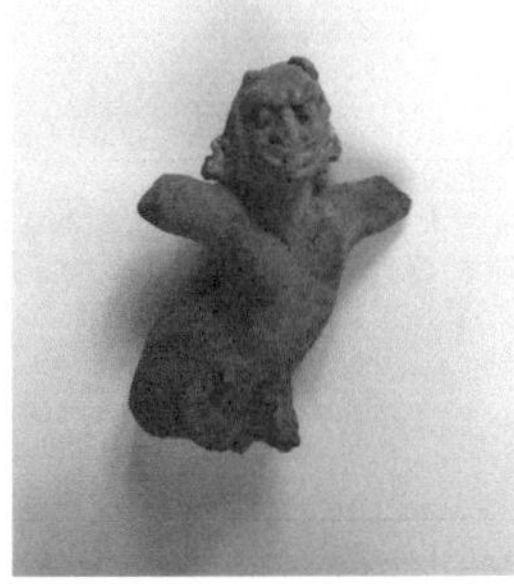

61 Jean-Luc Moulène, *Le Monde, Le Louvre, Crise* (*Crisis*), Paris, 2005, Cibachrome print under Diasec, 45.6 × 36.5 cm.

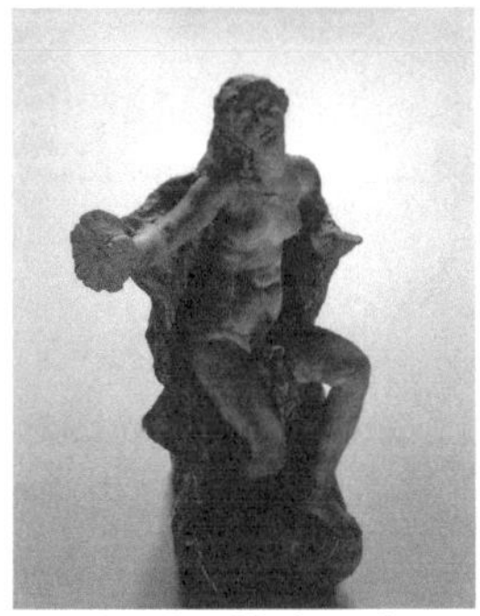

62 Jean-Luc Moulène, *Le Monde, Le Louvre, Vérité* (*Truth*). Paris, 2005, Cibachrome print under Diasec, 45 × 36 cm.

63 The photographs in Atlas are undated, but in some cases the date can be deduced from the registration information when the objects entered the collection.

In 1935 Walker Evans, working on site at the Museum of Modern Art in New York, made a series of photographs of sculptures. The context of these images was the *African Negro Art* exhibition organised by MoMA, which presented an extensive selection of some 603 objects borrowed from private and public American and European collections.[64] The show sidestepped the habitual ethnographic presentations of African art, in which artefacts would be arranged according to function, in favour of a modernist one that emphasised their formal and aesthetic qualities. In the context of MoMA, the exhibition was an acknowledgement of the importance of these productions for Western modernism.[65] The works in *African Negro Art* were sparsely distributed across four floors of the museum and displayed on plain white or wooden pedestals, or else in simple showcases against white walls.[66] Evans was commissioned to photograph a large number of the displays as an educational annex to the exhibition. In the course of six weeks, he produced 477 photographs that were assembled in a portfolio for distribution to museums and universities.[67] Out of this series, a selection of twenty-five images was printed in larger format (Evans called it 'poster size') to be exhibited in university and colleges throughout the United States.

Taking his pictures mostly during the museums' closing hours, Evans shot the objects in frontal or

64 Press release of the exhibition, MoMA archives, <www.moma.org/docs/press_archives/232/releases/MOMA_1934-35_0047_1935-03-06_10-3-6-35.pdf?2010>, retrieved 29 August 2013.

65 Concerning the exhibition and the Walker Evans' commission of photographs, see Virginia-Lee Webb, 'Perfect Documents', in *Perfect Documents: Walker Evans and African Art, 1935* (exhib. cat.), New York, The Metropolitan Museum of Art, 2000.

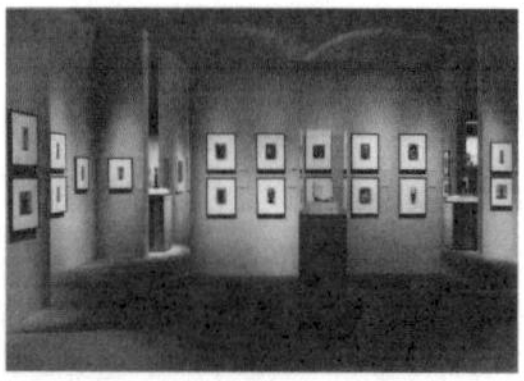

66 Installation view, *African Negro Art*, 1935, The Museum of Modern Art, New York.

67 Seventeen portfolios were produced and acquired by historically black colleges as well as museums, including the Victoria and Albert Museum, London, the Musée de l'Homme in Paris and the Peabody Museum at Harvard University.

three-quarter view, with a view camera and using even lighting that emphasised the surface texture. The plain coloured backdrops he selected bring the background of the picture to the front, flattening the image in contrast with the relief of the objects themselves. Masks and sculptures were photographed individually or in pairs and were occasionally accompanied by secondary views from the side or close up. In all cases, Evans framed his subjects tightly by cropping either the negative or the final print, thereby providing little clue as to the size of the objects.

Originally commissioned as an educational tool, Evans' photographs for *African Negro Art* were not considered part of the photographer's oeuvre by the authors of the first monographic studies of his work. Only in 2000 did the images reappear, as the subject of an exhibition at the Metropolitan Museum of Art entitled *Perfect Documents: Walker Evans and African Art, 1935*.[68] Reprising a phrase coined in the 1930s by Lincoln Kerstein, one of the photographer's earliest supporters, the curator of the 2000 exhibition, Virginia-Lee Webb, aimed at reassessing the importance within Evans' work of photographs that had been 'long overshadowed by their subject matter'.[69] Rather than merely a paid commission, Webb set out to explain, these images had a pivotal importance in the development of Evans'

68 *Perfect Documents: Walker Evans and African Art*, 1935, Metropolitan Museum of Art, New York, 1 February to 3 September 2000.

69 Webb, 'Perfect Documents', p. 45.

70 Walker Evans and James Agee, *Let Us Now Praise Famous Men*, Boston, Houghton Mifflin, 1941.

71 Webb, 'Perfect Documents', p. 43.

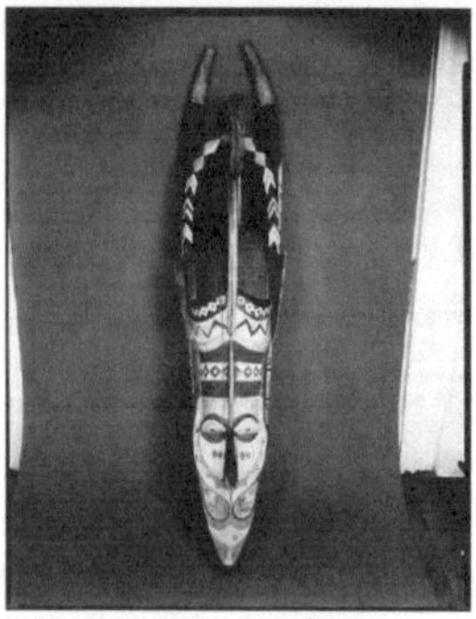

72 Walker Evans, *Mask (Banda Headdress), Africa, Guinea, Baga / Nalu peoples* (revised title and provenance, 2000), 1935, gelatin silver print, 22.2 × 7 cm.

73 For a particularly effective deconstruction of the modes of exhibition of African art, see Susan Vogel's curatorial work at the Centre for African Art, and her essay 'Always True to the Object', in Ivan Karp and Steven D. Lavine (eds.), *Exhibiting Cultures: The Poetics and Politics of Museum Display*, Washington and London, Smithsonian Institution Press, 1991, pp. 191–204.

self-defined 'documentary style'. Located chronologically between his depictions of nineteenth-century Victorian houses, initiated in 1931, and the photographs of the Depression-stricken South begun shortly afterwards for the FSA and eventually published independently with James Agee as the book *Let us Now Praise Famous Men,*[70] the *African Negro Art* photographs borrowed from the earlier works the frontal, tightly framed compositions that he would continue to construct in the later series. As much as they typify Evans' photography, the African art images were at the time seen as so realistic, argues Webb, that 'they were viewed as surrogates for the actual sculpture'.[71] In her reconstruction of this development, the formal characteristics of the images constituted a two-dimensional translation of the modernist aesthetic deployed in the 1935 exhibition, accentuating the formal qualities of the objects and isolating them from any sense of context or scale. The soft, even lighting, the tight framing and the avoidance of any sense of the onlooker's gaze being 'returned' rendered them available for the viewer as pure form and texture.[72] If post-colonial discourse has questioned the modernist presentation of non-western art objects, its visual translation in Evans' photographs remained, in *Perfect Documents*, immune to such critique.[73] The exhibition invited viewers instead to redirect their attention from the objects photographed to the formal characteristics of the photographs. The only suggestion of a space beyond the white cube that would reflect on the condition of production and presentation of the image came, somewhat surprisingly, in the form of an untrimmed Evans print of a Banda headdress, which Webb illustrates on the cover of the exhibition catalogue of *Perfect Documents*.[74] The photograph showed the mask resting vertically against the wall on a strip of paper or fabric that Evans used as a backdrop for his photograph; visible on either side are fragments of wooden parquet flooring and white stuccoed walls.[75]

Although Jean-Luc Moulène also uses a view camera and soft – but in his case natural – light, his treatment of the space around the Louvre statuettes is very different from the tight and symmetric compositions Evans produced. Even though the objects are placed in the middle of the frame, respecting a vertical axis, they each occupy space in their own way; some are cut off at their base, while others seemingly float in mid-air. Several appear to move forward toward the viewer, while others recede into the background. Rather than opting for a systematic framing that, like Evans' images, would easily permit a formal comparison, Moulène's variations of pictorial composition highlight the heterogeneity of his selection.

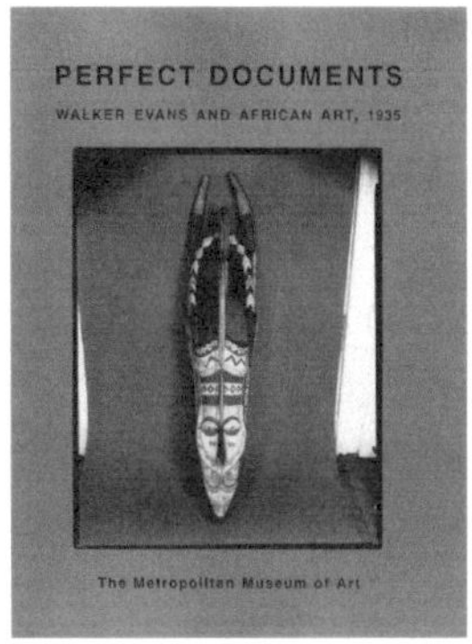

74 Virginia-Lee Webb, *Perfect Documents: Walker Evans and African Art, 1935*. Catalogue cover.

75 The catalogue states that the photographs were taken both at the MoMA and at the Pierre Matisse Gallery, then located in the nearby Fuller building. It does not specify to which location these architectural details belong.

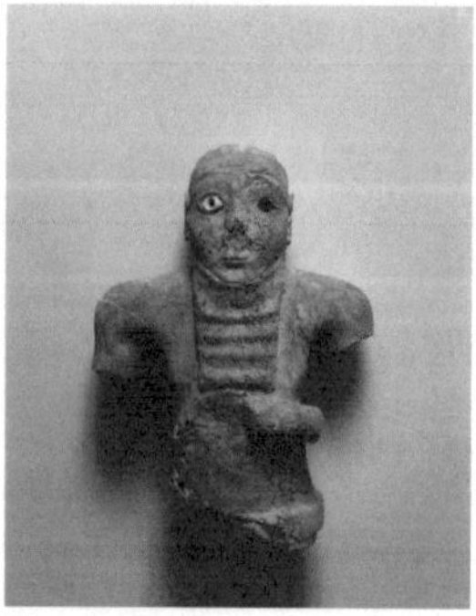
76 Jean-Luc Moulène, *Le Monde, le Louvre, Orant*, Paris, 2005, Cibachrome print, Diasec, mounted on aluminium, 50 × 40 cm.

But the greatest difference between the two series is that the sculptures shown in Moulène's photographs almost invariably and deliberately seem to return the gaze of the viewer, whilst Evans' often avert it. In the newspaper publication made at the same time as the exhibition, Moulène similarly made sure that the eyes of the statuettes would appear in the top third of the picture and would thus 'face' the reader, allowing the objects to 'look back' beyond the limit of the photographs, endowing them with an effect of 'presence'.[76] Evans, by contrast, avoided directing the gaze of his sculptures towards the viewer. He did this either by focusing not on the eyes but on the middle of the masks and sculptures, or by turning the sculpture away from the camera. In this way, he provided the viewer with unrestricted visual access to the object.

As pure form removed from any contextual information, the African sculptures in Walker Evans' photographs are the exact antithesis of those filmed two decades later by Chris Marker and Alain Resnais in their documentary on African art, *Les Statues meurent aussi* (*Statues Also Die*). In one sequence of this film, which was made in 1953 for the Paris-based Pan-African publishing house and gallery Présence Africaine, the filmmakers show a succession of sculpture heads and masks appearing and disappearing from a dark background, accompanied by the dramatic rhythm of the music.[77] Theatrically lit, the sculptures seemingly confront the viewer with an indomitable gaze. In quite another mode, these conquering expressions are commented on by an off-screen voice evoking the lost histories behind the masks and the relentless pursuit of knowledge and domination engendered by colonialism: 'Colonisateurs du monde, nous voulons que tout nous parle: les bêtes, les morts, les statues. Et ces statues-là sont muettes' ('Colonisers of the world, we want everything to talk to us: animals, the dead, statues. Yet these statues are mute').[78] With a use of montage that manifests the gap between image, music and sound, Marker and Resnais reveal what François Niney calls the 'verso of the image', its insufficiencies, the fact that 'every image conceals or calls for another one'.[79] Throughout the film a certain disjunction between image, sound and voice, along with purely visual montage, reveals this 'other side'. One brief scene, for instance, filmed at the Musée de l'Homme in Paris or at the Royal Museum for Central Africa in Tervuren (the two museum locations used in the film) tellingly juxtaposes a shot of vitrines containing ethnographic displays of African objects with a mock-up showing administrative and office paraphernalia similarly displayed and labelled in a glass case.[80] The other side of *Statues Also Die* is thus a combative critique of colonialism.[81] The film

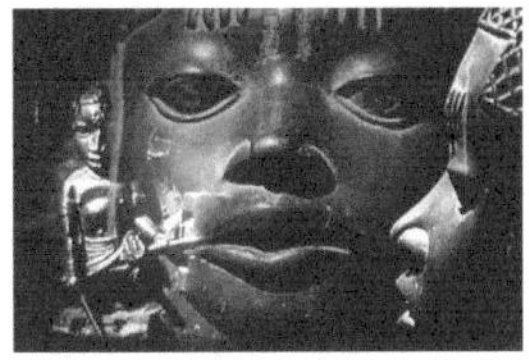

77 Chris Marker and Alain Resnais, *Les Statues meurent aussi*, 1953, black & white film, 30 minutes. Film still.

78 Chris Marker, *Les statues meurent aussi*, (film script) in Chris Marker, *Commentaires*, Paris, Seuil, 1961, pp. 7–23. Cited in François Niney, *Le documentaire et ses faux-semblants*, Paris, Klincksieck, 2009, p. 119.

79 Niney, *Le documentaire et ses faux-semblants* pp. 118–19.

80 This glimpse of glass cases containing everyday office tools can be compared to Walker Evans' quasi-contemporary 'Beauties of the Common Tool', a photo essay published in 1955 in the American magazine *Fortune*. In view of the similarities between these images and the *African Negro Art* photographs, it is possible to argue that an ethnographic reversal takes place in this series, as it does, far more vocally, in *Les statues meurent aussi*. In any case Evans' documentary style tends to resist unambiguous political readings.

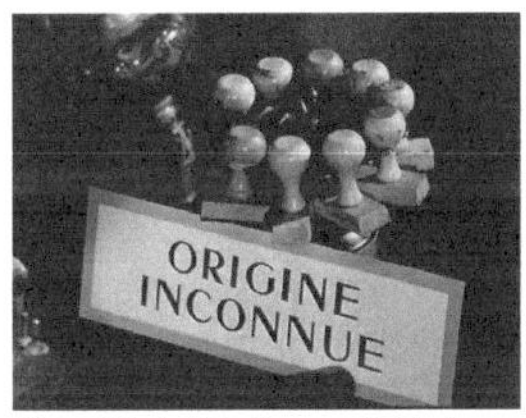

81 Chris Marker and Alain Resnais, *Les statues meurent aussi*, film still.

82 Nora M. Alter, *Chris Marker*, Chicago, University of Illinois Press, 2006, p. 60.

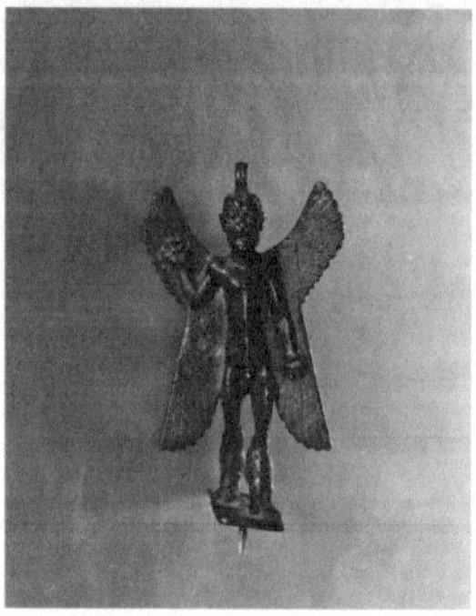

83 Jean-Luc Moulène, *LeMonde, le Louvre, Pazuzu*, Paris, 2005, Cibachrome print, Diasec, mounted on aluminium, 45 × 36 cm.

was in fact quickly recognised as such in France. After being shown in Cannes and receiving the Prix Jean Vigo, it was censored by the Centre National de la Cinématographie until 1963.[82]

If film can use montage, sound effects and voice-over commentary to show the reverse side of an image, photography must resort to other devices. In *Le Louvre*, Moulène makes a point of showing the metal screws protruding from the inside of statuettes (*Pazuzu*), the holes destined to welcome supporting rods, and the inventory numbers painted directly onto their surfaces.[83] These ubiquitous marks that are usually concealed in archival and documentary reproductions, indicate – more emphatically than the occasional limb that may have disappeared over time – the violence of the cultural appropriation enacted by the museum. Similarly, the airy composition of his photographs inscribes the sculptures within a continuous space that may stretch beyond the limits of the institution.

Moulène exceeds the illustrative capacity of the archival images in the digital database of the museum; he proffers a material and subjective alternative in the form of a tangible object that is also a multiple. If photography traditionally follows the grain of the museum and its white-cube aesthetic, which is true of the pictures in the Atlas database and even, somewhat differently, of Walker Evans'

African art photographs, Moulène's images rub against it. Like the film by Alain Resnais and Chris Marker, they show the verso of the image, creating a rupture in the museum's order. Working against the clarity of vision and the seamless realism of Walker Evans, Moulène's pictures, by directing the viewer towards the eyes of the sculptures, suggests that the object can look back, just like Marker and Resnais did before him. Needless to say, this is only a trick of the image. Just as the two filmmakers cannot undo the history of colonisation, so Moulène cannot give a new life to these museum objects: 'ces statues là sont muettes', as Marker wrote in the audio commentary of his film. In comparison with the closed world of Evans' portfolio of documentary photographs, Moulène, like the filmmakers, opens up the frame that Evans kept tightly shut. He opens it and shows us the frame, but also demonstrates that there is something beyond it.

When we think of the archive as the home of the document, and the museum as the home of the work of art, we subscribe to a cultural history that goes back to the eighteenth century, when art collections opened up to the public. The founding of the Louvre in 1793, in the aftermath of the French Revolution, and before that, the opening of the Sloane Collection – which later became the British Museum – and the Vatican brought to view objects emanating from private individuals, war loots, and royal collections.[84] 'Simultaneous with the opening of the galleries', writes Philip Fisher, 'is the beginning, in the work of Winckelmann on Greek art, of a systematic conceptual history'.[85] Soon museum displays materialised that newly developed history of art, hanging works according to school, to styles, to chronology. In this construction of the autonomy of art, the fine art museum detached itself from museums of civilisations and applied arts, with their more archival approach. In this sense, 'the Museum is more than a location. It is a script that makes certain acts possible and others unthinkable.'[86]

In borrowing and mimicking the formats of documents in their works, artists like Moulène metaphorically turn the museum into an archive, thus questioning the premises on which it was originally based. Today museums are undergoing a profound mutation that is fed by social, economic, and political factors, which force them to reconsider their mode of action, their routines of collecting and exhibiting.[87] In the Netherlands, the Tropenmuseum's reorganisation of photographic archives into collections, and the Van Abbemuseum's presentation of its own archives; in France, the instating of a research programme on the exhibition history of Centre Pompidou – all these are gestures that follow from and are inspired by artistic practices. In the

84 Fisher, *Making and Effacing Art: Modern American Art in a Culture of Museums*, Oxford and New York, Oxford University Press, 1991, pp. 7–8

85 Fisher, *Making and Effacing Art*, p. 7.

86 Fisher, *Making and Effacing Art*, p. 18.

87 On this re-thinking of the museum, see for example Catherine Grenier's recent plea for a re-invention of the museum in *La Fin des Musées?* Paris, Éditions du Regard, 2013.

process of re-thinking the museum as a collection of autonomous objects, the critical reflection on the document led by artists becomes an experimental model for the rethinking of the museum in the twenty-first century.

To place photographic reproductions of objects from the Louvre in the galleries of the Louvre itself raises questions about the visibility of art within its walls as well as beyond them, in the recent virtual extensions of the museum. The gesture of replacing sculptures by two-dimensional reproductions placed on pedestals as if they were the works of art, suggests a belief on the part of the artist that the dematerialization of art in the museum is already at work in the development of digital tools by the institution. Museums increasingly invite viewers (also called 'visitors') to 'browse' their collections and undertake 'virtual visits' of their displays. The proliferation of digital databases and other devices for online consultation, along with photographic reproductions, turns the museum into something of an archive or a library, and may reduce the art works themselves to mere samples of the diversity of the treasures it contains.[88] If that is the case, digitalisation would be a further step in the erasure of the unique presence or 'aura' of the work of art, as Walter Benjamin called it, which he attributed to the reproducible nature of photography.[89]

88 *Isis-Aphrodite*, 3rd cent. BC, terracotta, Department of Greek, Roman and Etruscan Antiquities; *Baal brandishing Thunder*, 14–13th cent. BC, Syria, bronze and gold, Department of Oriental Antiquities; Statuette of Demon Pazuzu, 1st millennium BC, Assyria, bronze, Department of Oriental Antiquities.

89 Walter Benjamin, 'The Work of Art in the Age of Mechanical Reproduction', in Hannah Arendt (ed.), *Illuminations*, New York, Schocken Books, 1969, p. 221.

What greater irony is there than to invite visitors to the museum and show them works of art as reproductions? In calling his work *Le Louvre,* Moulène suggests further that photography mirrors the museum's own ability to silence an object by cutting it off from its original cultural, historical and social identity and affixing to it a script of its own.

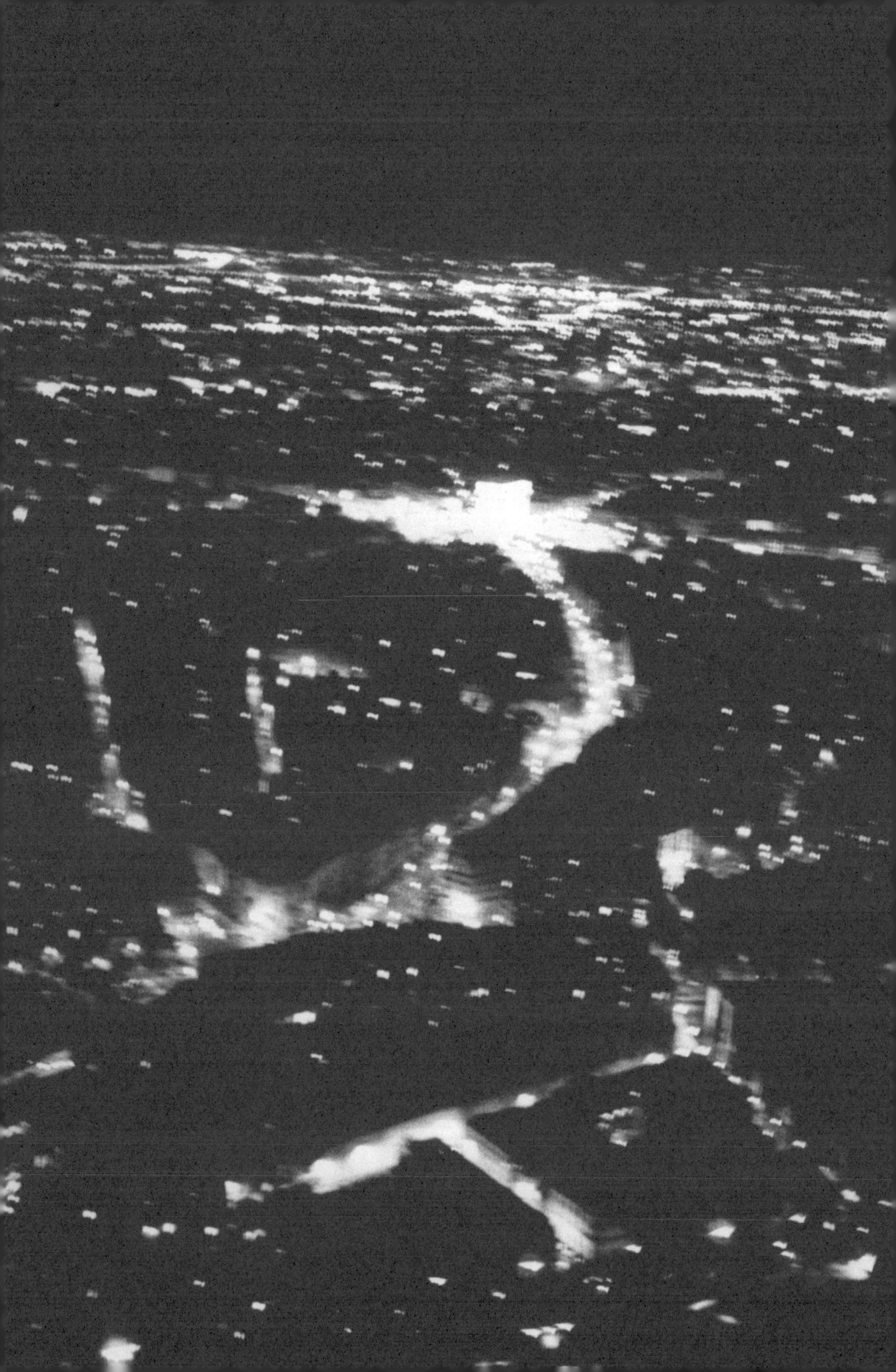

Two

(Dis)ordering the World

'By mechanical objectivity we mean the insistent drive to repress the wilful intervention of the artist-author, and to put in its stead a set of procedures that would, as it were, move nature to the page through a strict protocol, if not automatically.' In their history of objectivity in scientific representations, Lorraine Daston and Peter Galison describe the ultimately flawed attempts of scientists to use new technologies in the second half of the nineteenth century to objectively represent scientific phenomena.[1] Photography was one of the techniques they believed made it possible to move 'nature to the page' with little or no human intervention. Reading *Objectivity* in the context of Zoe Leonard's photographic work reveals both the artist's critical engagement with a technical history of the medium, through series of images that explore its boundaries and her interest in its social uses. There, by provocatively pitting against one another the quest for the objective image and the subjectivity of the photographer, Leonard shows how the gaze is always embedded historically.

1 Lorraine Daston, Peter Galison, *Objectivity*, New York, Zone Books, 2010, p. 121

Zoe Leonard, *Paris*, 1986, gelatin silver print, 78.7 × 56.5 cm.

2 Zoe Leonard, *Observation Point,* London, Camden Arts Centre, 31 March – 24 June 2012.

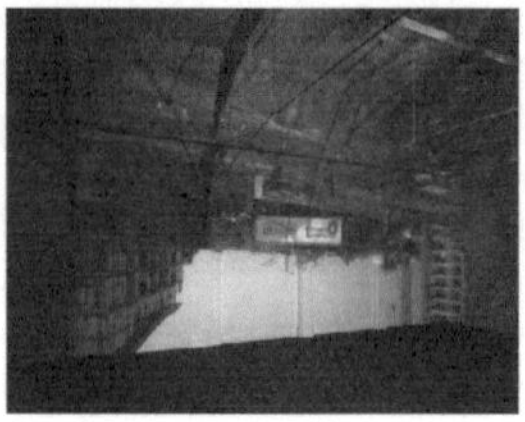

3 Zoe Leonard, *Observation Point*, Camden Arts Centre, London, 2012, exhibition view.

4 This was Leonard's second construction of a camera obscura in a gallery, after Galerie Gisela Capitain, Cologne in 2011, and before Murray Guy, New York, fall 2012.

Spring 2012. I am visiting Camden Arts Centre in London to see an exhibition of recent work by Zoe Leonard. The show is called *Observation Point* and it occupies three galleries that open onto a landing on the second floor of the building.[2] Visitors can choose to begin their visit with any of the three rooms; the one I enter first is pitch black forcing my eyes to accommodate slowly to the darkness. Making my way amidst people huddled in small groups, sitting on cushions scattered across the floor and speaking softly together, I discover a silent moving image projected onto a wall and spreading across the architectural details of the large Victorian room. Created by a small aperture fitted with a lens on the opposite wall, which turns the gallery into a large camera obscura, the image flows across the curved ceiling and spreads over the floor. Dim and monochrome at first, it grows in intensity, detail and colour the more I look, and reveals, in the low sunlight of April, the afternoon that quietly unfolds in the street below, but upside down, as a result of the way light rays pass through the lens.[3] An office block is being built, cars and people move in and out of the image in a continuous and captivating sequence, showing everyday activity at the intersection of Finchley and Arkwright Road.[4]

Extracting myself from the absorbing, silent environment only barely troubled by the muffled sound of the street, I walk across the landing to the second room and go in. It is painted entirely white and brightly lit by skylights. A dozen or so photographic prints are pinned onto the walls; each one shows a white circular patch of varying size and position, sometimes surrounded with a halo, on a velvet-smooth grey background.[5] *Available Light* is the collective title given to this series of photographs taken by the artist by directing the lens of her camera directly towards the sun.

Another door, a third gallery. Here I discover several piles of vintage postcards showing different views of the Niagara Falls (*Survey 2008–2012*).[6] They are probably a selection from the thousands that Leonard accumulated for a large mural installation she presented in the United States, at the Dia Art Foundation, a few years ago.[7] There – I remember once reading – the postcards displayed on the walls of the gallery mapped the site of the Niagara Falls across the space. In front of me, however, the postcards are stacked, presumably organised by view. The result evokes something of an orientation table in a natural site or the lair of an obsessive collector. Tacked onto one wall of the room, two postcards show a rocky landscape with a viewing point indicated by a sign that reads 'observation point', the phrase used as the title for the London exhibition.

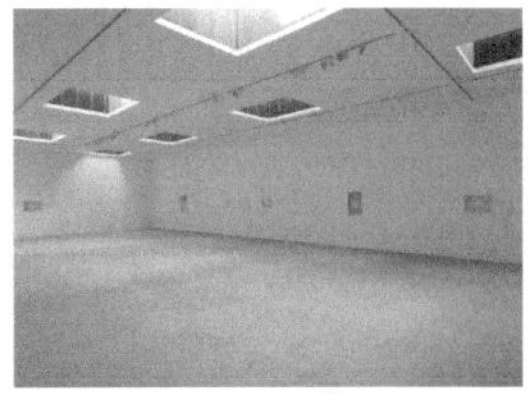

5 Zoe Leonard, *Observation Point*, Camden Arts Centre, London, 2012, exhibition view.

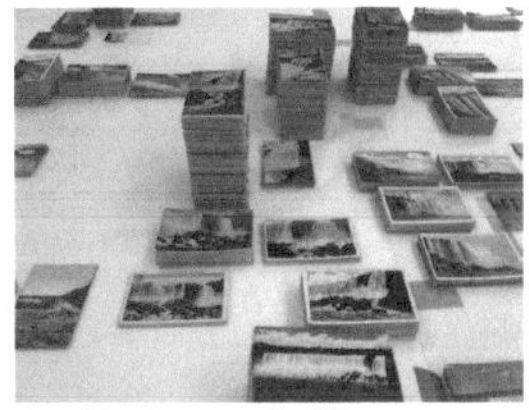

6 Zoe Leonard, *Observation Point*, Camden Arts Centre, London, 2012, exhibition view.

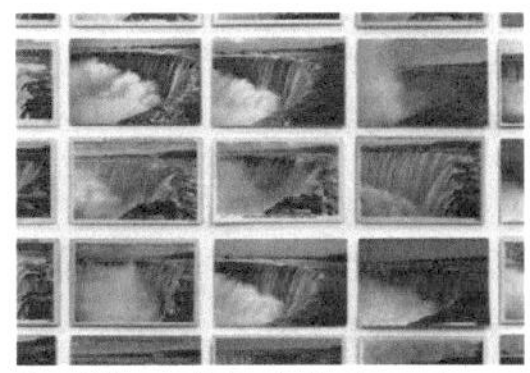

7 The wall installation at Dia:Beacon comprised some 4000 postcards. Zoe Leonard, *You see I am here after all*, solo exhibition. Dia:Beacon, New York, 2008, exhibition view.

The three rooms feel like a riddle facing a bemused Alice in Wonderland. However magical the atmosphere of the camera obscura may be, gathering together as it does a secret congregation of whispering onlookers, it seems necessary to leave it and to walk through the other two rooms and back again, as if only repeated and alternating visits to all three galleries will make it possible to solve the puzzle; as if the sum of the three rooms must exceed the story that each one tells on its own.[8]

This sum has something to do with questioning photography as a scientific process and as a technology: the camera obscura is a long-used optical device that organises the surrounding space into a two-dimensional view and thus dis-embodies vision; it is often considered as a prefiguration of photography. Here it can be understood and experienced by each visitor, although it is messier as well as more sensuous as the image is projected into a room rather than onto a flat, precisely delimited surface.[9] Next to it, *Available Light* pushes the crucial need that photography has of sunlight to its farthest and almost absurd point. Turning the camera lens towards the sun and registering *all* the 'available light,' the artist shows, in images such as *April 4, frame 2,* how the sun itself is impossible to capture on film, and how it can annihilate the photographic image rather than make it visible.[10] Looking at the postcard stacks

8 George Baker and Elisabeth Lebovici in particular have eloquently shared their experience of the camera obscura respectively in their New York and Venice versions. George Baker, 'The Relational Field of Photography', in: *Still Searching: An Online Discourse about Photography*, Fotomuseum Winterthur, 31 May 2013, <blog.fotomuseum.ch/2013/05/i-the-relational-field-of-photography/>. Consulted 20 August 22, 2013. Elisabeth Lebovici 'The Politics of Contemplation', in Zoe Leonard and Elisabeth Lebovici, *The Politics of Contemplation: From There to Back Again,* New York, Murray Guy, 2012.

9 Concerning the history of the camera obscura, see Jonathan Crary's *Techniques of the Observer*, who counters the general opinion and argues for a discontinuity between camera obscura and photography. Jonathan Crary, *Techniques of the Observer. On Vision and Modernity in the Nineteenth Century,* London and Cambridge, MA., MIT Press, 1990.

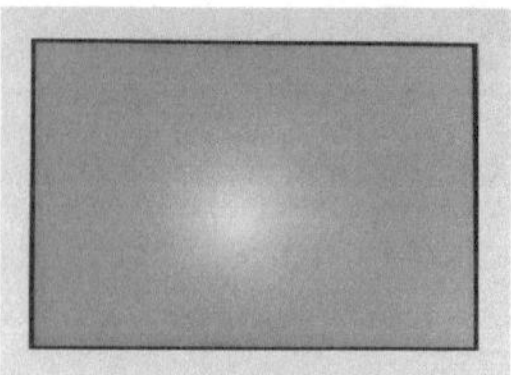

10 Zoe Leonard, *April 4, frame 2*, 2011, gelatin silver print.

of *Survey 2008–2012* in the same spirit, we can imagine they are here to testify to photography's power to fragment and flatten nature into an endless number of reproducible and portable pictures.
In short, these propositions invite us to consider the relationship between the various chemical, optical and technological rules and protocols of photography. This concern can be compared with a statement made almost twenty years ago in which the artist explained her attraction to photography:

> 'What attracts me in photography is not so much a fine arts approach but rather photographs as documents. Not only journalism but the other roles that photography has played outside of the art context: aerial reconnaissance photography, science and medical photography, family snapshots. All the ways in which human beings have documented the world in an attempt to order it, in an attempt to consume it or rule it or hang on to it in some sense.'[11]

What claimed Leonard's interest in 1993 was not so much the scientific and technical aspects of photography that seem central to the London exhibition of 2012, but rather the compositional rules developed within each discipline, through which a photograph can become a piece of evidence that is legible and usable within a particular environment. At the

11 Leonard refuted the association her interlocutor, critic Laura Cottingham attempted to make between her images and those of Edward Weston. Laura Cottingham, 'Zoe Leonard', *Journal of Contemporary Art*, vol. 6, no. 1, summer 1993, (interview), pp. 64–77.

12 Zoe Leonard, *The 1998 Bearded Lady Calendar, starring Jennifer Miller*, 1997. Spiral bound calendar, 6 pages, published by Kunsthaus Glarus. Edition of 500.

13 Lorraine Daston and Peter Galison, *Objectivity*. New York, Zone Books, 2010, p. 42.

time of her statement, she had already started to experiment with various kinds of applied photography, and produced documents that were legible and recognizable in a specific context. She had made aerial views and taken photographs of exhibits in science museums; shortly after she would create a photographic album retracing the fictional life of a Hollywood star (*The Fae Richard Archives*, 1993–1996) and take pictures of a performance artist, Jennifer Miller, who re-enacted some of the poses assumed by Marilyn Monroe in the infamous red velvet photo session (*Pin Up #1 Jennifer Miller does Marilyn Monroe*, 1995).[12]

In mentioning 'science and medical photography', Leonard conjures the particular fascination that photography once exerted in the sciences. In their study of the different historical notions of scientific objectivity as represented in scientific atlases, Lorraine Daston and Peter Galison recount how photography came to play an important role in the definition of 'mechanical objectivity' in the nineteenth century. They show how photography – along with several other techniques – was perceived as making it possible to produce scientific representations 'untouched by human hands', in the production of which subjectivity played no part.[13] This ideal of mechanical objectivity marked a rupture with an earlier, pre-photographic regime of scientific representation that Daston and Galison call 'truth to nature', in which scientific representation aimed at producing archetypes and synthesised views of scientific phenomena rather than illustrations of specific individual cases. Mechanical objectivity was developed in the context of industrialisation that brought with it the model of machines that work without thinking and, more specifically, without the involvement of a subjective mind. The automatic quality of the photographic image held the promise to provide accurate and truthful representations of natural phenomena and scientific experimentations, even though its weakness was precisely that it was limited to showing individual cases rather than archetypes. Although the authors are concerned with scientific discourse only, their discussion of scientific representations bears connection more broadly to the history of photography and the problematic question of objective representation it was once believed to achieve, for instance as Arago contended at the French Chamber of Deputies in July 1839 (see chapter 1). The history of mechanical objectivity is marked throughout by the intense and inevitably failed attempt by scientists to extirpate themselves from the subjective. Daston and Galison provide numerous examples of scientists eventually admitting defeat and acknowledging the flawed character of mechanical objectivity and of photography

14 Briony Fer, *Zoe Leonard File Note*, London, Camden Arts Centre, 2012. Non-paginated.

15 On this collective experience on the work see the texts by George Baker and Elisabeth Lebovici cited above.

as a tool to achieve it.

I see this relation between scientific objectivity and the inevitable – and perhaps propitious – intervention of the subjective as a thread running through Zoe Leonard's photographic practice. It was vividly exposed in the exhibition at Camden Arts Centre, where rules and principles of photography were systematically countered by personal agency. Hence the photographs of the sun break the first rule of photography, never to point the camera at the sun, as Briony Fer points out in the pamphlet accompanying the exhibition.[14] *Arkwright Road* turns the traditionally individual experience of the camera obscura into a collective one.[15] And the postcards, even though they are standardised representations of an experience each visitor believes to be unique, bear the idiosyncratic handwriting of those who once purchased and posted them. In turn – and Daston and Galison's descriptions of scientists reacting to photography show this vividly – the conflict between objectivity and subjectivity is not only played out at the level of chemistry, optics and technical reproducibility. Rather, it is also present in those other aspects of image-making in which Leonard expressed interest in her statement of 1993: framing, composition and use of light, which render a photograph both legible and usable as evidence in a particular administrative or scientific context.

The London exhibition *Observation Point* comes after two large-scale projects that Leonard had then recently completed: *Analogue* (1997–2008), a series of four hundred photographs of shop windows, bundles of clothing and market stalls taken around the world, and *You see, I am here after all*, a mural installation presenting some four thousand postcards of the Niagara Falls. Although they differ in scale from *Observation point*, the precise exhibition at Camden Arts Centre offers a key to reading these earlier, large projects. In the pages that follow, taking stock of this question of mechanical objectivity versus personal agency, I will examine how Zoe Leonard has articulated technical and institutional histories of photography, and how, through this, she has woven a critical reflection on objectivity and subjectivity.

Anatomical Models

I begin to explore these questions not with an example of Leonard's forays into an established scientific or vernacular photographic genre, but with one of her most arresting photographs of museum displays, a picture in which she demonstrates some of the rules and conventions of specific representation contexts, precisely while diverging from them. *Wax*

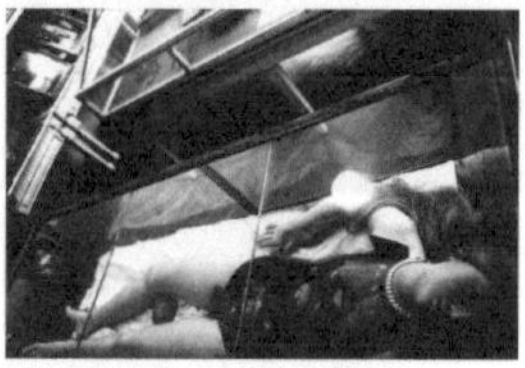

16 Zoe Leonard, *Wax Anatomical Model Shot Crooked from Above*, 1990, gelatin silver print, 77.8 × 116.8 cm.

Anatomical Model Shot Crooked from Above (1990) belongs to a larger group of black and white pictures the artist took in different museums across Europe and the United States in the late 1980s and early 1990s.[16] This particular one is part of a sequence of three images showing the same life-size female wax model resting in a glass case. They were taken in the Josephinum Museum, part of the Medical University in Vienna. The object photographed is one of the hundreds of anatomical and obstetric wax models that were brought to Vienna in 1786, purchased by Emperor Joseph II in Florence to serve as aids for medical training in Vienna. Leonard's photograph shows us the model lying on her back. The smooth greys of the photograph caress the wax skin and soften the modelling of the face, increasing its life-likeness. Her head is tilted to the left, towards the camera, her eyes are half-opened and her lips painted. Long blond hair flows on her shoulders and two rows of pearls adorn her neck. But contrasting with the calm submissiveness of her face, immediately below the pearl necklace, her torso is cut wide open to reveal her intestines, lungs, digestive system, and womb, meticulously rendered in wax. This disturbing sight is intensified by the viewpoint adopted by the artist, who presents the model 'Shot crooked from above', as the title of the work specifies. This contrasts with the relative tranquillity that emanates from the two other pictures in the series, for instance *Wax Anatomical Model Full View from Above,* which stresses the aspect of a 'sleeping beauty'.[17] The partial cutting off of a leg in the 'shot crooked from above' accentuates the grotesque mix of eroticism and gruesomeness of the model lying in her glass coffin. The oblique framing disturbs the composition of the picture: the glass case and the figure it contains look as if they are about to slide out of the frame, tipping over the entire room full of scientific samples and anatomic models on display. The reflection of the spotlight on the top of the glass case, the tilted angle of the image together stage – rather than merely suggest – an onlooker caught by surprise, hesitant as to how to approach the object with a camera. Leonard is all too aware of the ability of photography to enhance the already realistic appearance of the wax figure and so to validate its accurateness as a medical representation, but also to disseminate the representation beyond the walls of the museum. As she photographed the anatomical model, Leonard included in the image the surroundings that constitute, after the anatomical rendering of the human body, a second layer of representation: that of the museum narrative constructed through the display of objects placed in a certain order. Through her instable framing of the scene, Leonard created a dislocation between photography, the museum and the wax

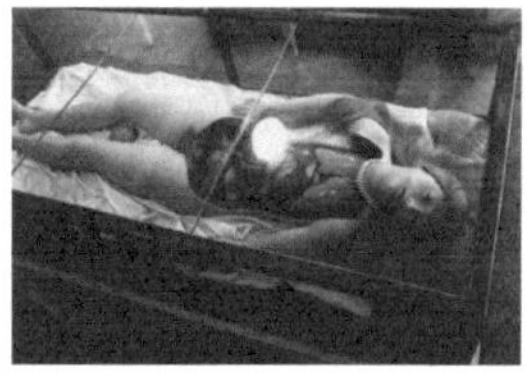

17 Zoe Leonard, *Wax Anatomical Model Full View from Above,* 1990, gelatin silver print, 78.7 × 118.7 cm.

18 Zoe Leonard, in Anna Blume, 'Interview with Zoe Leonard', *Zoe Leonard* (exhib. cat.), Vienna, Wiener Secession, 1997, p. 9.

model. Her photograph does not just 'reproduce' the anatomical model and the museum room and frame them as a legible object or a legible space. Instead, the awkward camera angle creates a clash, an incoherent juxtaposition of different representative systems amidst which the artists seems to asks what role photography can play in relation to them.

The crooked angle and the fragmentary view suggest instantaneity and speed, two characteristics habitually connected to street photography, with its dedication to accidental encounters, and its reliance upon the photographer's eye: her ability to discern the outstanding in the banality of the everyday. In a discussion with Anna Blume, Leonard evoked her affinity with a photographic practice that involved these characteristics:

> 'Part of why I like photography is that it is a form of observation. Just walking down the street I am amazed by how much of everything already exists. [...] I go out into the world and find things, images or situations that strike a cord in me. Like any good hunter or gatherer I am grateful that those things are there.'[18]

The image of the photographer as hunter is a classical trope in the discourse on photography. Leonard's words bring to mind the pictures the artist made in Alaska during a prolonged stay in 1996–1998, showing the leftovers of the destruction of animals by hunters (see for instance *Charlie's Moose*, 1995–1998, or *Bear Head on Ground*, 1996–1998).[19] In these images the violence of the subject matter contrasts precisely with the *absence* of a predatory gaze. Another trope of street photography is the carefree amazement at one's surrounding. But Leonard's images have none of the 'cool, gentle disdain' that Martha Rosler perceived in Lee Friedlander's pictures, or the narcissism usually associated with those of Garry Winogrand, two emblematical practitioners of the genre in the United States.[20] A third figure conjured in Leonard's remark is the nineteenth-century flâneur as social observer, the flâneur-as-writer that Susan Buck-Morss identifies in Walter Benjamin's writings, who diverts his readers with observations of street-life.[21] For Clive Scott, the flâneur is the prototype of a street photographer whose images do not address viewers to persuade them of something but instead turn them into witnesses of an instant.[22]

This sense that the viewer is a witness to the photographer's encounter, rather than addressed directly by her, radiates from *Wax Anatomical Model Shot Crooked from Above*. Leonard's sideways glance takes us in her stride as she brings together, with her camera, different systems of production of knowledge: the museum, with its artefacts

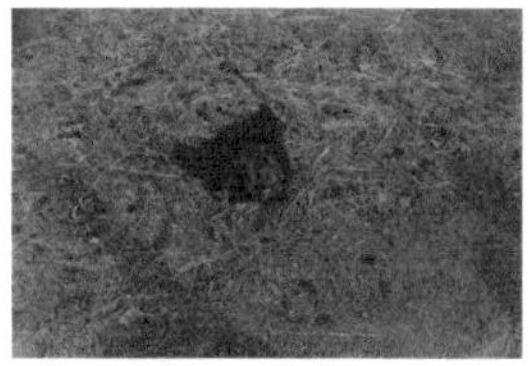

19 Zoe Leonard, *Bear Head on Ground*, 1996–1998, gelatin silver print, 63.5 × 91.8 cm.

20 Martha Rosler, 'Lee Friedlander, An Exemplary Modern Photographer', in Martha Rosler, *Decoys and Disruptions: Selected Writings, 1975–2001*, London and Cambridge, MA., MIT Press, 2004, p. 113.

21 Susan Buck-Morss, 'The Flâneur, the Sandwichman and the Whore: The Politics of Loitering', *New German Critique*, Second Special Issue on Walter Benjamin, no. 39, 1986, p. 112.

22 Clive Scott, *Street Photography. From Atget to Cartier-Bresson*, London and New York, I.B. Tauris, 2007.

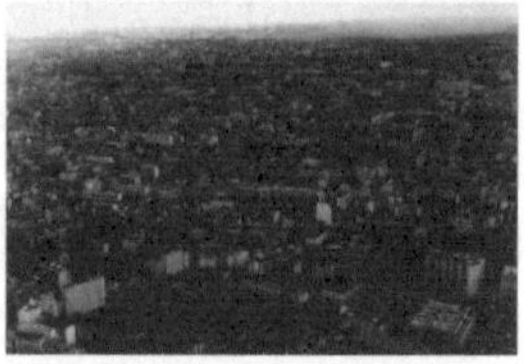

23 Zoe Leonard, *Untitled*, Paris 1989–1990, gelatin silver print, 40.6 × 50.8 cm.

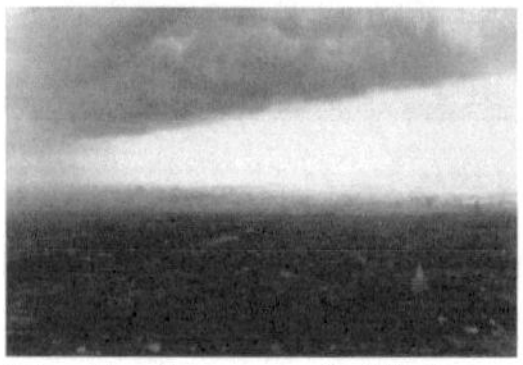

24 Zoe Leonard, *Untitled*, Paris 1989–1990, gelatin silver print, 40.6 × 50.8 cm.

organised in glass cases and cabinets, and the eighteenth-century wax model, that, following Daston and Galison, can be read as a pedagogical representation of the 'truth to nature' kind, representing a generic female anatomy rather than an individual and unique case. But as mentioned earlier, these representative systems are disturbed rather than comforted by the artist's camera. Instead of an instrument for 'mechanical objectivity', photography becomes a tool of dissension.

A similar sense of discord can be perceived in the extraordinary aerial photographs taken by the artist between 1986 and 1990, showing natural sites such as Cappadocia and the Niagara Falls and views of cities like Paris, Istanbul and Washington D.C. Some are taken from airplanes, and others from elevated points in a city. This is the case for a series of views of Paris taken between 1986 and 1990, by daytime and at night, in which the city is barely recognizable. *Untitled,* Paris 1989–1990 shows a seemingly haphazard accumulation of building blocks that almost obliterates the network of streets.[23] In other views, the sun casting its glow on the rooftops, the mist and the clouds further contribute to obscure the city below.[24] Two other pictures taken at night, presumably from the Eiffel Tower, reduce the Champ de Mars and the Avenue d'Iéna to an almost abstract pattern of glittery patches against a dark ground.[25] Leonard's fragmented, shimmering and illegible Paris is a far cry from the ideals of clarity that informed aerial photography in its early stages. Improved and generalised during World War I, it bore the promise of a comprehensive and direct, unencumbered vision, that became of prime importance in devising military strategies. In the inter-war period, aerial photography became a ubiquitous instrument with a variety of civil applications in the social sciences, ranging from geography to anthropology. (In France for instance, anthropologists Claude Lévi-Strauss and André Leroi-Gourhan created a laboratory of aerial photography at the Musée de l'Homme.) It was also an important tool for policy-makers and urban planners. In these different contexts, as Jeanne Haffner points out in her history of aerial photography in France, the 'view from above' was praised for its objectivity and the clarity of vision it provided.[26] The author cites a handbook for engineers from 1947 that makes these expectations clear:

> 'Vertical photography is an expressive image of the land, trustworthy and above all complete. It presents practically no dead angles: all the important details of topography are visible.'[27]

Haffner argues that the perfecting of aerial photography through developments in photography and

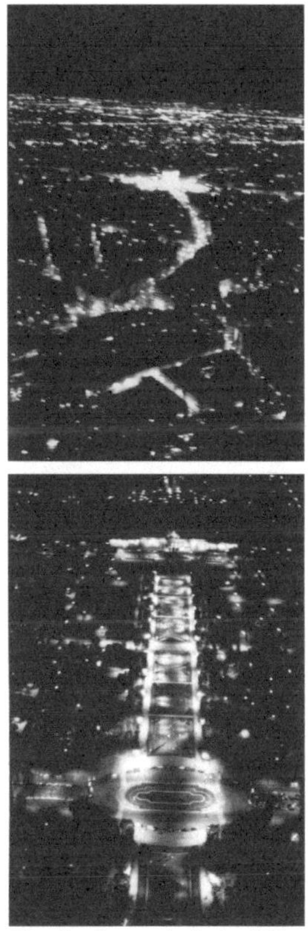

25 Zoe Leonard, *Paris*, 1986, gelatin silver print, 78.7 × 56.5 cm and Zoe Leonard, *Paris*, 1986, gelatin silver print, 87.6 × 62.2 cm.

26 Jeanne Haffner, *The View from Above: The Science of Social Space*, London and Cambridge, MA., MIT Press, 2013.

27 Institut Géographique national, *Collection de Stéréogrammes pour l'entrainement a l'identification des details sur les photographies aériennes à axe vertical* (1947), p.1, cited in Jeanne Haffner, *The View from Above: The Science of Social Space*, p. 75.

28 Jeanne Haffner, *The View from Above*, p. 109.

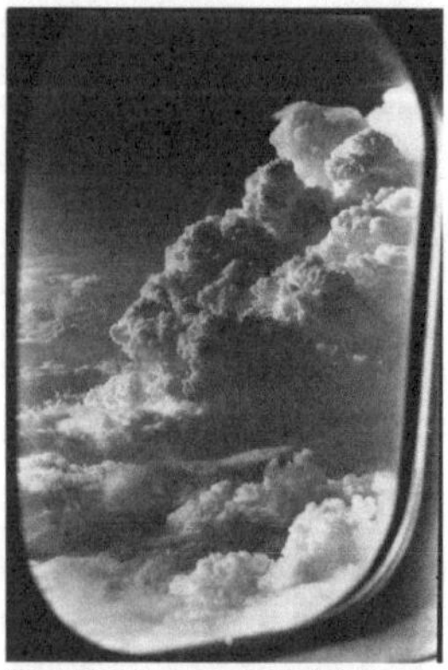

29 Zoe Leonard, *Untitled*, 1989, gelatin silver print, unique print, 25.4 × 20.3 cm.

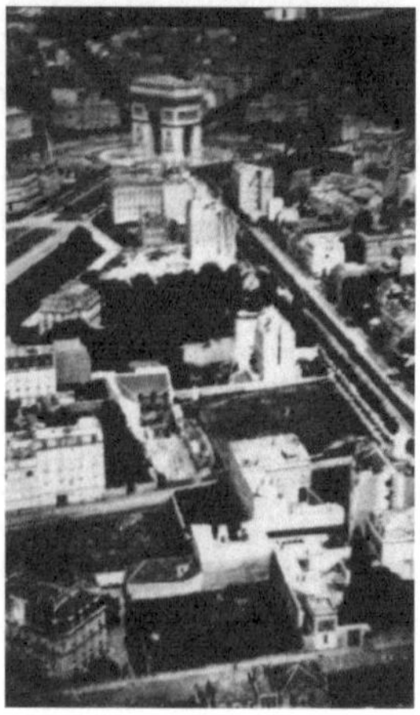

30 Nadar (Gaspard Félix Tournachon), *The Arc de Triomphe taken from a balloon*, 1868.

aeronautics (climaxing in the 1960s with the first satellite views) came to signify 'the repressiveness of state-controlled urban planning'.[28]

It its precisely from this technical proficiency and the alleged objectivity of the satellite view that Leonard distances herself in her own aerial views. Instead of showing overall, unencumbered views, her photographs of Paris include ephemeral atmospheric elements: clouds, rays of light, the steamy air after a rain shower. And when she takes them from the air, it is the rounded shape of the airplane window that becomes a prominent framing device.[29] Leonard's views of Paris are taken from a relatively low vantage point; in some photographs this seems to be the second floor of the Eiffel Tower – at some 115 metres above the ground only slightly higher than the views of Paris taken by Nadar in the late 1860s from a hot air balloon, culminating at about eighty metres above ground level.[30] Like Nadar's photographs of Paris, Leonard's pictures are fragmentary, showing the organic growth of the city rather than its predetermined planning. And when the horizon appears in the upper part of the image, the aerial view tilts towards the landscape format. This low-tech approach to aerial photography, reminiscent of its earliest years in the 1860s, also brings to mind what Le Corbusier called the 'law of the meander'; the law that enabled the architect to develop a critique of capitalism, taking as justification the chaos of cities revealed by the view from above:

> 'With its eagle eye, the airplane looks at the city. It looks at London, Paris, Berlin, New York, Barcelona, Algiers, Buenos Aires, São Paulo. Alas what a sorry account! The airplane reveals this fact: that men have built cities for men, not in order to give them pleasure, to content them, to make them happy, but to make money!'[31]

31 Le Corbusier, *Aircraft* (Studio Publications, 1935), p. 11, cited by Jeanne Haffner, p. 46.

Here, then, it is the history of photography that brings together the technical aspect of the medium with the disciplinary one. Leonard's photographs articulate the relation between discipline and technique through the conjuring and layering of multiple histories. Nowhere is this articulation more developed than in one of her most extensive projects to date, *Analogue* – a kind of atlas that tells different narratives, uses different photographic genres and is simultaneously steeped in the history of photography.

Analogue

Analogue is a collection of over four hundred photographs documenting small-scale local commerce and parallel circuits of global exchange. In its first

32 On this subject, see Margaret Iversen 'Analogue: On Zoe Leonard and Tacita Dean', *Critical Inquiry*, vol. 38, no. 4, summer 2012, pp. 796–818.

presentations at the Wexner Center for the Arts in Columbus, Ohio and at Documenta 12, Kassel in 2007, it took the form of small prints assembled in grids displayed on gallery walls. Yet it also exists in other modes of presentation: a book of colour plates and text, an archive of images and a series of individual prints. These different aspects make up for the complexity of a project that is already inscribed within its title. Can *Analogue*, be taken unambiguously to refer to the now obsolete technique of analogue photography, which the artist has always continued to use?[32] Or can it be understood as that original belief in photography as providing a visual equivalent, an analogy to the world around, something that made photography, for a while, appear as if it could be an exemplary tool in the search for objective representation in the sciences?

Leonard has traced the origins of *Analogue* back to 1998, when she began to record on camera the local shops gradually disappearing from the streets of her New York neighbourhood. From there she moved to a systematic exploration of a visual language of retail that ran parallel to the world of high-street chains and logos, one that included family-run, discount or small specialist stores bearing hand-painted logos and promotional signs. Exhibited together in sequences of twelve and more images, the photographs all display a black edge – a marker indicating that the negative had not been cropped. This acts as a frame enclosing the shop fronts and the seemingly unlimited permutations of everyday objects within their displays. The square prints are arranged in grids, allowing the eye to travel up, down and diagonally, noting recurrences and subtle visual puns. So pervasive is the format that when Leonard's camera moves from urban window display to warehouses and then to rural market stalls, the black edge of the negative continues to suggest an invisible shop window, home to an intricate and ever varying assemblage of forms, textures and colours. The organisation of her images in grid-like compositions on the wall might recall a layout often used by Bernd and Hilla Becher to present their photographs of factories, water towers and petrochemical installations. In their work as well, individual pictures inside the grid respond to one another, yet the effect here is very different. Typological classifications in *Analogue* tend to emphasise difference instead of similarity, idiosyncrasy rather than order, as the rows of pictures reveal certain combinations of objects: ironing boards always come in fours, but mattresses and washing machines in threes, toeing the sidewalk and teasing the passer-by.[33] Chests of drawers, still wrapped in plastic, are heavily discounted, already obsolete.[34] Shop windows flaunt spectacular compositions of washing-up liquid and Kleenex boxes, while white

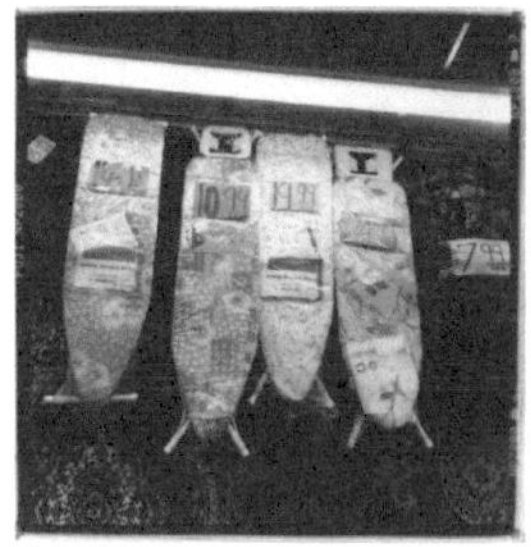

33 Zoe Leonard, *Nostrand Ave., Brooklyn*, 2003, C-print, 28 × 28 cm.

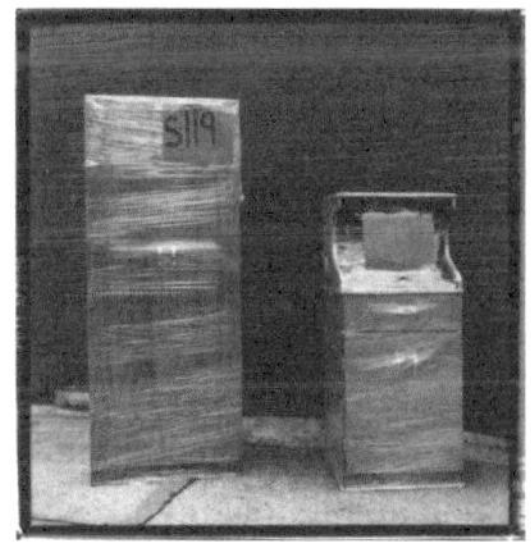

34 Zoe Leonard, *Leonard St. Brooklyn*, 2004, C-print, 28 × 28 cm.

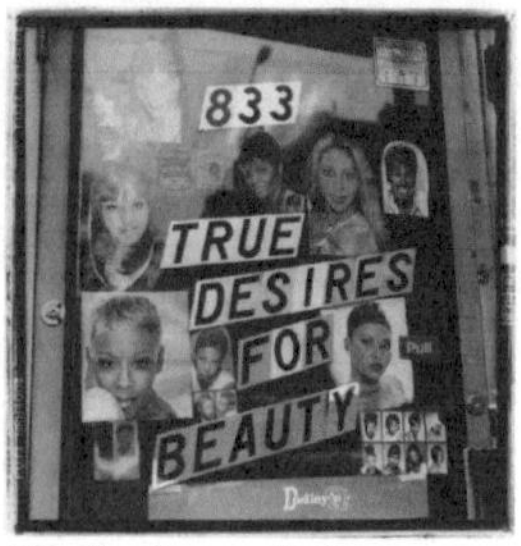

35 Zoe Leonard, *Crown Heights, Brooklyn*, 2001, C-print, 28 × 28 cm.

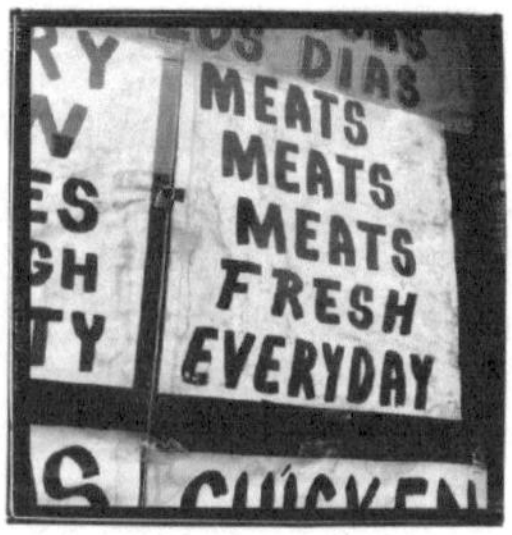

36 Zoe Leonard, *5th Ave., Brooklyn*, 1999, C-print, 28 × 28 cm.

pumps (once-worn wedding shoes?) are a constant of market displays, like a silent running gag.

Along with this visual play of objects, Leonard's camera captures the verbal and visual games created by shop signs, their absurd poems and illogical slogans: TRUE DESIRES FOR BEAUTY, says a sign in the window of a beauty parlour; MEAT 'N' MORE, reads a sign above a butcher's shop.[35] MUST SELL ALL MAKE OFFER, reads another, MEATS MEATS MEATS FRESH EVERYDAY, proclaims a fourth one, that reads like a dada sound poem.[36] Photographed on storefronts, collected and assembled in sequences, these signs also recall those ready-made poems that Louis Aragon sampled on the walls of cafés in the Passage de l'Opéra and gathered in his book *Le Paysan de Paris* (*Paris Peasant*) from 1926. Price lists of spirits in a café and of seats in a theatre, expropriation orders in shop windows created an arbitrary poetry made out of fragments of everyday life. This kind of poetic collage was a marker of surrealism as André Breton defined it in the first *Manifesto* of the movement in 1924:

> 'Everything is valid when it comes to obtaining the desired suddenness from certain associations. The pieces of paper that Picasso and Braque insert into their work have the same value as the introduction of a platitude into a

> literary analysis of the most rigorous sort. It is even permissible to entitle POEM what we get from the most random assemblage possible [...] of headlines and scraps of headlines cut out of the newspapers.'[37]

Armed with 'a practical mind – and a little Kodak', Louis Aragon put Breton's ideas into practice.[38] Reprising the posture of the flâneur or perhaps the street photographer, he combined this with a pastiche of positivism: the expression Aragon uses is 'un esprit positif', and the English translation 'practical mind' fails to convey the possible allusion to positivism.[39] Aragon minutely described the shops, cafés and cheap lodgings housed in the passage that was soon to be demolished and replaced by a stretch of the Boulevard Haussmann. Like many of the local stores photographed by Leonard in the early stages of her project in New York, the Passage de l'Opéra in Paris no longer existed when *Paris Peasant* was published in 1926, meaning that this radical surrealist text simultaneously became a documentary record of 'old Paris'. Despite this, the weight placed on this scientific quality of the project suggested by the phrase 'practical mind' should be taken with more than a pinch of salt. Positivism of course was one of the *bêtes noires* of surrealism. In the opening pages of the *manifesto,* André Breton took aim against the

37 André Breton, *Manifestoes of Surrealism,* Ann Arbor, University of Michigan Press, 1969, p. 41.

38 Louis Aragon, *Paris Peasant* (1926), London, Jonathan Cape, 1971, p. 69.

39 Louis Aragon, *Le Paysan de Paris* (1926), Paris, Gallimard, 1953, p. 71.

'positivism-inspired realism' of the French novelist Anatole France and offered 'psychic automatism' as an alternative to it. This he famously defined as the verbal expression of 'the actual functioning of thought. Dictated by thought, in the absence of any control exercised by reason', exempt from any aesthetic or moral concern.'[40] The productions of psychic automatism can thus be defined, following Walter Benjamin in his essay on surrealism, as 'documents', unaltered records of the mind, productions in which the distinction between the aesthetic and documentary is abolished.[41] In this configuration, Breton explained, the surrealist poets whose names he enumerated in the text, became no more than 'recording instruments'. In Aragon's *Paris Peasant,* this translated into alternations between a descriptive and a visionary mode. Colourful sequences recording in detail the architecture, the passers-by and the history of the passage, on occasion, suddenly lapsed into personal recollections or hallucinatory visions narrated in the same breath.

Leonard's camera, we might say, is just a 'recording instrument', helping her to observe, like a street photographer, minute accidents that occur daily in the city. She captures on film 'inconceivable analogies and connections between events,' similar to those that the surrealists perceived in Paris. However, what Leonard's camera records,

40 André Breton, *Manifestoes of Surrealism*, p. 26.

41 'Anyone who has perceived that the writings of this circle are not literature but something else – demonstrations, watchwords, documents, bluffs, forgeries if you will, but at any rate not literature – will also know, for the same reason, that the writings are concerned literally with experiences, not with theories and still less with phantasms.' Walter Benjamin, 'Surrealism: The Last Snapshot of the European Intelligentsia', Susan Sontag (ed.), *One-Way Street and Other Writings*, London, Verso, 1979, p. 225.

undergoes classification.[42] She not only presents a collage of those 'ghostly signals', but also organises her findings into series of images presented as grids.

42 Walter Benjamin, 'Surrealism', p. 231.

In favouring the incident, street photography often produces only single images, whereas documentary photography, by contrast, tends to work with series. The serial mode is a way for documentary photographers to underscore the seriousness of their engagement with a theme or a subject matter. It is a form of modesty, as the photographer claims not to say all within a single image, but it also has a pedagogical function: like a picture atlas, a documentary series is aimed at teaching or instructing through a series of images.

In *Analogue,* Leonard combines urban wandering and accidental encounters with a rigorous filtering and organisation of results. She merges the visual language of street photography – taking the viewer as a witness and relying on the instantaneous and the fragmentary – with the cooler, more distanced and authoritative language of documentary photography, which seeks to educate, alert or persuade its viewer. *Analogue* begins on a local scale, only to grow beyond it to become a research project investigating the changing forms of commercial display from 1998 to 2007, along with its local economics and (geo)politics – recessions and rehabilitations, shops closing down and moving out. Having begun with recording the changing situation of local shops in the Lower East Side of Manhattan, Leonard eventually trailed off to pick up a different yet contiguous strand. In this second narrative, she followed bundles of used clothes collected in Brooklyn and sent off to other parts of the world. She observed and recorded second-hand retail in places such as Kampala, Mexico City, Warsaw and Budapest. From charity shops to market stalls, her photographs track an economy derived from gleaning, similar to what Agnès Varda showed in the opening scene of *Les Glaneurs et la glaneuse* (2000): people picking up leftover vegetables from market stalls about to close. In Leonard's project, that ancestral rural tradition of picking up wheat left over after the harvest, which Varda chronicled, has taken on a global and economic turn. Moving from warehouses in Brooklyn to markets in Uganda, *Analogue* follows bundles of clothes from charity to re-sale.

In this strand, the project invites comparison with that great documentary narrative of global economic circuits that is Allan Sekula's *Fish Story* (1989–1995). This work consists of two slide projections and 105 photographs presenting views of container ships, shipyard workers, sailors and harbours that include Rotterdam, Hong Kong and Los Angeles, interspersed by text panels. It is the result of a five-year investigation that led Sekula around the world to visualise an international market economy that is usually perceived as immaterial and abstract. Mapping the economy of the sea, Allan Sekula provided a tangible view of global exchange.[43] But where *Fish Story* is driven by an interest in global capitalism and its effects on people, and is underpinned by a didactic narrative and militant if at times melancholic tone, the story recounted in *Analogue* progresses sideways: never does it address the viewer head-on with the assurance of a demonstration. It proceeds instead through analogies of form and the repetition of objects and through interwoven thematic strands that occasionally merge or dissolve altogether. While both projects are tales of the globalisation of trade, Sekula's story is truly global, while Leonard's *Analogue* is rooted in New York, and often more specifically in that great portal for immigration that has been the Lower East Side. However, the focus on New York enables Leonard to point out the circularity of the journey made by some of the goods she represents: they are sold in shops set up by immigrants from around the world and later resold or donated to some of the countries where those shop owners originate from; the juxtaposition of displays of New York shop windows and Polish or Ugandan market stalls suggests so much.

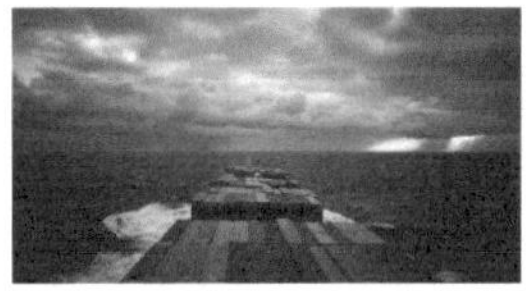

43 Allan Sekula, *Panorama. Mid-Atlantic, November 1993*, from *Fish Story* 1989–1995.

The particular quality of Leonard's images also points at an important difference with Sekula's work.

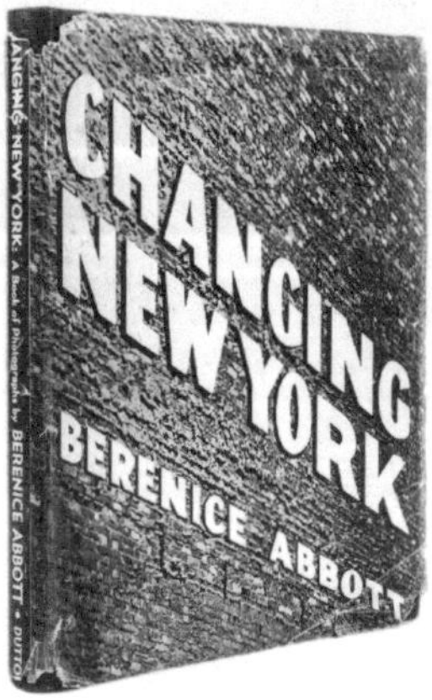

44 Berenice Abbott, *Changing New York*, New York, E.P. Dutton, 1939, book cover of original edition.

Whereas his practice, as many of his writings on photography and documentary show, stemmed from a narrative and descriptive perspective that breaks away from any aestheticizing documentary format, Leonard's work is infused with earlier photographic and literary traditions.

A lingering presence amidst the photographs of New York shop fronts is Berenice Abbott's documentary work on New York from the 1930s. Working with assistants and with the aid of scripts, Abbott captured in her book *Changing New York* (1939) the transformations in the popular culture and architecture of the city.[44] In this she was following the footsteps of Eugène Atget in Paris around 1900, whose work she discovered when working in Paris as an assistant to Man Ray and later greatly contributed to disseminate.

There is nothing elegiac or fetishist in Zoe Leonard's dedication to earlier photographers: her allusions to Abbott, Atget, Aragon and Evans, among others, do not form a referential surplus but rather point to something that runs deeper throughout *Analogue*. As much as the project maps the highs and lows of independent commerce in Manhattan, it also traces a history of photography as a technique, a cultural object and an institutional practice.

This concern with photographic history becomes explicit in Leonard's essay for the book version of *Analogue*. Written in the first person singular, 'A Continuous Signal' – a title that refers to the dictionary definition of 'analogue' reproduced in the essay – presents a collage of quotations from writers, photographers and art historians. The text steers through the history of photography, beginning with early definitions of the medium as document and moving through to its applications. Charles Marville (1816–1879) and Atget are evoked through their own words and that of their exegetes, alongside texts about the exploration of the territory of the United States through photography in the nineteenth century. Photography's role in colonialism and its use in ethnography are evoked by academics alongside writers such as Aimé Césaire and V.S. Naipaul, and are followed by reflections by modernist writers and photographers on their skill and trade. The words of Berenice Abbott and Gisele Freund intertwine with those of Marcel Proust, Virginia Woolf and James Baldwin; they form a fascinating kaleidoscope in which recognisable citations alternate with lesser-known ones. All similarly constructed in the first person singular, these quotations take on an oddly personal character, as if they were the voice of the artist herself.

The literary form used by Leonard, with its peculiar mix of intimacy and distance, recalls the literary tour-de force that Georges Perec achieved in his novel *Un homme qui dort* (*A Man Asleep*, 1967), an autobiographical work paradoxically composed entirely of literary quotations. In a similar way, the use of quotations all written in the first person singular is an invitation to read and apprehend Leonard's project through the voices of a multiplicity of photographers, writers, and artists. But more than an interpretative key to the images, it provides a clue as to the way in which Leonard conceives photography. Drawing on Perec's idea of an impersonal autobiography, we might read 'A Continuous Signal' as a biography of Leonard's *Analogue*. As a biography, the collage of quotations offers clues and information on its object. It draws a multi-faceted portrait of photography in different periods and places.

Leonard repeated this technique in *You see I am are here after all*, the completion of which followed closely that of *Analogue*. In the book accompanying the installation of pictures of Niagara Falls at the Dia Art Foundation in Beacon, she reproduced the messages written on the back of the postcards (the title of the work itself is derived from one of these notes). This collage of random messages creates a micro-history of the Falls through the many different perceptions and occurrences of its visitors. In the case of *Analogue*, 'A Continuous Signal' brings to light the archaeological underpinnings of Leonard's practice. More than the variety of sources of the

quotations, it is the very principle of collage that is significant here. For Georges Perec, collage signified 'the will to place oneself in a lineage that takes all of past writing into account. In that way, you bring your personal library to life, you reactivate your literary reserves.'[45] The use of quotations in 'A Continuous Signal' makes the viewer aware of the historical dimension of formal aspects of photography.
Zoe Leonard's *Analogue* reflects upon the construction of visual traditions in the field of documentary photography.

The composition of the photographs in *Analogue* is remarkably consistent. The world appears to be mapped out and reconfigured into a series of visual signs on shop fronts, reduced to a similar format and arranged in a way that emphasises formal analogies and disruptions. Indeed, the systematised frontal shots and close-up views in the first sections of *Analogue* stress the flatness of the image, and suggest an exhaustive scanning of the city for the purpose of a purely descriptive process. Moving outside of the Manhattan grid towards different geographies, the frame becomes looser, the viewpoint less frontal. The camera may reveal here some space around a market stall and point down towards the floor to record a disparate collection of objects scattered across an old blanket.[46] In these surroundings, unfamiliar to the artist, the camera seems to

45 Georges Perec, cited by David Bellos in *Georges Perec: A Life in Words*, Boston, David R. Godine, 1993, p. 347.

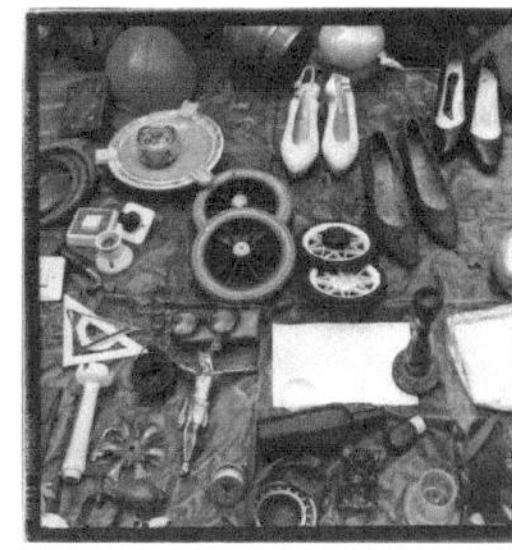

46 Zoe Leonard, *Praga Market, Warsaw*, 1999, C-print, 28 × 28 cm.

47 On these characteristics see Olivier Lugon, *Le Style documentaire d'August Sander à Walker Evans 1920–1945*, Paris, Macula, 2001, chapters 2 and 3.

48 Berenice Abbott, cited by Bonnie Yochelson in Berenice Abbott, *Changing New York*, New York, The New Press, 1997, p. 14

search for a position, to hesitate between what would be a more informative shot, both contextual and focused on its object, and a more systematic frontal view reminiscent of the images made in New York. This visual construction repeats the features of clarity, frontal view and seriality that have characterised documentary photography, features that Evans and Abbott drew from Atget.[47] Just as the essay 'A Continuous Signal' literally integrates the voices of past photographers, Atget, Abbott and other figures in Leonard's personal library are 'brought to life' and appear to speak through Leonard in her particular choices of subject matter, editing and framing. As she takes in the multiple historical narratives of documentary photography, she similarly takes on and interrogates the visual conventions that have come to define the document and the documentary.

To the question, then, of what documentary photography can be today for a contemporary artist, Leonard's work answers that above all it is a genre permeated by history. In *Analogue*, photographers of the past fit into one another like Russian dolls. Documentary photography is a genre in which Walker Evans discovers Eugène Atget through Berenice Abbott, and in which Abbott notes that she wanted to 'do in Manhattan what Atget did in Paris', equipping herself with a view camera similar to his.[48]

Decades later, picking up after Abbott, Evans and the surrealists, Leonard returns to Atget, making perceptible both a layering of allusions and a process of historical and cultural translation from one vision to another.

The images that make up *Analogue* suggest both the nineteenth-century French idea of 'documentary', as well as its later Anglo-American counterpart. The first occurrences of the term 'documentary' in French dates from 1876, when it was used to characterise the Orientalist paintings of Eugène Fromentin and what was then perceived as their ethnographic exactness.[49] Long before documentary became a genre, mostly in film and photography, the term documentary thus served to describe images or texts that provide information. Only in the 1920s and 30s did the term move from adjective to noun. Thanks to filmmaker and critic John Grierson, and subsequently Walker Evans and the WPA photographers in the United States in the 1930s, it evolved into a genre in which debates about realism, aesthetics and morality were of prime importance.

This awareness of photographic conventions is also built into the three presentation formats of *Analogue* – a photography book, an archive and a series of forty individual dye-transfer prints. While this threefold existence might result from practical concerns, it also corresponds to historically signifi-

49 Paul-Émile Littré, *Dictionnaire de la langue française*, tome 2, Paris, Le club français du livre, 1957, p. 1789.

cant modes of preservation and circulation of photography. The archive refers to the collecting of photographic documents for investigative and recording purposes that originated in the nineteenth century. The photography book is the format that enabled the widest distribution of documentary photography, as opposed, for instance, to reportage or studio portraiture, in the twentieth century. The exhibition print, finally, points to the presentation of photography as art in the museum space, and refers to the enlargement of photographs to accommodate the posture of the standing viewer and the scale of the museum wall – an argument put forward by Hilla Becher to explain the different sizes of the photographic prints she made with Bernd Becher, where the size of the images doubled from grid assemblages to single pictures on the wall.[50] By contrast, the dimensions of the images in Leonard's *Analogue* are relatively similar in each mode of presentation. This suggests that while the work reflects on the different purposes of photography, it may be read as a homogeneous collection of images and – although strictly speaking it is neither – as an archive or an atlas.

We seem to be looking both at a nineteenth-century French *fond d'archive* and a contemporary database. The narrative that emerges through the dates given for each photograph and the temporally

50 Hilla Becher in Jean-Pierre Krief, *Bernd et Hilla Becher. Contacts* (film), 14 minutes, Arte France, 2002.

homogeneous sequences recall the classification by provenance and acquisition date of a *fond d'archive*. But this organisation, which historically was believed to yield the most coherent information, is supplanted in other thematic series in *Analogue*, resulting from permutations and rearrangements of documents culled from various sources and over different periods of time. These later series open up wider potential readings. Their instability – so different from the stable strategies of a *fond d'archive* – is reminiscent of the principle of the database, in which categories can be called upon for particular requests, creating ever-changing orderings of documents. The integration of divergent forms of the archive echoes the coexisting strands of a project that explores not only the historical and geographical mutations of capitalism but also a multitude of local and global micro- histories identified by collections of shop signs, advertising posters, flags and hand-painted logos. In this, *Analogue* epitomises the changing idea of the archive from a closed body of information for select users to an open database whose existence is defined by and dependant upon its public visibility, as epitomised by the extensive presentations of the project in Kassel, Madrid and elsewhere.

But if we try to read *Analogue* as an atlas, we should following the characteristics defined by

51 Lorraine Daston and Peter Galison, *Objectivity*, p. 22.

Daston and Galison – insist on different issues than those pertaining to the archival. Atlases, they write, 'are systematic compilations of working objects [...] For initiates and neophytes alike, the atlas trains the eye to pick out certain kinds of objects as exemplary.' And a few lines further: 'the atlases drill the eye of the beginner and refresh the eye of the old hand.'[51] As an atlas, *Analogue* might be said to visually teach us about shop signs or window displays in certain parts of the world and at a certain epoch. It is like Atget's collection of images of wrought iron balustrades or shop signs that might be used to study stylistic variations of specifically defined objects. But to the comparison of objects across a particular field, Leonard adds a temporal dimension. This becomes evident when we compare *Analogue* to *You see, I am here after all.* In the presentation of this work at Dia:Beacon, 4000 postcards of the Niagara Falls were displayed across the vast galleries; the effect of this mapping of the site through thousands of identical views was to train the eye – not so much in the different views of the site, as these are mostly standardised, but in identifying the small variations of colour and texture that each era imprints on a postcard. A sky that is grey at times and blue at others, green bushes that are subdued or highlighted, perhaps through the use of filters or different films. Looking across the walls or in the pages of the book that repeats detailed views of the installation, those small variations within time chink at the homogeneity of representations.[52] In other words, *Analogue* and *You see, I am here after all* both function as archives and atlases: we travel through time as well as through space; we learn about different ways of seeing and different objects, but also about how these both diverge from and echo one another through time. And it is in this way, ultimately, that Leonard bridges the gap between the elusive objectivity of scientific representation and the agency of the thinking self: through the deep-seated awareness of a history of photographic forms that acts as a pair of lenses through which we look out at the world and the objects in it.

52 Zoe Leonard, *You see I am here after all*, New York, Dia Art Foundation, 2010.

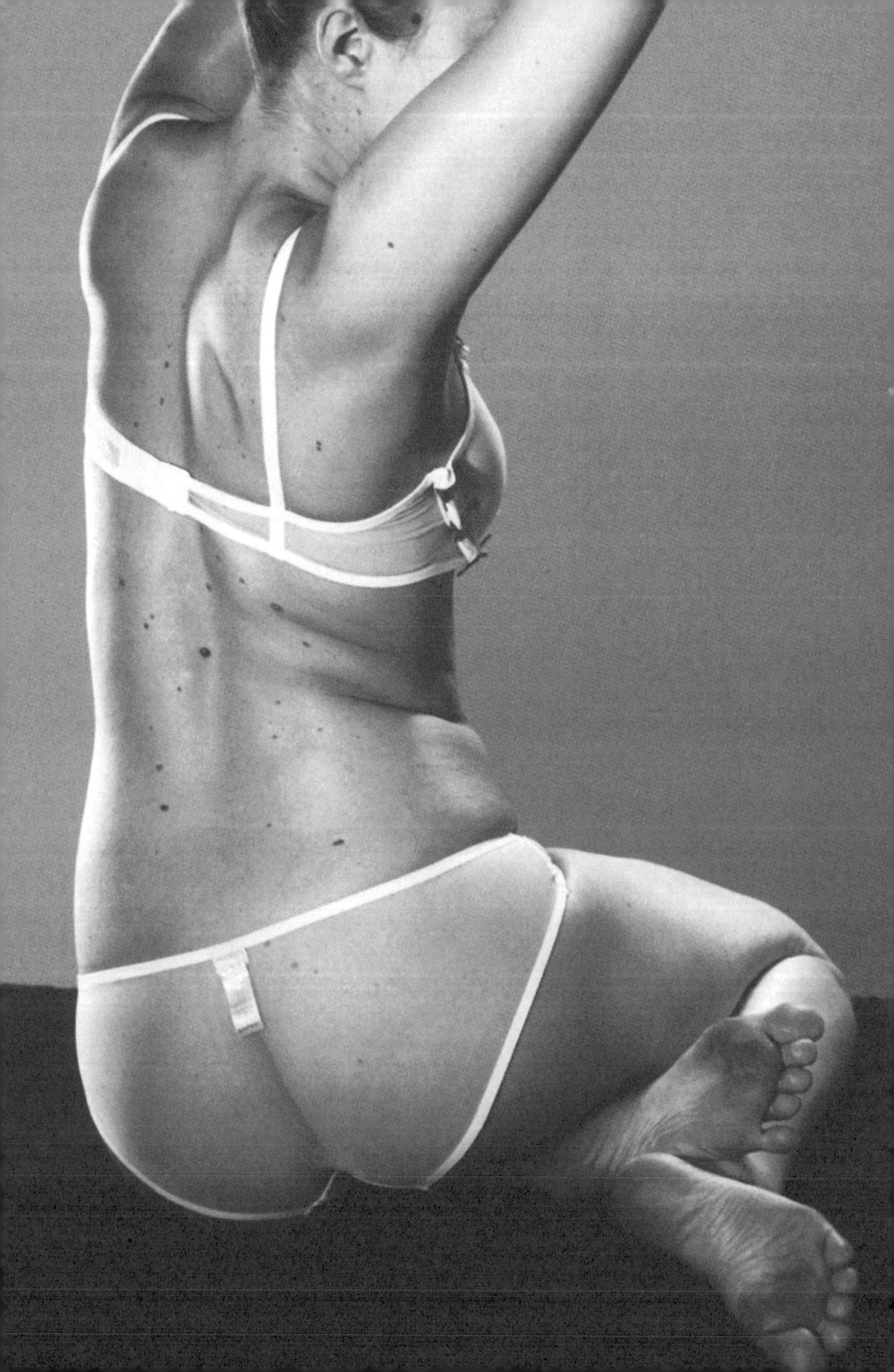

Three

Industrial Images

In 1934, reacting against the ubiquity of creative photography – and more widely, to the affinity of the medium with mass-produced objects, Walter Benjamin, in a lecture entitled 'Der Autor als Produzent' ('The Author as Producer'), called for its mobilization in favour of political responsibility. 'What we must demand from the photographer is the ability to put such a caption beneath his pictures as will rescue it from the ravages of modishness and confer upon it a revolutionary use-value.'[1] Whether we take it literally or not, this call for text anchoring the image returns in photo-conceptualism, where it becomes the subject of word play and ambiguity. Looking back at these different ideas concerning the relation between text and image, Christopher Williams reflects upon the legibility and illegibility of photography and its relation to industry.

1 Walter Benjamin, 'The Author as Producer' (1934), in Victor Burgin (ed.), *Thinking Photography*, London, Macmillan, 1982, p. 24.

In his photographs from the series *For Example: Dix-Huit Leçons Sur La Société Industrielle*

Christopher Williams,
Untitled (Study in Yellow/Berlin)
Dirk Schaper Studio, Berlin,
June 21, 2007 (No.1), 2008,
C-print, 50.8 × 40.6 cm.

(2003–), Christopher Williams brings together a heterogeneous ensemble of objects that includes, among others, chocolate bars and rubber tyres, photographic equipment, shower screens and a chestnut tree branch. Sometimes accompanied by a human presence – a smiling model or manicured hands presenting objects to the camera – each item is shot individually against a luminous white background. The imposing size of the pictures – framed, they measure just short of a square metre in size – suggests they should be interpreted in relation to traditional pictorial genres: still-life, portrait and landscape. Yet both the everyday quality of the objects depicted as well as the sharp outlines and bright colours of the photographs evoke, rather than fine art, categorisations borrowed from the realm of applied photography. What we see closely resembles fashion photographs, pack-shot images destined for sales catalogues, and technical pictures for user manuals. Blown up and lifted out of the context of the magazine page or shrunk in size from the billboard, these pictures have found their way into the art gallery. As applied photography, the images recall the interdependence that exists between mass-produced industrial objects and optimally lit, technically flawless photography. In this context photography not only illustrates the objects but turns them into commercially desirable things, a process that is indispensable in the circuit of production and consumption that ensures the growth of industrial societies.[2]

Might this be one of those 'eighteen lectures on industrial society' given by the artist, as the title of his work suggests? When asked about the reference to Raymond Aron's 1963 classic comparative study of industrial development in capitalist and socialist societies after 1945, *Dix-Huit Leçons Sur La Société Industrielle (Eighteen Lectures on Industrial Society)*, Williams replied that this title corresponded well to 'the Cold War programme that I wanted to explore.'[3] Pressed for clarification the artist expressed a keen interest in 'the restructuring of cultural life in the post-War period and in particular the Americanisation of European popular culture'. The explanation that Williams gives here, in particular the choice of the term 'programme', perhaps suggests a concerted endeavour on his part to create an iconography of popular culture and everyday life in the era of the Cold War. This in turn grants *For Example: Dix-Huit Leçons Sur La Société Industrielle* a documentary quality, as though the project aimed to collect and present visual documents and record an epoch, arranged into an archive or a documentary narrative. Perhaps it is this interpretation that the interviewer had in mind when he described Williams' work as 'a series *about* the Cold War.'[4]

2 On the relationship between industrial object and photography, see Thomas Seelig and Urs Stahel (eds.), *The Ecstasy of Things: From the Functional Object to the Fetish in 20th Century Photographs*, Göttingen, Steidl, 2004.

3 Raymond Aron, *Dix-Huit Leçons sur la société industrielle*, Paris, Seuil, 1963. 'Christopher Williams in Conversation with Mark Godfrey', *Afterall*, issue 16, 2007, p. 63.

4 'Christopher Williams in Conversation with Mark Godfrey', *Afterall*, issue 16, 2007, p. 63. My emphasis.

5 Williams calls the selections of images he presents in each show 'revisions'. The first exhibition of the series took place in 2005 under the title: *For Example: Dix-Huit Leçons Sur La Société Industrielle Archéologie, Beaux-Arts, Ethnographie, Théatre-Vérité, Couleur Europeénne, Couleur Soviétique, Couleur Chinoise Variétés,* Contemporary Art Gallery, Vancouver, Canada. In 2011, the 15th revision of the series was presented in Leverkusen under the title: *Christopher Williams. For Example: Dix-Huit Leçons Sur La Société Industrielle (Revision 15),* Museum Schloss Morsbroich, Leverkusen. The thirteen intervening exhibitions of the work took place in different commercial galleries, contemporary art galleries and museums around the world.

This project would no doubt be a feast for a cultural historian wishing to investigate such an iconography. Yet Williams' pictures are not photographic documents to be used as testimonies of an epoch; they are works of art that cite commercial photography. This becomes clear if we look at his pictures in the context of an exhibition rather than a book. The choice of images as well as the method of display are carefully worked out in each of the exhibitions of the series so as to obfuscate any thematic or chronological reading from one image to the other.[5] Hung low on the walls, the pictures at first exude a cool muteness. It is only after a while that they begin to speak; the pointing fingers and hands that hold objects in the pictures for instance begin to draw the viewer's attention to the usefulness and practicality of these objects. Images converse with one another and extend the discussion across the rooms and beyond, calling on other art works and objects apart from those immediately present and thereby creating a seemingly endless constellation of references and ideas.

While they do not form a documentary series *about* the Cold War, Williams' photographs are nonetheless concerned with the era of the Cold War and, in particular, with the role that documents play in representing historical events and material culture. We might ask, for example, how visual documents can be used to testify, represent or otherwise contribute to the edification of historical constructions, or what the role is of photographic technology in this process. To answer such questions requires us to understand the way Christopher Williams has played with the idea of the document in different contexts and how his ideas have developed over time. As there is a distinction between his early work from the 1980s and his most recent series, in the first part of this chapter I look at how Williams has processed the legacy of conceptual art through an interest in the archive and the document as evidence. In the years that follow, and particularly in the collection of photographs entitled *For Example: Die Welt ist Schön,* Williams displaces his investigation of the document from post-conceptualism to the interwar debates around art photography and applied photography. This interest is carried forth in more recent years, in *For Example: Dix-Huit Leçons Sur La Société Industrielle.* Returning to that series in the last part of this chapter, I interpret the artist's specific interest in the Cold War period in relation to a wider commercial and photographic culture.

Dislocating Evidence or The Document after Conceptual Art

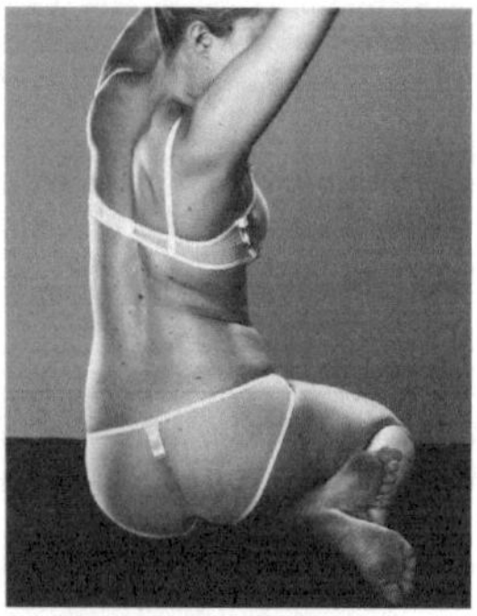

6 Christopher Williams, *Untitled (Study in Yellow/Berlin) Dirk Schaper Studio, Berlin, June 21, 2007 (No.1)*, 2008, C-print, 50.8 × 40.6 cm.

To introduce Williams' critical revision of conceptualism and its use of the document, I begin, as in the chapter on Zoe Leonard, with reading a work that has a synecdochic value for his oeuvre, unfolding, as it does, a conceptual twist as well as a constellation of references that make it a summary of many of the artist's interests. *Untitled (Study in Yellow/Berlin) Dirk Schaper Studio, Berlin, June 21, 2007 (No. 1)* seems something of an oddball amidst the other pictures from the series that include figures.[6] The photograph shows a lingerie model sitting down, stretching up and displaying a translucent white set of underwear in a flattering pose. Yet instead of looking into the camera as one might expect, only the back of the model is presented to the viewer, revealing nothing of her head or face but the nape of her neck. What we can however see is a bare back speckled with prominent moles, yellow clips holding the bra in place, the label of the underpants, and the conspicuously dirty soles of her feet.

Whereas a view from the front might have evoked a lingerie advertisement or a photograph from a mail order catalogue documenting the available stock, this reversed image, resulting from a 180-degree rotation of the camera angle, prohibits any such identification. Instead it suggests a stolen image or a 'behind the scenes' view of a commercial photo shoot – altogether a different kind of visual document.

This peculiar image thus seems to belong to two distinct photographic genres in which different ideas of the document are at work. It is at once a commercial photograph awkwardly turned back to front and also a behind-the-scenes view documenting the production of a commercial image. To me, the dirty feet and uneven skin of the model are reminiscent of Colette's powerful depiction of the unseen side of show business in *L'Envers du music hall* (*Music Hall Sidelights*, 1913), where she described the dribbling make-up and strained limbs of the performers, invisible to the pleasure-seeking audience during the show, and only revealed in the dreary aftermath of the performance. If we take into account the clips used for tightening the bra, we could see the photograph as an ironic perspective on the simulacra of fashion photography and its concern with a perfection of appearances, and thus even as an image of the underside of capitalism.

However, as an art work the reversing of the image in *Untitled (Study in Yellow/Berlin)* summons different associations: the picture here is 'wrong' as a professional image. The principle here is similar to the way in which John Baldessari played with

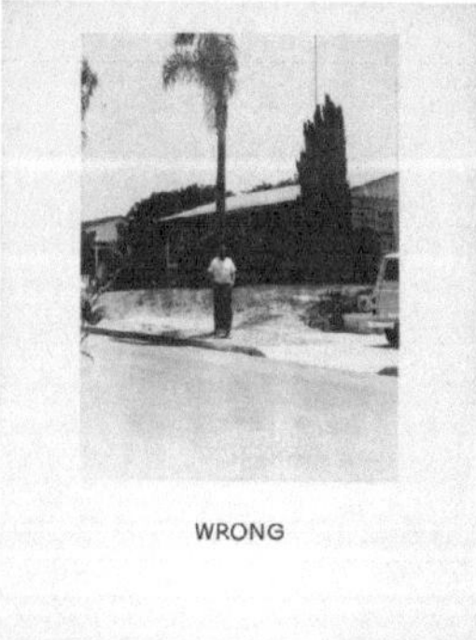

7 John Baldessari, *Wrong* (1966–68), 149.86 × 114.3 cm. The Los Angeles County Museum of Art.

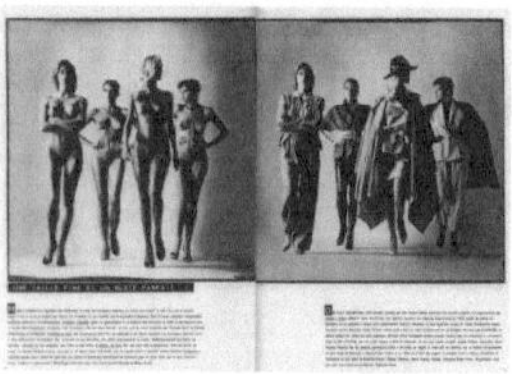

8 Helmut Newton, *They are Coming*, 1981, diptych part of a series of six photographs published as illustrations for the article by Lorraine Bolloré, 'Silhouette 82', *Vogue Paris*, November 1981, pp 164–165.

amateur photography rules in the late 1960s, in works like the series *Wrong* (1966–68), which defy the basic compositional rules of photography.[7]

Yet the awkwardness of what might be 'wrong' in Williams' photograph *Untitled (Study in Yellow/ Berlin)*... is slightly different. For here the technique itself is not wrong: despite presenting a view of the back of the model, the picture is otherwise flawless, and as professional as the front or 'right' side would be. The picture thus incorporates a contradiction: while the view from the rear seems to undermine any authority that a putative view from the front would convey, at the same time the very quality of the picture eliminates any sense of it being a stolen image or an amateur-quality snapshot, therefore rendering the image purposefully unresolved. Such ambiguousness recalls the strategy employed by Helmut Newton who, in the 1970s and 1980s, famously extended his professional fashion shoots in order to take a few extra pictures 'for himself' in the same settings and with the same models, thereby creating an 'artistic' variation of his commercial images. In the most famous of these, a diptych known under the title *They're Coming!*, he staged a naked version that exactly mirrored a 'dressed' photograph of four women walking towards the photographer. Both pictures were circulated commercially.[8] Newton's procedure somewhat cynically exploits the fine line between commercial and art photography, conceiving of the two genres as distorted mirrors of each other. Yet at the same time the procedure also refers to the tradition of the nude in Fine Art. Williams likewise refers to different genres. By reversing the image he displaces the subject matter of his photograph, transforming the lingerie model into an artist's model in the studio.

The title of Williams' work underpins this reading. *Untitled (Study in Yellow/Berlin)...* does not give the technical specifications of the object represented (the lingerie), unlike some of Williams' other photographs (see infra). The artist has instead opted for a title that alludes to the tradition of modernist painting, exemplified by Whistler's 'harmonics', 'symphonies' and 'studies' in colour. Williams himself has pointed to possible references in his own work to the realm of Fine Art, mentioning in particular the work of Francis Picabia.[9] Indeed there is a similarity between the pose of the model in the present photograph and some of Picabia's saucy nudes of the early 1940s, while the see-through lingerie reads as a witty reference to the transparency effects in some of Picabia's earlier paintings from the mid-1930s.[10] Moreover, in invoking Picabia's nudes that were painted after erotic photographs published in so-called 'girlie' magazines, Williams brings the viewer straight back to the world of commercial

9 Christopher Williams, in conversation with the author, Amsterdam, 30 August 2010.

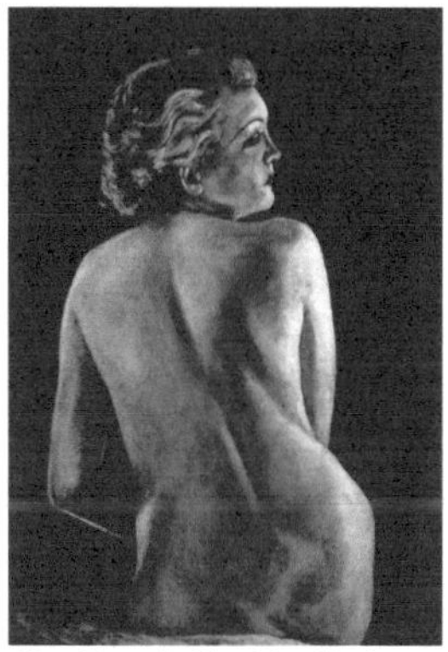

10 Francis Picabia, *Nu de dos*, 1942–1944, oil on wood, 105 × 75 cm.

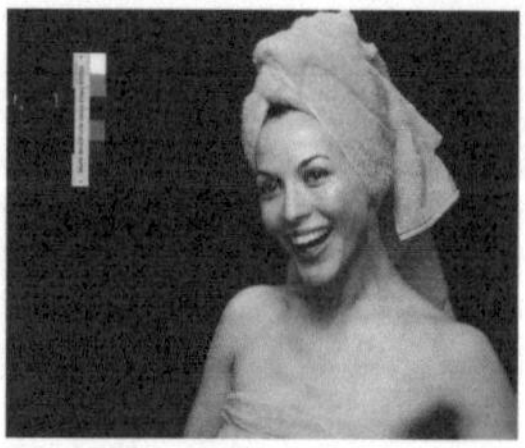

photography. The 'study in yellow' loses some of its Whistlerian high art associations and becomes a technical verdict on the image. As there is precious little yellow immediately visible in the image (aside from the clips holding the bra) the reference to the colour in the title can be taken instead as an indication of a faulty balance of colours that would make the photograph unacceptable for commercial circulation.[11]

The interplay between Fine Art and commercial photography that appears in the title and the pose of the model also rehearses some of the themes that appeared in French art criticism in the second half of the nineteenth century, when critics seemed caught in a wrestle between allegory and realism in nude painting. For example, when one of Courbet's nudes was described as 'a washerwoman masquerading as a nymph',[12] and critics spoke of the 'yellow stomach' and dirty feet of Manet's *Olympia*, they expressed bewilderment in the face of the shedding of allegory in favour of a realism that brought painting dangerously close to photography, as bathers became laundresses, and goddesses prostitutes.[13] These markers of the realist revolution were indeed shared with early photographic depictions of the female nude in French photography in the 1850s. In the time before the technology and skills existed to provide the public with idealised depictions of the female body,

11 Yellow is recurrent in Williams' images and seems to refer both to the cover of Georges Bataille's journal *Documents* (see note 13, *infra*.) and also to the colour of packaging of the photography firm Kodak, which is the subject of several images. See for instance: *Kodak Three Point Reflection Guide, Copyright 1968 Eastman Kodak Company, 1968. (Meiko laughing), Vancouver, B.C. Wednesday, April 6, 2005*, 2005, C-print, 50.8 × 61 cm, in which the towel wrapping the model's hair is bright Kodak yellow, while the colour is missing from the colour guide strip.

12 Eric Homberger, 'The Model's Unwashed Feet: French Photography in the 1850s', In Peter Collier and Robert Lethbridge (eds.), *Artistic Relations: Literature and the Visual Arts in Nineteenth Century France*, New Haven and London, Yale University Press, 1994, pp. 130–143.

13 Jules Claretie, 'L'Artiste', 15 May 1865, reprinted in George Heard Hamilton, *Manet and his Critics*, New York, W.W. Norton & Co, 1969, p. 73.

some of the earliest commercial nude photography also featured dirty feet and slippers left lying around, which lent these pictures, taken in barely disguised domestic settings, a home-made or candid character.[14]

Although there are no slippers in Williams' photograph and the setting is that of the aesthetically neutral space of a photography studio, furnished only with a dark-coloured and slightly crumpled rug, the dirty feet and uneven skin colour of the model connect the work to that early history of commercial photography and its rapid expansion – 'industrial madness', as Ann McCauley calls it – in the Paris of the Second Empire.[15] By calling up that earlier history at the same time as evoking the Cold War era, Williams invites us to read this picture in relation to another, later moment of 'industrial madness'. It was a century later that the context of unprecedented economic growth in Western Europe during the 1960s and 70s led to the rapid development of mass media, including the expansion of television, the rise of advertising and the growth of commercial photography as a dominant form of visual communication.

By reversing his image, Williams destroys the document as a stable vector of meaning and thereby invites the onlooker to open up to the possibility of another view into more instable and multiple realities. The two sides of the image – one virtual, the

14 Eric Homberger, 'The Model's Unwashed Feet: French Photography in the 1850s'.

15 Elizabeth Ann McCauley, *Industrial Madness: Commercial Photography in Paris, 1848–71*, New Haven, Yale University Press, 1994.

other materialised – correspond to different purposes of documentation that each conjure particular networks and contexts of production, circulation and interpretation. Together they evoke different and coexisting frameworks and socio-economic contexts of photographic practice. The 180 degree rotation of the camera angle can be read metaphorically as the shift from industrial to post-industrial or information society; in photographic terms it signals a shift from analogue photography to the endlessly modifiable digital image. It is in this sense that *Untitled (Study in Yellow/Berlin)...* works as a synecdoche for all of Williams' photographic work.

The rotation of the camera angle that makes *Untitled (Study in Yellow/Berlin)...* so complex and ambiguous an image reprises directly a rotation that takes place in a photo piece created by Williams at the outset of his career. In this work, consisting of four photographs and a lengthy title, the artist staged a famous public figure seen from the back. This piece is key to understanding how Williams works through the legacy of photo-conceptual art practices of the preceding two decades, in particular taking up questions of evidence, deskilling and the archive.

Made in 1981, and first presented at the time he was completing his studies at the California Institute of the Arts (CalArts), this work bears an unusually long and site-specific title that both provides a set of instructions to the artist and a series of clues for the viewer to interpret the work. I give here the title it assumed when the work was presented in the exhibition *Under the Big Black Sun, California Art 1974–1981* in 2011–2012: *SOURCE: The Photographic Archive, John F. Kennedy Library, Columbia Point on Dorchester Bay, Boston, Massachusetts, 02125, USA; CONDITIONS FOR SELECTION: There are two conditions: the photograph or photographs must be dated May 10, 1963, and the subject, John F. Kennedy, must have his back turned toward the camera. All photographs on file fulfilling these requirements are used. TECHNICAL TREATMENT: The photographs are subjected to the following operations: rephotography (4 × 5" copy negative), enlargement (from 8 × 10" to 11 × 14" by use of the copy negative), and cropping (1/16" is removed from all sides of the rephotographed, enlarged image). PRESENTATION: Under the Big Black Sun: California Art 1974–1981, 1 October 2011 – 13 February 2012, The Museum of Contemporary Art, Los Angeles, Christopher Williams, 1981.*[16]

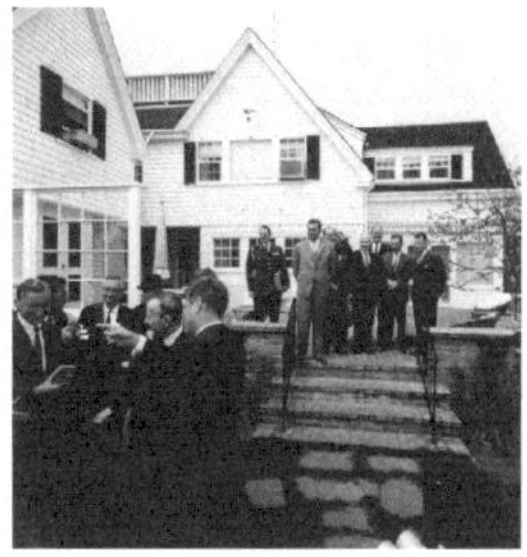

16 Christopher Williams, *SOURCE: The Photographic Archive, John F. Kennedy Library, Columbia Point on Dorchester Bay, Boston, Massachusetts, 02125, USA; CONDITIONS FOR SELECTION: There are two conditions: the photograph or photographs must be dated May 10, 1963, and the subject, John F. Kennedy, must have his back turned toward the camera. All photographs on file fulfilling these requirements are used. TECHNICAL TREATMENT: The photographs are subjected to the following operations: rephotography (4 × 5" copy negative), enlargement (from 8 × 10" to 11 × 14" by use of the copy negative), and cropping (1/16" is removed from all sides of the rephotographed, enlarged image). PRESENTATION: Under the Big Black Sun: California Art 1974–1981, 1 October 2011–13 February 2012, The Museum of Contemporary Art, Los Angeles, Christopher Williams, 1981.* Detail, 1981, Chromogenic print, 27.8 × 27.8 cm.

At first view the work I will abbreviate as *SOURCE: The Photographic Archive*... seems to rehearse a number of motifs and procedures usually identified with conceptual art of an earlier generation, and which include: arbitrarily determined selection criteria; separation between the idea and its

17 Sol LeWitt, 'Paragraphs on Conceptual Art', *Artforum*, summer 1967, pp.79–83.

18 The work is usually described as comprising four photographs, although only the two same ones generally appear in publications.

realisation that is achieved by following the instructions provided; and the favouring of the idea over the completed object. In this piece Williams is working through a legacy that he was directly acquainted with, as Douglas Huebler, Michael Asher, and John Baldessari were teachers at CalArts at the time Williams studied there. By repeating a classic format of text and image work familiar within conceptual art, Williams encourages the viewer to favour the textual aspect of his work, the part which describes most directly the idea behind the project, or 'the most important aspect of the work', as Sol LeWitt noted in his 'Paragraphs on Conceptual Art'.[17] Following this logic, the photographs themselves are present merely in order to materialise or testify to the result of the selection process described in the text. This relation between text and image, typical of conceptual art, over-determines our first approach to the four pictures.[18] They show a group of men in suits standing outside a house, on the porch and in the garden. One of them is John Fitzgerald Kennedy. He is inconspicuous yet clearly recognizable, seen from the back, and appearing in a corner of each image. The pictures are unremarkable save for their inclusion of Kennedy and thus their sole virtue seems to be that they match the criteria described in the title. The images are made redundant by the caption even if they respond to that most straightforward purpose attributed to photography, namely to faithfully record an object or an action and thereby provide material evidence of its existence at a given moment.

This idea of the 'anti-photograph' appeared in some of the early accounts of the use of photography by conceptual artists with an interest in the linguistic aspects of conceptualism.[19] The idea of the 'anti-photograph' corresponded to the keenness of certain artists (for example Ed Ruscha) to downplay the importance of the medium, which they often regarded as just a convenient tool for recording and presenting an idea or a process. Other artists working within conceptual art, however, developed an often humorous reflection on the technical properties of photography. The idea that, beyond providing visual evidence, it could be used to reflect on the paradoxes and ironies of a media-saturated world was central to a number of artists, including notably those of Eleanor Antin, Jan Dibbets, John Hilliard and Douglas Huebler. Huebler's text and photo work *Duration Piece #31 Boston* (1974), for example, reconsiders the notion of the 'snapshot'.[20] This work paradoxically foregrounds the duration of the image by manipulating the shutter speed of the camera so as to represent moments from two different years within a single image, as the text in the work explained:

19 Nancy Foote, 'The Anti-photographers', *Artforum*, September 1976, pp. 46–54.

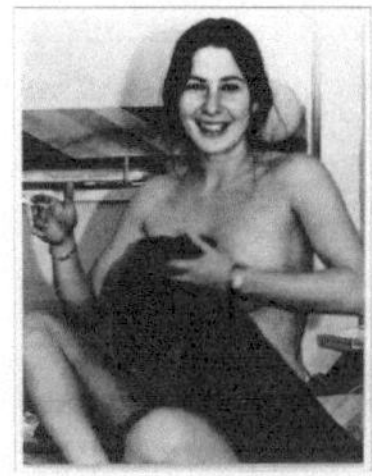

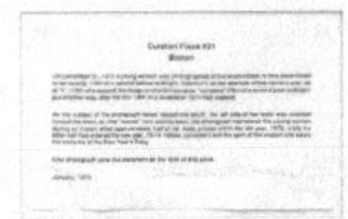

20 Douglas Huebler, *Duration Piece #31 Boston*, 1974, typewritten sheet of paper and black and white photograph.

21 See <www.jfklibrary.org>, retrieved 6 July 2014.

> 'On December 31st, 1973, a young woman was photographed at the exact instant in time determined to be exactly 1/8th of a second before midnight. Inasmuch as the aperture of the camera was set at "4" (1/4th of a second) the image on the film became "complete" 1/8th of a second past midnight: put another way, after the first 1/8th of a second of 1974 had elapsed. [...]'

In this work Huebler explored the technical limits and abilities of the camera as evidenced in the photographic process. By contrast, Williams, in SOURCE: *The Photographic Archive...* uses found photographs and thereby shifts the focus from technical aspects of the camera to the photographic print itself. He subjects his prints to reframing, cropping and re-photographing thus enabling different angles and details of the image to appear.

By deciding to work with found photographs possibly taken by an official White House photographer as documentation, and by selecting these images from an archival library that presents itself today as 'the nation's official memorial to President Kennedy,' Williams is not only exploiting the technical properties of photography.[21] He also approaches photography as a cultural object. As such, the caption of SOURCE: *The Photographic Archive...* bears resemblance in more than one way to an early text and photo work by John Hilliard. Hilliard's *Cause of Death* (1974) takes a thoroughly tongue-in-cheek approach to the uses and abuses of photography by the print media. The work consists of four almost identical photographs each showing a human figure covered in a light-coloured sheet and lying on rocky ground.[22] Each image is accompanied by a single word caption above the image that corresponds to the variations of framing of the photographs and the resulting interpretation that could be derived from each variation. The different ways of cropping the images mean that each reveals a detail of the surrounding landscape, which is obliterated from the other views: a boulder, a cliff, the seashore and a campfire. Underscoring these elements, each photograph is accompanied by a single word that provides a succinct 'cause of death'. These are respectively: 'crushed', 'fell', 'drowned' and 'burned'. In *Cause of Death*, Hilliard presents a straightforward case-study to demonstrate the inability of a photograph to convey anything but partial information. At the same time, the subject matter chosen by the artist openly alludes to the way in which photography is subject to manipulation by the media for sensationalist purposes. Like Hilliard, Williams demonstrates an interest in photographic manipulation by reframing photographs so as to alter their possible meaning. His choice of subject is all the more significant since

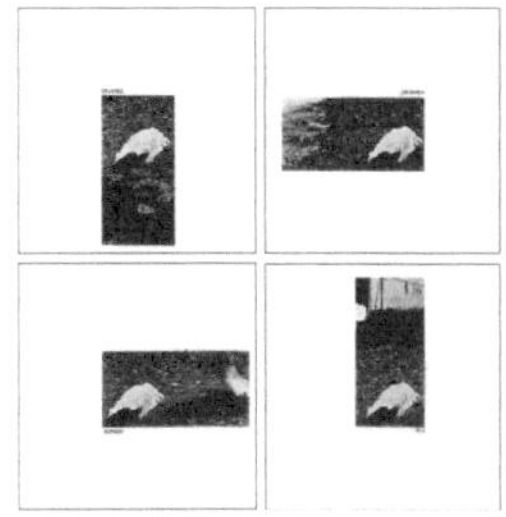

22 John Hilliard, *Cause of Death*, 1974.

Kennedy, often referred to as the most photographed person of his time, achieved a success in the 1961 elections that has been attributed to his innovative and persuasive use of the media. Yet whereas Hilliard encourages a detached reading of his four photographs that display deadpan, or slapstick humour, in contrast, and despite their apparent lack of drama, the photographs selected by Williams have a highly emotional content. For although the effect and purpose of the cropping and reframing is conspicuously absent from the lengthy description in the work's title, the resulting images clearly manifest a disquieting impression of foreboding, focusing as they do on the back of the head of the American president some six months before he was assassinated, shot in that specific part of his body. Moreover, unlike Hilliard, who posits the viewer as the distant and critical recipient of a news item, Williams manipulates his photographs in order to position us in the place of the camera operator and, by analogy, in the place of the killer.

Even if Tom Crow rightly noted that Williams' precise knowledge of the history of the movement 'put[s] his enterprise on an equal footing with the written histories of conceptual art,' *SOURCE: The Photographic Archive...* is not a textbook reading of conceptualism. Instead, it consciously undermines and turns inside out some of the best-known motifs and procedures of the movement; in particular the trope of photographic documents used as straightforward evidence.[23] For instance, the act of creating an emotional response on the part of the viewer not only reverses the cool and usually distant aesthetic of much photography-based conceptual art. It also creates an unbridgeable gap between text and image. Here the photographs critically exceed their function of simply providing visual proof of the process described in the caption. The viewer is encouraged to construct a chain of associations, anticipating the drama that would unfold six months later in Dallas.

23 Thomas Crow, *Modern Art in the Common Culture*, New Haven, Yale University Press, 1998, pp. 216 -217.

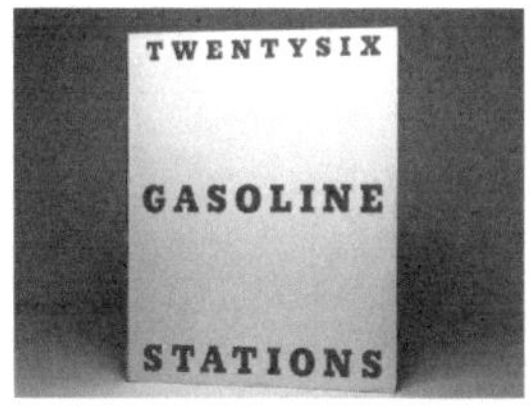

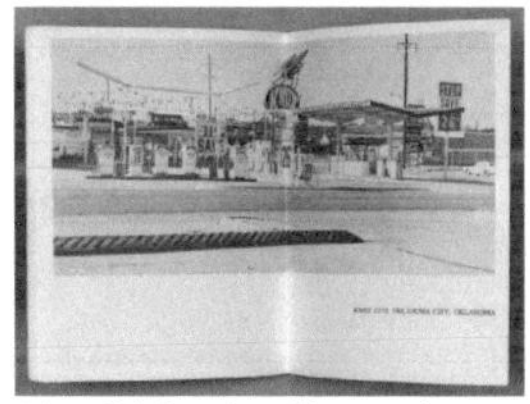

24 Ed Ruscha, *Twenty-Six Gasoline Stations* (1962). Cover and double page.

Just as Williams inverts the usual photograph/text hierarchy of conceptual art, he also reverses another conceptual trope, namely the phenomenon of deskilling. In a 1995 essay on conceptual art and photography, Jeff Wall identified how artists resorted to unskilled types of photography – principally the imitation of amateur photography – and explained the importance of this gesture, however paradoxical it appears, in the process of turning photography into a legitimate medium in contemporary art. Wall refers to the photo books by Ed Ruscha from the 1960s and takes the 'dull, boring and insignificant' images of *Twenty-Six Gasoline Stations* (1962) as a prime example.[24] He argues that it was only by side-stepping the culturally established traditions of art photography, notably the idea of photographic

25 Jeff Wall, 'Marks of Indifference: Aspects of Photography as or in Conceptual Art', in Anne Rorimer and Ann Goldstein (eds.), *Reconsidering the Object of Art*, Los Angeles, Museum of Contemporary Art, 1995, pp. 247–267.

quality, that artists were able to reinvent the medium of photography for the express purpose of contemporary art, turning it into 'an autonomous medium'.[25] Deskilling, Wall argued, was key in this process of establishing photography as an independent art medium. Yet as the author also noted, this could last just as long as amateur photography remained devoid of technical finesse – as long as a culture prevailed that was exemplified by Kodak's famous slogan, devised as early as the 1890s, 'You press the button, we do the rest'. In other terms, deskilling could constitute a valid aesthetic choice only until a culture of skilled amateur photography, with its photo-clubs and publications, would emerge. Although *SOURCE: The Photographic Archive...* hints at conceptual ideas of deskilling, by listing instructions in the form of a series of rules that could potentially be followed by anyone, the process also suggests an indirect reskilling in the sense that the artist adopts tools used in the magazine industry: re-photographing, cutting, reframing and enlarging. Acting as a picture editor, Williams ventures here into the territory of professional photography, establishing a dialogue that would only become more important in subsequent works such as: *For Example: Die Welt ist Schön*, (1998–2002) and *For Example: Dix-Huit Leçons Sur La Société Industrielle* (2003–).

By selecting and manipulating the four photographs included in this work, Williams appropriates and inverts conceptual art practices, thereby commenting on the use of press photography in the media. Yet the work also reflects on the particular 'source' from which the documents were 'borrowed', namely the photographic archive of the John F. Kennedy Library. *SOURCE: The Photographic Archive...* anticipates several of his later works which also examine the subject of the archive. A 1990 photograph of a storage room at the Getty Center in Los Angeles presents the archive as a material object: a specific space filled with clearly labelled books in standard bindings and numbered archive boxes aligned in rows of shelving, as well as other cardboard boxes containing, we imagine, not yet classified or oversize documents.[26] Williams' photograph does not evoke the archive as a closed and complete system in which documents are duly accumulated and classified. He presents it as an open-ended system in which documents are in transit rather than fixed, as suggested by the almost empty shelves in the foreground of the image, the trolley containing books, and the cardboard packing boxes. A year earlier, in another work entitled *Angola to Vietnam**, Williams had presented a different idea of the archive altogether: no longer a place where documents are put to rest and their 'meaning is

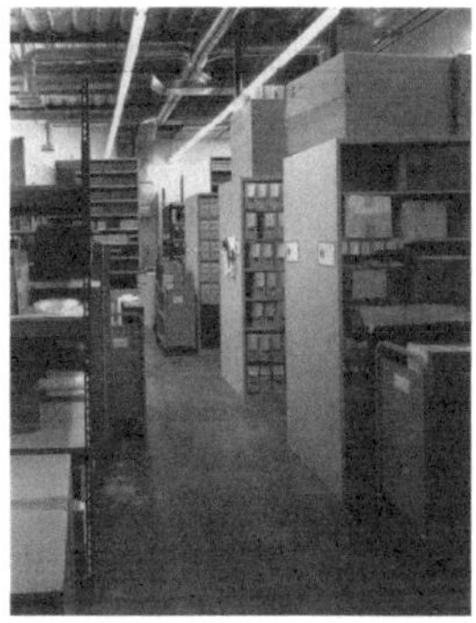

26 Christopher Williams, *The Archives of the History of Art/ The Getty Center for the History of Art and the Humanities/ 4503B Glencoe Avenue/ Marina Del Rey, California 90292/ TEL 213 822-2299 FAX 821-94091990*, 1990.

27 Allan Sekula, 'Reading an Archive' (1983), in Brian Wallis (ed.), *Blasted Allegories: An Anthology of Writings by Contemporary Artists*, New York, The New Museum of Contemporary Art and Cambridge, MA., MIT Press, 1987, pp. 114–127.

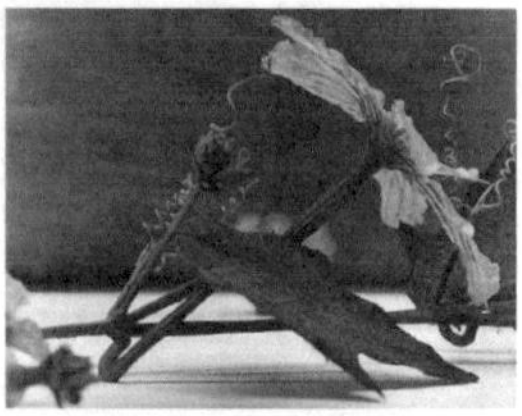

28 Christopher Williams, *Vietnam (from Angola to Vietnam) 1989, Blaschka Model 272, 1892. Genus no. 8594. Family, Cucurbitaceae. Luffa cylindrica (Linn.) Roem.* 1989. gelatin silver print, 28 × 35.5 cm.

29 Allan Sekula, 'Reading an Archive' (1983), in Brian Wallis (ed.) *Blasted Allegories: An Anthology of Writings by Contemporary Artists,* New York, The New Museum of Contemporary Art and Cambridge, MA., MIT Press, 1987, p. 118.

suspended', but instead a site that can be read in terms of world politics.[27] In *Angola to Vietnam**, Williams juxtaposed black and white photographs of a selection of twenty-seven botanical glass models of exotic plants with parts of an inventory released by Amnesty International listing countries in alphabetical order, from Angola to Vietnam, for which data on political disappearances had been collected during the year 1985. Williams breaks the original taxonomy used for these 847 glass specimens of plants in their original home in the Collection of Blaschka Glass Models in the Botanical Museum of Harvard University, and instead makes a selection that bears no logic in relation to its purpose and organization.[28] At the same time, Williams also short-circuited the Amnesty International list by reprocessing it in a form that, similarly,, had no logical relation to the human rights issues at stake. Brought together, two distinct archival orders offer themselves up for examination. While archives impose an order on objects or, as Allan Sekula wrote, they 'embody the power inherent in accumulation, collection and hoarding as well as that power inherent in the command of the lexicon and rules of a language,' *Angola to Vietnam** subverts that power by scrambling the very lexicons of the archives it referred to, thereby deconstructing the very order the archive is supposed to impose.[29]

The attitude to the archive presented in SOURCE: *The Photographic Archive...* lies somewhere between the normative view expressed in the photograph of the Getty Center and the deconstructionist one of *Angola to Vietnam**. The work does not present the archive as an open-ended yet impenetrable accumulation of knowledge, but neither does it directly confront its authority and organisation. Rather, by extracting a small selection according to specific criteria, William brings into relief the modes of organisation of an archive. He simultaneously probes the conditions under which information contained in its holdings can produce knowledge and demonstrates how such knowledge can subsequently be used. There is a paradox here. The photographs from the Kennedy archive appear to be inconsequential, as the event they document is not mentioned and the American president is not clearly visible. Yet at the same time these photographs are crucial if we consider they contain a premonition, albeit an obscure one, of the assassination that would take place six months after they were taken. The work invites us to view the arbitrariness of the process of archival accumulation and simultaneously the fact that such a system is unable to make use of the information it blindly compiles.

In these respects, SOURCE: *The Photographic Archive...* can be compared to another

30 Mike Mandel and Larry Sultan, *Evidence* (1977), New York, DAP, 2003.

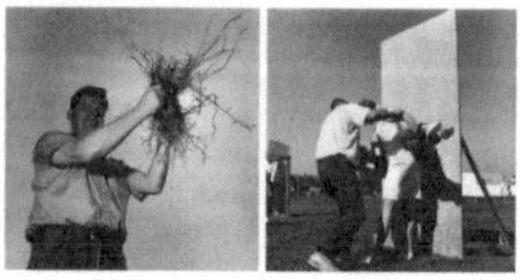

31 Mike Mandel and Larry Sultan, *Evidence*, double page spread of the book.

late-conceptualist work: Mike Mandel and Larry Sultan's exhibition and book *Evidence*, which compiles photographs from the archives of different American government agencies, educational institutions and corporations, including the General Atomics company, the San Jose Police Department and the United States Department of the Interior. The book, published in 1977, presents one image per page without any caption, following the conventions of a classical photography book.[30] The images – made according to specific professional standards and conventions of photographic documentation, and produced as records of activities and situations, test results, crime scenes and so forth – have become illegible. The book thus presents a sequence of strange, obscure, and at times funny situations. The strangeness is emphasized by the selection and montage of the pictures in the book.[31]

The occasionally comic effects created by the selection of the pictures and their de-contextualization suggest that it was perhaps works such as *Evidence* that Allan Sekula had in mind when writing his 1983 essay 'Reading an Archive'. There he deplored the 'depoliticization of photographic meaning' in the work of some of his contemporaries, without naming names. As he suggests, by extracting documents from the archive and presenting them out of context, Mandel and Sultan make it impossible for the viewer to explore the 'imaginary economy' of the photographs, the way in which they construct, transform, and restrict historical and social memory. As photographer and writer Joan Fontcuberta later noted: '*Evidence* pulverized the very notion that photography was the proof of something, the support of some evidence. Because we should have asked ourselves: Evidence of what? Perhaps evidence only of its own ambiguity. What remains, then, of the document?'[32]

32 Joan Fontcuberta, 'Evidence of What?', *The Harvard Photography Journal*, vol. 9, 'Fantastic', <www.hcs.harvard.edu/~hpj/evidence.htm>, retrieved 27 January 2012.

The question of what remains of the document may equally be asked of Williams' SOURCE: *The Photographic Archive...*, even if the choice of photographs distinguishes the two projects from the outset. In *Evidence*, the strangeness of the photographs is countered by the recurring visual conventions of documentation photography – plain backgrounds, measuring instruments, explicit gestures of pointing hands – which together form a visual language for displaying evidence commonly used across the range of institutions listed in the publication. By contrast, Williams' idiosyncratic selection of photographs eschews the categorizations that would commonly be associated with the presentation of a famous subject like JFK, namely portrait or news photography. Thus, whereas *Evidence* addresses typologies of documentation photography across a variety of archives, SOURCE: *The Photographic Archive...*

draws attention to the indiscriminate archival practice of collecting documents. Aside from this difference, both works focus on the emotional and material extra-diegetic space of the photograph. *Evidence* triggers the imagination of the viewer who might attempt to link the caption-less images to the archives they were extracted from, and Williams' photographs exude an atmosphere of suspense when viewed in connection to Kennedy's impending assassination. In this way, both works stress the importance of the psychological dimension of photography for the viewer, and question the purely factual dimension of each photographic representation.

The idea of evidence is thus displaced and becomes fortuitous. It is shown to depend on the particular and changing conditions that imprint meaning on visual documents. *SOURCE: The Photographic Archive...* reads in retrospect like a statement of intent. The selection of a subject presented from the rear becomes a metonymy for turning a document back to front or inside out to reveal its inner instability. The work presents a situation in which an object is caught between appropriation and representation; between the archive and the work of art. These ambiguities form the departure point from which Williams has subsequently developed his extensive photography-based projects.

Reskilling Photography

The process of indirect reskilling that Christopher Williams introduced in *SOURCE: The Photographic Archive...* takes on a new dimension in *For Example: Die Welt ist Schön*, a photographic series that occupied the artist from 1998 to 2002. As I noted previously, in his essay 'Marks of Indifference, Aspects of Photography in or as Conceptual Art', Jeff Wall pointed out that as amateur photography became increasingly technically competent, the amateur-like photography of conceptual art lost much of its subversive power and became a somewhat ubiquitous visual style, thus provoking a process of technical reskilling exemplified by Wall's own artistic work. Yet the obsolescence of the black and white, low quality snapshot was not only caused by the new technical proficiency of amateur photography. It was also an indirect consequence of shifts in the place of photography within the cultural field. The 1970s saw the birth of a market for vintage photography, as renewed efforts were made to write its history, and early photography was rediscovered, including the work of Atget. All this resulted in a change in the place of photography in cultural institutions. Photographs previously appreciated for their informative quality and kept as documents in library archives were now transferred to art and print

33 Christopher Philips and Douglas Crimp brilliantly dissected this phenomenon in their essays: Christopher Philips, 'The Judgement Seat of Photography', *October*, vol. 22, autumn, 1982, pp. 27–63, Douglas Crimp, 'The Archive's New/The Museum's Old Subject', *On the Museum's Ruins,* Cambridge MA. and London, MIT Press, 1993, pp. 66–83.

34 Jeff Wall, 'Marks of Indifference: Aspects of Photography as or in Conceptual Art', in Anne Rorimer and Ann Goldstein (eds.), *Reconsidering the Object of Art*, Los Angeles, Museum of Contemporary Art, 1995, p. 266.

collections.[33] Institutions such as the Victoria and Albert Museum in London and the New York Public Library decided that their photographs had more than a straightforward documentary value and could be turned into objects of collection endowed with aesthetic qualities, while the Musée d'Orsay in Paris, which opened in 1986, began, from 1979, to accumulate a variety of nineteenth-century photography for its collection. Documents thus turned into art objects, and the artistic act of retrieving photographic documents from an archive was made obsolete. In this respect, the early work of Williams is, like Sultan and Mandel's *Evidence*, situated at the very last moment when such an appropriation and displacement from the archive to the gallery was credible in an aesthetic sense.

For Jeff Wall who had produced his own share of deskilled photo-conceptual documents, such as his early *Landscape Manual* (1969), the demise of deskilled photography opened up the possibility of a 'restoration' of 'the picture form' in contemporary art photography.[34] Along with some slightly younger artists such as Thomas Struth and Andreas Gursky, Wall has come to exemplify this reskilling of photography in contemporary art, involving the uses of complex production processes – for example the construction of elaborate studio sets – to produce photographic works that evoke, both in size and ambition, nineteenth-century monumental painting.[35] Wall indeed once expressed his desire to create 'an art as solid as the great museum art of the past.'[36] Williams' attitude to reskilling is different from that of Jeff Wall. In *SOURCE: The Photographic Archive...*, he appropriated the tools of the magazine industry. In *For Example: Die Welt ist Schön,* instead of refining his own technical skills, Williams, again, appropriates them by working with a range of specialised professional photographers who operate the camera for him (or with him). As a result, rather than creating a dialogue with monumental painting, he develops a critical exchange with different kinds of industrial and commercial photography. In the process of making *For Example: Die Welt ist Schön,* Williams would bring his own photographer onto a professional photo set and ask him to stand to one side of the 'official' photographer and take pictures. The photographs created in this manner bear the signs of this slight shift in the angle of the shot. Something is just not quite right in the images, as evidenced for example in the tense look on the face of models attempting to respond to several cameras at the same time.[37]

The collaboration with professional photographers continued in *For Example: Dix-Huit Leçons Sur La Société Industrielle.* For some images from this series, the artist appointed studio

35 Jean-François Chevrier has developed the notion of photographic tableau in relation to Jeff Wall and in dialogue with nineteenth century painting. See in particular Jean-François Chevrier, 'The Adventures of the Picture Form in the History of Photography' (1989), in Douglas Fogle (ed.), *The Last Picture Show: Artists Using Photography 1960–1982,* Minneapolis, Walker Art Center, 2003, pp. 113–128.

36 Jeff Wall in Jean-Pierre Krief, *Jeff Wall – Contacts* (film, 14 minutes), Arte France, 2000. On the production process of Wall's photographs and the connection between reskilling and the development of a 'museum' art, see Julian Stallabrass, 'Museum Photography and Museum Prose', *New Left Review* no. 65, September–October 2010, pp. 93–125.

37 Concerning Williams' hiring of a photographer to intervene on a photo set and the result of this procedure, see Timothy Martin, 'Undressing the Institutional Wound', in *Christopher Williams. For Example: Die Welt ist Schön (Final Draft),* Rotterdam and Basel, Museum Boijmans Van Beuningen and Kunsthalle Basel, 1997.

photographers specialised in particular types of photography: a food photographer for the Ritter Sport chocolate bar images, a fashion and cosmetics photographer for his pictures of women in underwear. These studio photographers are credited in the titles of Williams' images: 'Fotostudio Axel Gnad, Düsseldorf', 'Dirk Schaper Studio, Berlin' and so on. While this use of professional resources echoes the conceptual art practices previously discussed, Williams' approach to photography in these works is more than a gesture of distancing between the artist and the work of art. By placing his camera next to the professional photographer and re-directing the lens towards a viewpoint which diverges from the image that the commercial photographer would make, or by asking a studio photographer to photograph an object in a different manner but with the same image quality as a commercial shot, Williams affects not only the production process but also the viewer's experience of the resulting images.

At first glance, his works suggest archetypes of commercial photography, and their quality resides precisely in the ability to efficiently convey the information. In other words, the way in which they are produced means that Williams' images closely identify with particular kinds of 'visual documents' that surround us in everyday life, documents whose purpose is to explain, promote, show and inform.

One of the photographers that Williams has worked with, Dirk Schaper, sums this up humorously on his website, describing his USP (Unique Selling Point) as 'Unique Selling Photography'.[38]

Yet can any photograph ever really be said to 'document' something, even if it is produced to enhance as much as possible the specific qualities of the object it represents (think for a moment of food photography)? This is the question that Williams asks by adopting commercial production formats to produce works of art for display in art galleries and museums. This is also the question Walter Benjamin raised when, citing his friend Bertolt Brecht, he claimed: 'A photograph of the Krupp works or of the AEG tells us next to nothing about these institutions'.[39] By asking what kind of information can be provided by taking pictures of an individual object or a close-up of a machine, Benjamin questioned the ability of photography to provide information of any kind, again citing Brecht: 'less than ever does the mere reflection of reality reveal anything about reality'. In this passage of his 'Kleine Geschichte der Photographie' ('Small History of Photography'), published in 1931, Benjamin attacked a certain trend in photography that was then enjoying critical and commercial success; he targeted in particular the work of Albert Renger-Patzsch, albeit without naming him.[40] Three years later, in 'The Author as

38 See <www.schaper4usp.com/unique-selling-photography/>, retrieved 12 January 2012.

39 Walter Benjamin, 'The Author as Producer'. The Brecht citation is from 'Der Dreigroschenprozess: Ein Soziologisches Experiment' (1930), in *Werke*, W. Echt (ed.), Frankfurt am Main, Suhrkamp, 1992, t. XXI, p. 469.

40 Walter Benjamin, 'A Small History of Photography', in Susan Sontag (ed.), *One-Way Street and Other Writings*, London, Verso, 1979, p. 255.

41 Walter Benjamin, 'The Author as Producer', p. 24.

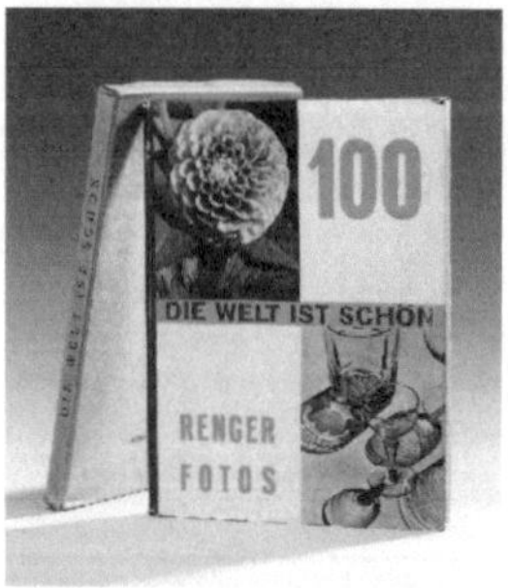

42 Albert Renger-Patzsch, *Die Welt ist Schön*, Munich, Kurt Wolff, 1928, Dust jacket.

43 Walter Benjamin, 'A Small History of Photography', p. 255.

Producer' Benjamin was more explicit: he described the photo book that Renger-Patzsch had published two years earlier under the title *Die Welt ist Schön* (*The World is Beautiful*) as having succeeded in 'turning abject poverty itself, by handling it in a modish, technically perfect way, into an object of enjoyment'.[41] The book brought together one hundred photographs with subject matters ranging from natural elements to everyday objects and industrial structures. Renger-Patzsch often took close-up views that dramatically isolate the objects from their surroundings, reducing them often to harmonious abstract patterns and geometric forms.[42] The book was a success from the time it appeared. It was reprinted several times and is now considered as a prime example of Neue Sachlichkeit (New Objectivity) photography. Benjamin meanwhile derided 'The world is beautiful', as the 'watchword' of a kind of creative photography that could 'endow any soup can with cosmic significance but cannot grasp a single one of the human connections in which it exists'. In terms echoing those of Brecht, Benjamin denounced a type of photography more concerned with 'commercialisation' than preoccupied 'knowledge seeking' and added that the true face of this 'commercial' art was 'advertisement and association.'[43] He pitted this against the work of Karl Blossfeldt, Germaine Krull and August Sander whom he praised in the preceding pages of his essay. Taking his cue from Brecht's belief that, instead of attempting to literally replicate the real, 'something must be built up, something artificial, posed,' Benjamin argued that photography should 'demystify' and 'construct' rather than *promote*, taking the photomontages of John Heartfield as a counter-example.'[44]

44 Bertolt Brecht, as cited by Walter Benjamin, 'A Small History of Photography', p. 255.

This complete dismissal of Renger-Patzsch with the aid of Brecht's rhetoric is not completely convincing. At the beginning of his article, Benjamin praised the kind of technical progress in cameras that had enabled Blossfeldt to create his close-up views of plants (albeit a very different subject matter), extolling the very technical experimentation with a photo camera that he was prone to dismiss in the close-up photographs of Renger-Patzsch. Moreover, if indeed the gap between creative photography and advertising was narrow, Renger-Patzsch was certainly not alone in bridging it. The space between avant-garde and applied photography was increasingly explored by artists such as Sasha Stone and Germaine Krull, who were both highly regarded by Benjamin. Sasha Stone is best known today for his photomontage on the cover of the original edition of Walter Benjamin's *One-Way Street* (1928) and for his photographs of female nudes, although he also produced photography-based posters for theatres and advertising

45 Christopher Williams, in conversation with the author, 30 August 2010, Amsterdam.

46 For an analysis of the series in relation to Albert Renger-Patzsch as well as German New Objectivity in general, see Timothy Martin, 'Undressing the Institutional Wound', in Christopher Williams, *For Example: Die Welt ist Schön (Final Draft)*, Rotterdam and Basel, Museum Boijmans van Beuningen and Kunsthalle Basel, 1997, pp. 14–87.

images; Krull is known for the fashion photographs she took for couturier Paul Poiret as well as for her modernist compositions.

Benjamin may also have been prejudiced by the carefree connotations of the title of Renger-Patzsch's book, imposed by his publisher against the will of the photographer, who allegedly preferred the more neutral 'Die Dinge' (The Things). Referring to this anecdote, Christopher Williams has suggested that his choice to cite the title of Renger-Patzsch's book in the title of his own series *For Example: Die Welt ist Schön,* might have been motivated by a desire to somewhat redress an unjust condemnation of the earlier work by Benjamin.[45] In adding the prefix 'for example', the artist nonetheless suggests that Renger-Patzsch is but one of several works of Weimar photography that he was seeking to invoke with his work.

This is not the place for a close reading of the affinities with and references to Weimar era photography in Williams' *For Example: Die Welt ist Schön;* such an analysis has been conducted elsewhere.[46] Yet even more than correcting an unfair judgement, both *For Example: Die Welt ist Schön* and Williams' subsequent project *For Example: Dix-Huit Leçons Sur La Société Industrielle* appear to proceed from a close critical engagement with the terms posed by Benjamin and Brecht's critique of photography. In the work of Williams the differences between artistic and commercial photography are translated into strategies of displacement. They are materialised in visual incongruities that disturb the smoothness conveyed by the images at first sight – imperfections that do not become visible until the viewer has slowed down to examine each photograph not as a sample of a photographic genre (fashion, architecture, product), but as an individual work of art.

In the opening of this chapter, I showed how the 180 degree rotation of the camera angle in *Untitled (Study in Yellow/Berlin) Dirk Schaper Studio, Berlin, June 21, 2007 (No.1)* could be understood as a way of confronting two views of the same subject matter. The question of what kinds of information a photographic document can provide is articulated by the shift between two views – in this case, one imaginary (the frontal lingerie shot), the other one materialized in the actual photograph. Other groups of photographs by Williams present a shift of perspective between different images, as in the case of a series of eight photographs from 1993 showing views of the dam of Grande Dixence, in Switzerland, an engineering masterpiece and one of the largest dams in the world. The eight views of the dam, which belong to the series *For Example: Die Welt ist Schön*, alternate between different registers. Some

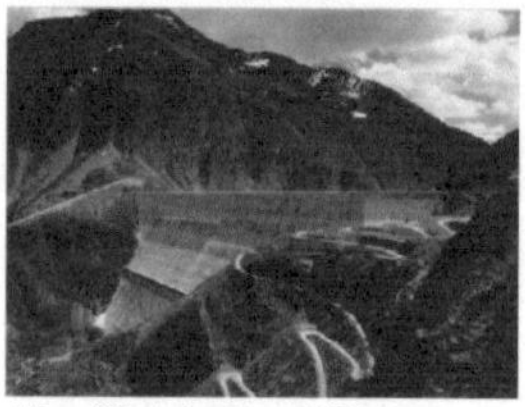

47 Christopher Williams, *Grande Dixence, Val de Dix, Switzerland, August 2, 1993 (No 1)*, 1993, gelatin silver print, 28 × 35.5 cm.

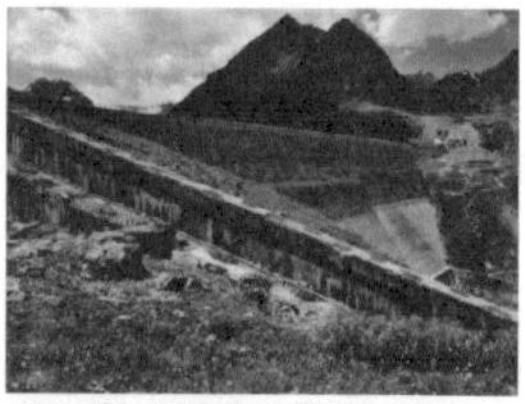

48 Christopher Williams, *Grande Dixence, Val de Dix, Switzerland, August 2, 1993 (No 6)*, 1993, gelatin silver print, 28 × 35.5 cm.

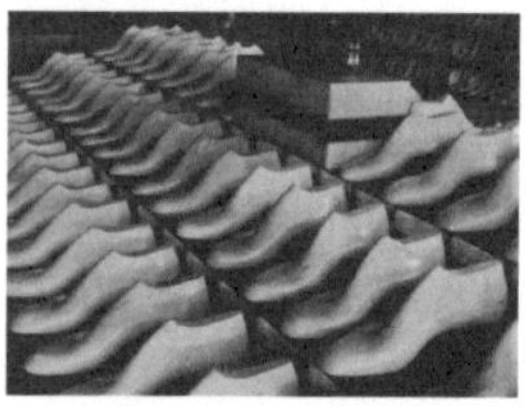

49 Albert Renger-Patzsch, *Shoe Forms, Pattern Room In Fagus-Werk Shoe Farm & Stamping Tool Factory*, published in *Die Welt Ist Schön.*

depict it as a vertiginous wall, others as a spectacular ribbon of concrete slicing through a lush landscape.[47] The latter images would be in line with promotional views of the site (which is also a tourist destination). But other photographs in this series move away from the celebratory and the spectacular, and focus instead on the aging concrete around the edges of the dam, showing areas where rubble mingles with weeds.[48] These different photographic registers are not only the result of the physical displacement of a camera operator searching for the best viewpoint. They also reveal potentially divergent purposes that could be attributed to the photographs: touristic promotion for some, technical survey for the others. Together, the photographs also record the personal experience of the artist walking over the dam. This juxtaposition of different sorts of applied and artistic photography echoes the ambivalence of the subject matter depicted: the dam is an 'ouvrage d'art' in French; that is, it is not exactly a work of art, but neither is it simply an engineering work. The photographs correspond thematically to the same kind of aesthetic glorification of industry that some of Renger-Patzsch's photographs sought to convey – for instance, his images of industrial objects depicted in factories.[49]

A second strategy that recurs in Williams' photographs is the intentional and often humorous inclusion of 'faulty details', which are sometimes barely perceptible, yet when noticed completely reconfigure the reading of the picture. A bright yellow cardboard box from the German Post is shown half open and presented against a white background, framed and lit as if presented as an item in a catalogue. It seems to be brand new until one notices the worn flaps of the box that show the package has in fact previously been sealed and then opened.[50] Using a similar approach, *Untitled (Study in Red) Dirk Schaper Studio, Berlin April 30, 2009* (2009) shows a close-up view of a foot modelling a sock, raised so as to show the brand, 'Falke' knitted on the sole.[51] A closer view of the image reveals imperfections on the bare skin of the model. As in the photograph depicting the rear side of the model in white underwear, these imperfections would make the shot unusable for any professional purposes unless it was subjected to digital retouching.[52]

Less visible to the naked eye are the imperfections in several photographs that show stacks of Ritter Sport chocolate bars.[53] Here Williams stacks unwrapped bars of chocolate sliced open to reveal their different fillings. The chocolate bars have been sliced with a machine, which leaves visible cutting marks and shows the uneven filling of the chocolate bars. Such details differentiate Williams' photograph from otherwise identical yet digitally composed

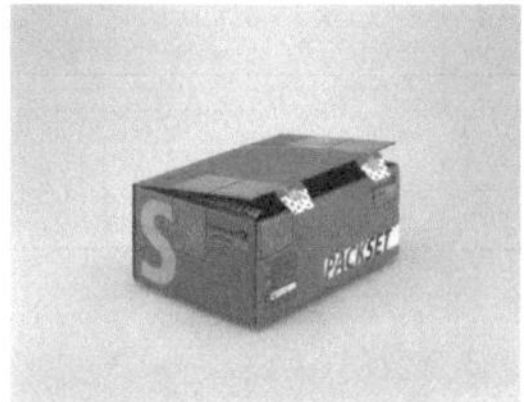

50 Christopher Williams, *Packset (small 25 × 17 × 10 cm) Deutsche Post, Euro Express. (Kleben Sie den ausgefüllten Versandschein hier auf. Lassen Sie sich beraten und wählen Sie die beste Versandart für Ihr Pakset). Douglas M Parker Studio, Glendale, California. April 14, 2003.* 2003, Dye transfer print, 40.6 × 50.8 cm.

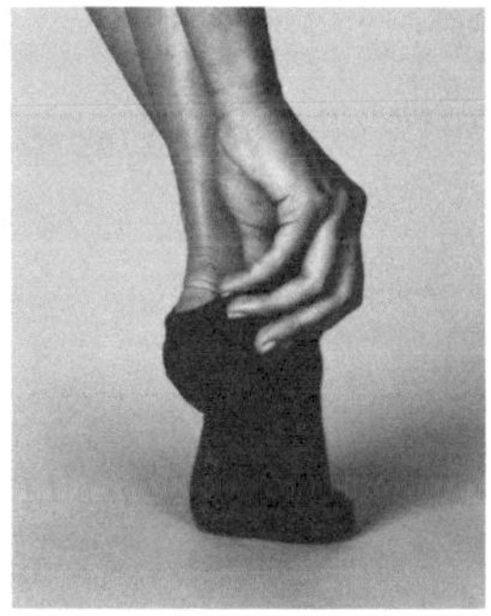

51 Christopher Williams, *Untitled (Study in Red) Dirk Schaper Studio, Berlin April 30, 2009*, 2009, Archival pigment print, 35.5 × 27.9 cm.

52 On the subject of digital retouching see Christopher Williams in Julie L. Belcove, 'Working Practice: Christopher Williams', *Introspective*, January 2011. Consulted online: <16fdn9ufhox41fwkc1azw8b1bio.wpengine.netdna-cdn.com/wp-content/uploads/2011/10/110101-CW-Introspective-Belcove.pdf>. Retrieved 13 August 2014.

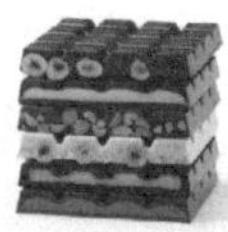

53 Christopher Williams, *RitterSport. Von oben nach unten / from top to the bottom. 100 g Tafeln / 100 g Bars. Offizieller Produktname / Official Product Name / EAN Code Bar / UPC Code for Case / Bars per Case. Voll Nuss / Whole Hazelnuts / 4000417019004 / 050255013005 / 10. Joghurt / Yogurt / 40004170270 09 / 050255027000 / 12. Voll Endnuss / 4000417262202 /... / 10. Weisse Voll Nuss / White Whole Hazelnuts / 4000417013002 / 050255013003 / 10. Marzipan / Marzipan / 400041725005 / 050255025006 / 12. Cappuccino / Cappuccino / 40004172300 03 / 0550255230042 / 12. Fotostudio Axel Gnad, Düsseldorf, October 21st, 2008* [No. 1], 2009, digital pigment print, 50.8 × 61 cm.

54 Williams recalls that a direct juxtaposition of the original and remade Ritter sport photographs occurred in March and April 2010 in Berlin and then Cologne when posters for Ritter Sport appeared on billboards across the city at the same time Williams was showing his own photographs at Galerie Gisela Capitain. (Interview with the artist, Amsterdam, August 2010.)

images produced for advertising purposes by the Ritter Sport chocolate manufacturer. By using analogue photography to remake digital images, Williams subverts the values traditionally associated with advertising photography. One such value is the truthfulness of the product suggested by a close-up view that mimics its real presence in the space of the consumer. This truthfulness collapses in the advertising image once we know it is a digital construction, and the deceit becomes visible when the advertisement is juxtaposed with Williams' 'remakes'.[54]

It was the truthfulness of the photographic image and its capacity to reveal social interactions that Benjamin found lacking in the photographs of Renger-Patzsch. Williams also explores these issues through the relationships he establishes between text and image. The muteness of the pictures that confront the viewer entering an exhibition of his work is counterbalanced by a flow of information and references that is generated by captions, press material (often supervised or authored by the artist) and, more obliquely, by the informed readings made by critics and curators in the essays that accompany Williams' exhibitions, which thus, whether voluntarily or not, become relays in the circulation of specific references.

Mark Godfrey's extensive survey of *For Example: Dix-Huit Leçons Sur La Société*

Industrielle is a case in point.[55] His essay provides an impressive political, economic and art-historical contextualisation for Williams' photographs. Additionally, it gives information about the references of specific works. Godfrey points out, for instance, the large number of photographs referring to France and its colonial empire as it was shrinking in the 1950s and 1960s, and the numerous allusions to Germany and the consumer culture of the period of reconstruction and the *Wirtschaftswunder* ('Economic miracle'). He also identifies specific allusions in Williams' photographs to Capitalist Realist paintings by Sigmar Polke and Gerhard Richter, the cinema and video work of Jean-Luc Godard and the imagery of advertising designer Charles Wilp, among other things. While some of these references are straightforward, others are more convoluted and stem from explanations provided by the artist (as in the case of photographs involving a model that Williams claims to have been chosen following the criteria set by Jacques Tati for the casting of his 1967 film *Playtime.*[56]) When the artist releases such specific information, it inevitably becomes a part of the work itself even if it is not visible in the photograph. This accumulation of information contradicts the apparent formal simplicity of the picture.

By presenting his images in a large format, hanging them low on the wall, framed and under a glass

55 Mark Godfrey, 'Pop? Progresso Fotografico? Radio Daniele? Christopher Williams? Kodak Color? Kapitalistischer Realismus?', *Christopher Williams. Program*, Baden Baden, Verlag der Buchhandlung Walther König, 2010, pp. 77–87.

56 'Christopher Williams in conversation with Mark Godfrey', *Afterall*, no. 16, 2007.

pane – in other words as objects – the artist grants them the ability to stand on their own. The captions that accompany the images do not occupy the same space; this is also the case when the pictures are reproduced in exhibition catalogues, with the captions usually listed separately. This strategy suggests that the images should be seen as autonomous. Yet at the same time the artists often provides lengthy captions for the pictures suggesting precisely the opposite, namely that photographs need to be accompanied by information that cannot be visualised. The captions provided are mainly of two kinds; they range from short indications providing the time and place of production and little else (save for the mentions 'untitled', or 'study') to lengthy listings of all technical details of the object represented in a given image. Despite their precision these longer captions are nonetheless often slightly 'off kilter'. Either they reproduce information that the attentive viewer can see in the image itself, or they provide an overwhelming number of factual details that are of little or no use to the viewer attempting to understand what the picture might be about. The excess of information turns the purpose of the caption inside out. Instead of guiding the viewer, it silences the image. In this sense, Williams' photographs entertain an ambiguous relationship with the demands that Benjamin made in 'The Author as

Producer'. While some of his images can be said to share the 'modish' character of the creative photography of Renger-Patzsch, his captions, unlike those of his predecessor tend towards an over-detailed specialisation that evokes the industrial context of production. This can be interpreted as meeting Benjamin's demand that the photographer 'put such a caption beneath his pictures as will rescue it from the ravages of modishness and confer upon it a revolutionary use-value'.[57] In other images however, Williams eschews the technical perfection of a Renger-Patzsch, but gives them more conventionally 'artistic' titles ('study in...'), as if to suggest that the subject of art and politics is more complicated than what Benjamin's militant tone in that essay suggests.

57 Walter Benjamin, 'The Author as Producer', p. 24.

From 'Programme' to 'Program'

One specific group of images plays a particular role in making visible the gap between applied photography and contemporary art. These are pictures that show photographic equipment. Although such images are less conspicuous in *For Example: Die Welt ist Schön*, they recur with increased frequency in *For Example: Dix-Huit Leçons Sur La Société Industrielle*. Williams has described the triptych showing three views of a Kiev 88, a Soviet replica of

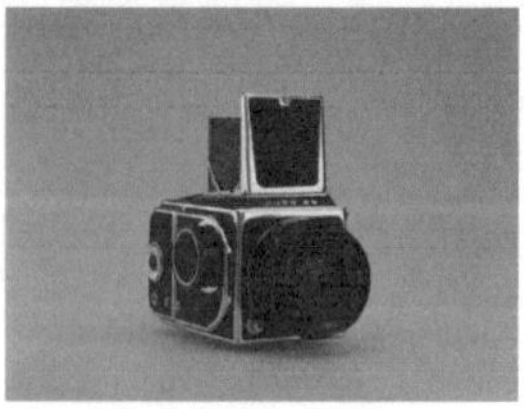

58 'Christopher Williams in Conversation with Mark Godfrey', *Afterall*, no. 16, 2007, p. 64. Christopher Williams, *Kiev 88, 4.6 lbs. (2.1 Kg) Manufacturer: Zavod Arsenal Factory, Kiev, Ukraine. Date of production: 1983–87, Douglas M. Parker Studio, Glendale, California. March 28, 2003, (no.1.)*, 2003, dye transfer print, 40.6 × 50.8 cm.

59 *Weimar Lux CDS, VEB Feingerätewerk. Weimar, Price 86.50 Mark GDR. Filmempfindlichkeitsbereich 9 bis 45 DIN und 6 bis 250000 ASA, Blendenskala 0,5 bis 45, Zeitskala 1/4000 Sekunde bis 8 Stunden, ca. 1980. Models: Ellena Borho and Christoph Boland, November 12th, 2010*, 2010, digital pigment print, 61 × 50.8 cm.

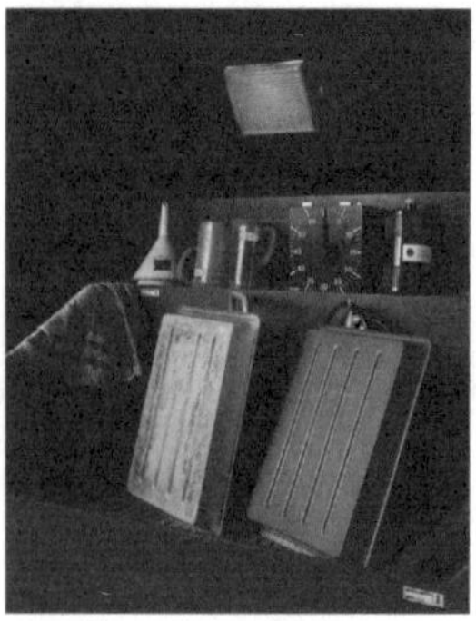

60 Christopher Williams, *Fachhochschule Aachen, Fachbereich. Gestaltung, Studiengang: Visuelle Kommunikation, Fotolabor für Studenten. Boxgraben 100, Aachen, November 8th, 2010*, 2010, pigmented inkjet print, 61 × 50.8 cm.

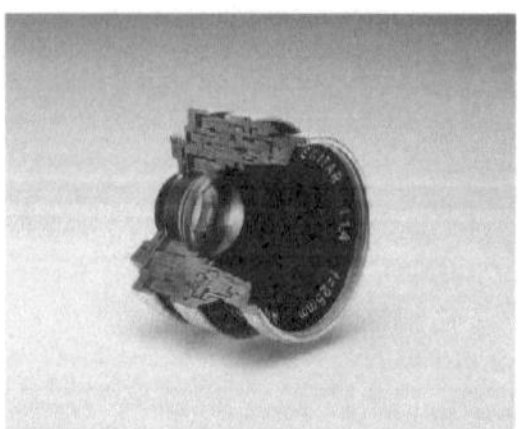

61 *Cutaway model Switar 25mm f1.4 AR. Glass, wood and brass. Douglas M. Parker Studio, Glendale, California, November, 17, 2007 – November 30, 2007*, 2008, chromogenic print, 50.8 × 61 cm.

the famous Hasselblad photo camera as the inaugural work of the series.[58] Following this inaugural triptych are individual images showing close-up views of camera parts set against blurred backgrounds which suggest that a fashion shoot is taking place, for example in *Weimar Lux* CDS, VEB *Feingerätewerk...*, (2010) which focuses on a light meter.[59] Pictures such as this one might have been made almost as an afterthought at the end of a studio session. Other pictures from this group show the context in which photography is produced: *Fachhochschule Aachen, Fachbereich* (2010), depicts brightly coloured utensils used for processing analogue film in a photo lab in Aachen.[60] More spectacular are several photographs of cameras and zooms lenses isolated against white backgrounds, some of them sliced open to reveal their shiny insides.[61] Photographs such as these function with a double-entendre: on one level, they are visually attractive and clearly result from a technical tour-de-force that will command the admiration of technically learned viewers. At the same time, they constitute a kind of *mise en abyme* of the photo camera and, by extension, of the entire photographic process itself.

Some of the photographs of equipment are obscure, either because they reveal rapidly changing technology and chronicle the gradual disappearance of analogue photography, as in the image from the

Aachen photo lab, or because the equipment is too professional and specific for generations of individuals who are now used to simplified (and increasingly digital) cameras. These pictures of cameras and zoom lenses bisected or otherwise sliced open, are derived from drawings in camera manuals and transposed to real cameras. The objects become mysterious, both resulting from the displacement of the concept from instruction guide to art photograph, and also because this dissection provides no further information about the camera (for the layman at least). Despite the overt exposition of its insides, the workings of the camera still remain obscure: it is, as Vilém Flusser put it, a 'black box' that conceals its workings.[62] This is even the case when this box occasionally takes the form of a transparent Polaroid camera.[63]

To read these pictures of cameras as a *mise en abyme* of the photographic process directs the focus of *For Example: Dix-Huit Leçons Sur La Société Industrielle* away from the descriptive and the iconographic, and more towards the technical realm, perhaps even intertwining the two approaches. Williams' interest in exploring a 'cold-war programme' might therefore be understood as the rationale behind a project that closely questions photographic forms and genres and their histories. This intention becomes clearer if, with reference to

62 Vilém Flusser, *Towards a Philosophy of Photography*, London, Reaktion Books, 2000, p. 16.

63 *Polaroid 660 [promotional non functional] with completely transparent plastic housing. Produced for promotional use for display and demonstration purposes. Lens: 116mm f/11, single-element plastic Automatic focus; uses Polaroid Sonar AF system. Minimum focus: 3ft. Electronic shutter: range 1/4–1/200 sec. programmed automatic exposure system; built-in electronic flash, with automatic flash, exposure for all pictures. The camera was introduced in 1981 with an original product price of $95.00 and worked with the Polaroid 600 Film family which all have the following characteristics in common: ASA 600 film speed, self-developing, packaged 10 prints to a pack including a self-contained battery to power camera. Actual image area: 3 1/8″ × 3 1/8″ [7.9 × 7.9 cm] Fotostudio Axel Gnad, Düsseldorf February 09, 2009*, 2009

64 Christopher Williams refers to this aspect of Flusser's theory in his interview with Mark Godfrey, op. cit. p. 68.

Vilém Flusser, we read the last word in the phrase 'cold war programme' not as 'programme' but instead as 'program'. This latter spelling occurs time and again on the covers of catalogues, folders and books accompanying the exhibitions of Wiliams' *For Example: Dix-Huit Leçons Sur La Société Industrielle*. The distinction here is not only between British and American English. In both languages, 'program' refers to computer programming, and it is this meaning that Flusser uses by analogy in his philosophical study of photography. For Flusser, the camera or 'black box' is the hardware shell containing the software or 'program', which in turn contains the sum of all possible photographs that can be made with this camera. And just as a software program is produced for a specific purpose, so too is the photographic program which is determined not only by its most direct authors but also in a dialogue with the different circles that contribute to shaping and disseminating it.[64]

> 'The camera memory has been programmed by people employed in the photo industry, and the photographer dialogues [sic] with those people. But those people have, in their turn, elaborated that program in a dialogue with the industrial program, which is a memory which contains a vast amount of virtual camera programs.

> The program of the photo industry is, in its turn, programmed by people who are employed in elaborating the programs of the industrial park of a country. The programme of that industry complex is, in its turn, programmed by people who are elaborating the economic, cultural, political and ideological program of a society. And this program is again further developed at some "higher" level. In all of these programming processes, people are involved with ever more complex "artificial memories", with ever more complex hard and soft apparatus. In the last analysis, therefore, the photographer is in dialogue with a transhuman hierarchy of progress. This is a dialogue with a memory which is only partly human, and partly autonomous of human decision, or namely "automatic".'[65]

65 Vilém Flusser, 'First Lecture, 23 February 1984: "Photo Production"'. École de la Photographie, Arles. In *Flusser Studies,* no. 10, November 2010, double issue, online journal, <www.flusserstudies.net/pag/archive10.htm>, retrieved 19 January 2012.

By resorting to the metaphor of computing, Flusser, writing in the early 1980s, makes a case for the way in which photography, far from reproducing natural vision, can instead be seen as the result of a layered system which, circle after circle, determines conventions of reading that ensure the homogeneity and legibility of photographic documents. The vision of photography he outlines is that of conventional photography as it exists and is perpetuated in professional, industrial, scientific contexts.

In *For Example: Dix-Huit Leçons Sur La Société Industrielle,* Williams develops less a *programme* than a *program*. The series of images and other elements in the work is not only a reflection on the visual culture of the Cold War, the German *Wirschaftswunder* or the French *Trente Glorieuses,* presenting photographs as documents whose value lies in the subject they depict. It also provides a reflection on the conditions of production and perpetuation of these conventionalised forms of visual documents. Dating the objects that Williams depicts from the Cold War era, they are thus twice historicised: once as objects dating from that specific epoch and once as objects photographed using a technology that is now almost obsolete. Moreover, the intertwining of iconographic and technical interests explains why Williams does not limit his repertory to objects immediately recognisable as period objects. By inserting representations of objects produced more recently, and establishing a dialogue between analogue photography and digital images, Williams points to an epoch that has now entirely disappeared, with commercial photography – even more than other domains – having surrendered to digitalization. By going against the grain of these post-industrial images, Williams becomes what Flusser calls in his lectures a 'true photographer', an artist whose task is not to add photographs that fit into a prescribed *programme,* but rather to disturb the *program* and propose alternative images:

> 'This is the reason why the true photographer is committed to opposing automation. His or her aim is to force [the] apparatus to somehow invert its program like a glove, and have it produce that which is unexpected from the point of view of the program.'[66]

66 Vilém Flusser, 'Second Lecture on March 15, 1984: "Photo Distribution"' École de la Photographie, Arles. In *Flusser Studies,* no. 10, November 2010, double issue, online journal, <www.flusserstudies.net/pag/archive10.htm>, retrieved 19 January 2012.

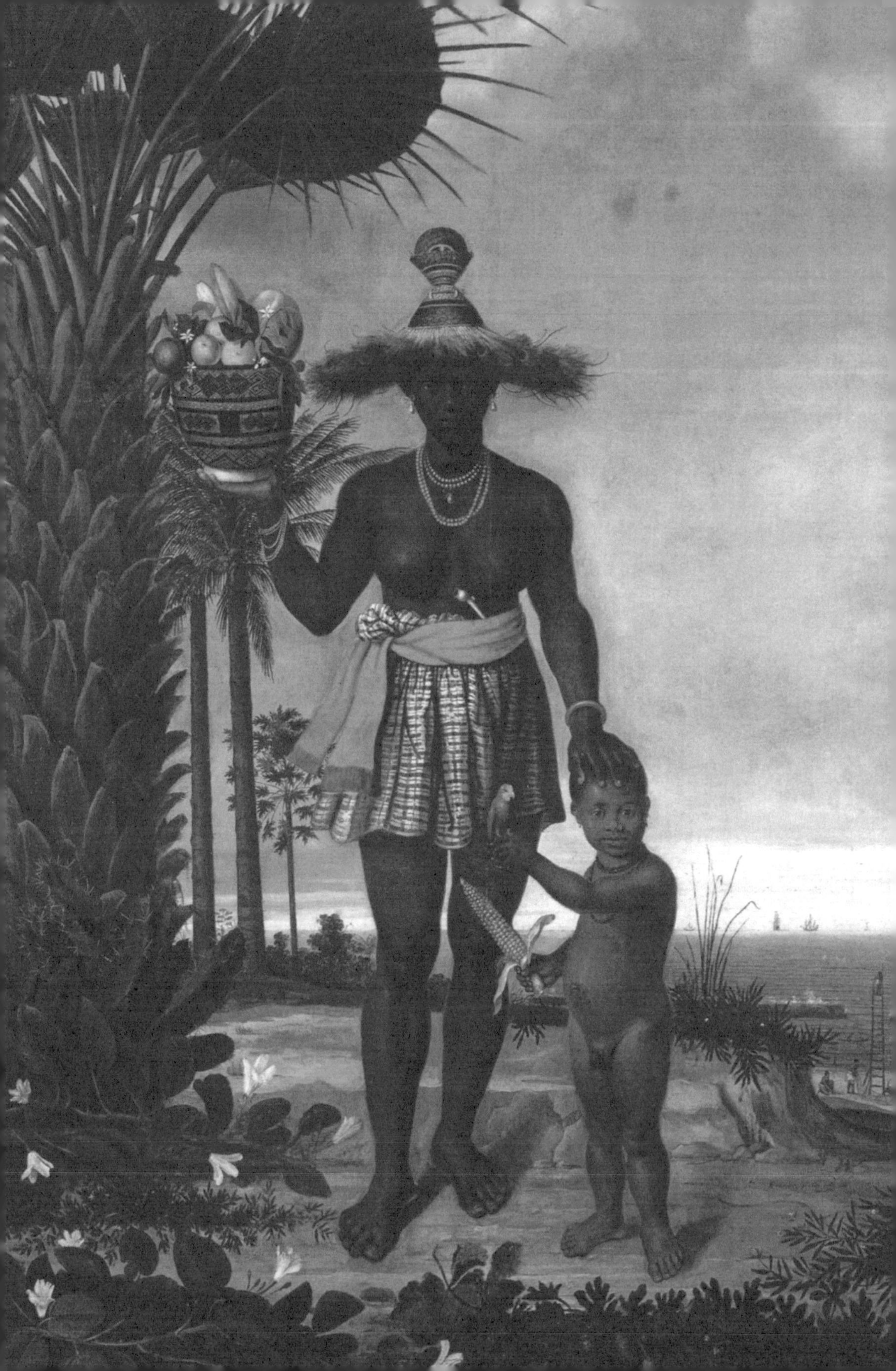

Four

Decolonising the Archive

The advent of what she calls 'the era of the witness', in the 1970s, marks for Annette Wieviorka a rupture in the figure of the witness in society.[1] Witnessing no longer responds to an inner necessity but rather to a pervasive social imperative; it has become a widespread discursive form, present everywhere, from tribunals to reality television. This omnipresence of the witness challenges the work of the historian and disturbs the balance between witness, written documents and archives.

In their work on colonial pasts, particularly those of Belgium, Congo and the Netherlands, Fiona Tan, Sven Augustijnen and Wendelien van Oldenborgh appropriate the tools of the historian – early film footage, paper archives and the voice of a witness – only to turn them around and question their authority. Echoing the plea by Ann Laura Stoler to pay attention to the forms of the colonial archive, they resort to human presence as a way not only to question the figure of the witness, but to pull apart the authority of the colonial archive – in other terms, to decolonise the document.

1 Annette Wieviorka, *The Era of the Witness* (1998), Ithaca, NY., Cornell University Press, 2006.

Albert Eckhout, *African Woman and Child,* 1641, oil on canvas, 282 × 189 cm, Copenhagen, National Museum of Denmark.

2 The film collection is now part of EYE Film Institute Netherlands.

3 I am discussing here the film as it was presented at Stedelijk Museum Amsterdam in the display entitled *Temporary Stedelijk 1*, which opened in August 2011. The film was projected on a screen roughly 3 by 4 metres large, in a 200-square metre room that was otherwise empty.

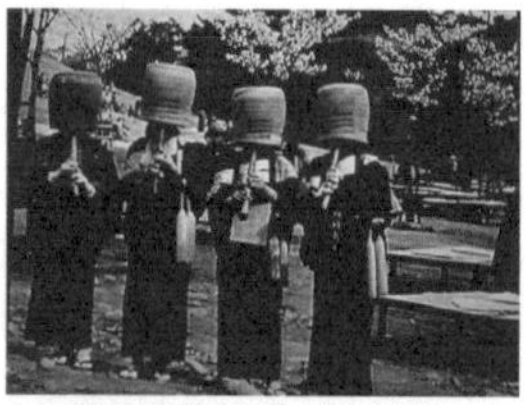

4 Fiona Tan, *Facing Forward*, 1999, video installation, 11 min, b&w/tinted, stereo, projection ca. 2.7 × 3.9 m. video still.

A room in the Stedelijk Museum in Amsterdam shows *Facing Forward* (1999), a single-screen video installation by Fiona Tan. The eleven-minute film is projected onto a wall measuring three by four metres in an otherwise empty room. What we see is a montage of footage dating from the early twentieth century, excavated from the archives of the Netherlands Film Museum, with a voice-over reading of fragments from Italo Calvino's *Invisible Cities*.[2] Undated and unidentified, the sequences show groups of people from different parts of the world, a world that was then largely colonised.[3] Flickering black-and-white and tinted film sequences show groups of people from different, unspecified countries. In one scene, which gives the appearance of being a rehearsed act, women walk towards the camera playing musical instruments.[4] In another, a group of indigenous men and colonial militaries pose for a portrait, standing and sitting in a formal arrangement, as the camera slowly pans the scene horizontally. The film then cuts to a sequence likewise showing tribal men and women filmed in a slow horizontal camera motion, but now in a tropical forest. Another scene, another place: a mobile camera, probably mounted onto a car, films a crossroads and then the sidewalks and façades of buildings in a colonial town somewhere in Southeast Asia, capturing a diverse population in an everyday context.

The attitudes of those captured by the camera vary widely from one fragment to another, ranging from indifference to shyness and curiosity. Some individuals perform for the camera, while others submit reluctantly to it. Some expected it and others simply happened to pass through its frame.[5]

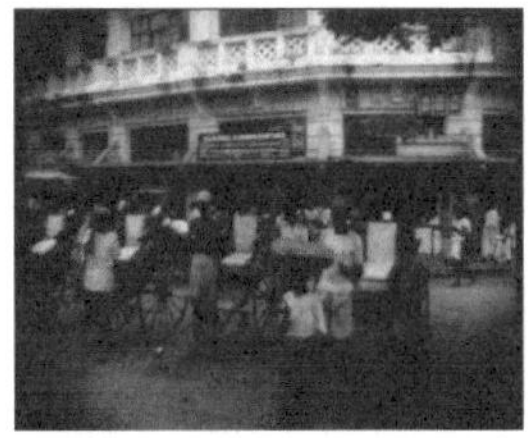

5 Fiona Tan, *Facing Forward,* 1999, video still.

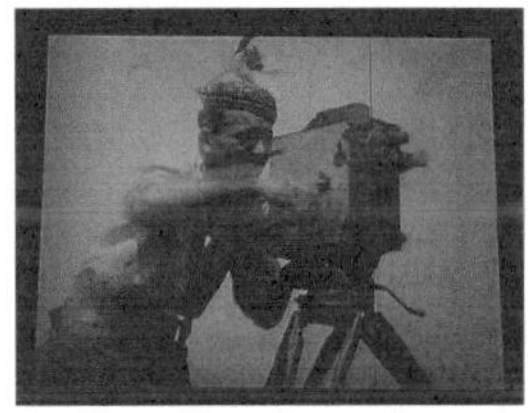

6 Fiona Tan, *Facing Forward,* 1999, video still.

The different responses to the camera mirror our own uncertainties as viewers about how to look at and respond to these images when we first encounter them in a museum gallery. If the people who have been filmed often do not know how to respond to the camera – well, neither do we. There are no captions or lists of sources informing us about the mix of different genres: ethnographic document, military colonial footage, or personal recording. The mirroring effect between the images presented and ourselves looking at them is brought full circle when a short sequence appears showing only one person, a European man manipulating a hand-wound camera directed at us. Dressed informally in slacks and a white shirt and sporting a feathered headband, he smiles the brazen smile of the Western explorer seeking adventure in distant places.[6]

The immediate seduction of *Facing Forward* resides in the viewer's discovery of previously unseen footage that Fiona Tan found, selected, edited and compiled into a film. Once you start watching, it is impossible not to scrutinise the gestures, costumes and questioning glances of the people in the film. You cannot help guessing where, when and for what purpose the images were originally made. Can my visual literacy make up for the factual ignorance with which the artist has saddled me? That question grows acute, I feel, each time the film cuts to the man with a movie camera who mischievously turns his camera onto us, laughing. The life-size scale of the projection intensifies my identification with the filmed individuals: standing in the museum gallery I am put on the spot and become the target of the image hunter, who can read my face like an open book. Soon after, however, I resume my position as a viewer seeking to identify the images that pass before me, trying to identify the genres of the films. Inevitably, I turn into a visitor to the colonies, a soldier and an ethnographer.

By turning the feathered image hunter on us, Fiona Tan reverses the aim of the camera. She makes us aware of the power structure inherent in any film image and shows us the complexity of dealing with colonial documents. Deprived of dates, facts, locations and other contextual information, we are forced to rely on what we see. We must carefully follow the movements of the cameras, look at the way people are placed in front of them, and be attentive to their gestures, expressions, clothing and settings. In short, while extracting whatever information we can from the images, we must also seek to ascertain how information is produced. The kind of attention Fiona Tan elicits from us in *Facing Forward* recalls the attitude that Ann Laura Stoler urges on scholars of colonial history when she bids them to ask themselves 'what insights about the colonial might be gained from attending not only to colonialism's archival content, but to its particular and sometimes peculiar form'.[7] Referring to the critique of the document developed by such historians as Carlo Ginzburg and Natalie Zemon Davis, Stoler exhorts scholars to work 'along the archival grain' and to study at close range the ways in which archival documents are produced within colonial administrations.[8] She frames the 'challenge' posed to historians in the following terms:

> 'We are just now critically reflecting on the making of documents and how we choose to use them, on archives not as sites of knowledge retrieval but of knowledge production, as monuments of states as well as sites of state ethnography.'[9]

Stoler's focus resonates with the commitments found in a growing body of literature in the social sciences devoted to the colonial archive, that 'supreme technology of the late nineteenth-century imperial state'.[10] Working on the Dutch East Indies

7 Ann Laura Stoler, 'Colonial Archives and the Arts of Governance', *Archival Science*, no. 2, 2002, p. 87.

8 Ann Laura Stoler, *Along the Archival Grain: Epistemic Anxieties and Colonial Common Sense*, Princeton, Princeton University Press, 2009.

9 Stoler, 'Colonial Archives and the Arts of Governance', p. 90.

10 Stoler, 'Colonial Archives and the Arts of Governance', p. 87.

11 Stoler, 'Colonial Archives and the Arts of Governance', p. 96.

12 Arjun Appadurai, 'Number in the Colonial Imagination', in *Modernity at Large: Cultural Dimensions of Globalization*, Minneapolis and London, 1996.

13 Thomas Richards, *The Imperial Archive: Knowledge and the Fantasy of Empire*. London, Verso, 1993.

and the British presence in India, Arjun Appadurai and Thomas Richards show how colonial bureaucracy operated as a tool for running the colonial empires of European states as well as forces that 'bolstered the production of those states themselves'.[11] Further, they have shown how these 'information-hungry machines', as Stoler calls colonial states, obsessively compiled masses of 'secret reports, special commissions, statistics and surveys of all sorts', giving colonial powers 'the illusion of bureaucratic control' over vast territories and populations.[12] Richards compellingly speaks of 'imagination' or a 'fantasy' of empire.[13]

These authors rely primarily on written documents. Other historians have pointed out how film archives can be subjected to a treatment similar to the one described by Stoler in the context of the Dutch East Indies. In 1971 Marc Ferro, a pioneer of the use of film in historical studies, argued that film (including newsreels, documentaries and feature films) could reveal the mechanisms of a given society. 'The effect of film', he wrote, 'is to de-structure what several generations of men of state and thinkers have built into such a beautiful harmony. It destroys the alter image that every institution and every individual composes for itself in the face of society. The camera reveals their real functioning and tells more about each one of these than they could want.

It unveils secrets and shows the undersides of a society and its lapses.'[14]

14 Marc Ferro, 'Film, A Counter-analysis of Society? (1971), in *Cinema and History*, Detroit, Wayne State University Press, 1986, p. 29.

Fiona Tan seems to be in agreement with Ferro's thesis that the camera can reveal – unbeknownst to the maker of the film or the individuals being filmed – the obverse of the professed purpose of a document: indeed, the repeated viewing of the looped footage does not only make the postures and gazes from the filmed individuals available for analysis, but also reveals the uncertainties of the camera operators in the early days of filmmaking – the camera that pans a group assembled as for a photo portrait, the men and women moving in front of a fixed camera, the camera mounted on a car that sweeps the scenery around like a dreamy passenger with no specific aim.

And yet, however much we attempt to take on the distanced look of the scholar to analyse the images before us, Tan's installation immerses us into the filmic material: the large screen, the surrounding sound and the repeated sequence of the man with the feathered headband turning his camera on us all make it impossible to remain at bay. No longer just viewers, we get involved in the film montage and become something of a witness, a witness of our own reading of these events. This involvement of the viewer, the impossibility to take distance is paradoxically what makes it possible to break open the colonial document, to expose it, to decolonise it.

This is what, using different strategies, Sven Augustijnen and Wendelien van Oldenborgh also do in their films. Augustijnen follows, in *Spectres* (2011), a Belgian adventurer turned scholar who retraces the steps of his investigation into the circumstances behind the assassination of Congo independence leader Patrice Lumumba in January 1961. In *Maurits Script* (2006) Van Oldenborgh brings together a group of people to read aloud and discuss documents from the archives of the seventeenth-century Dutch colony of Brazil. They gather in the Mauritshuis, originally built as a home for Johan Maurits of Nassau during the years he was governor of Brazil, and examine some commissioned paintings that today still hang in the Mauritshuis museum in The Hague.

Spectres: A 'Cinema of Bodies'

Sven Augustijnen's *Spectres* opens with a scene shot from the inside of a car driven by a formally dressed grey-haired man. He steers into a single-lane countryside road and drives through a bright green landscape, in intermittent conversation in French with the woman seated beside him, while rolling titles take us to a different time and place, summarising the complex and violent events that attended the liberation of what is today the Democratic Republic of the Congo.[15] It evokes the short 200-day period from the Declaration of Independence pronounced by King Baudouin of the Belgians on 30 June 1960 in Kinshasa (then Léopoldville), immediately followed by the legendary and controversial speech of the first prime minister of the independent Congo, Patrice Lumumba, to the assassination of Lumumba in Katanga, in shadowy circumstances, on 17 January 1961. As the car drives on through the Belgian countryside, the on-screen text continues and presents the main protagonist of the film, Jacques Brassinne. He is introduced as a 'privileged witness of these events' who subsequently completed a doctoral dissertation in which he attempted to elucidate the circumstances of – and assess the responsibilities for – Lumumba's death. His dissertation was dedicated, the text concludes, to Harold d'Aspremont Lynden, *chef de cabinet* and later Minister of African Affairs in Belgium during this period.

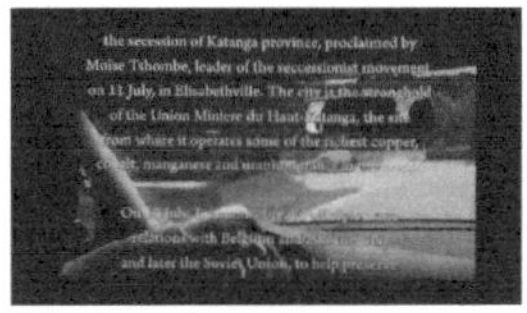

15 Sven Augustijnen, *Spectres*, 2011, HD video, colour, stereo sound, 104 min, video still.

The rolling titles give way to the first measures of Bach's *Johannes-Passion* (*St John Passion*). The music accompanies the car as it enters the grounds of a castle under a menacing sky. As the passengers climb out of the car, they are met by a dog, children and finally the lord and lady of the manor. The camera jitters as its operator tags along and films the social rituals and small talk that begin this visit to the countryside.

These very first minutes convey a clear suggestion: we are about to see a 'cinema of bodies', a term Gilles Deleuze used to describe the work of John Cassavetes. This is a type of film in which 'the story is secreted by the characters' and the action is propelled by the bodies of the protagonists.[16] It is a kind of cinema that Augustijnen was familiar with from the start, through his early collaboration with choreographer Alain Platel and his dancers on the film *Iets op Bach* (*Something on Bach*, 1998).[17] Always operating the camera himself, in later works he chose to focus on one or two protagonists whom he follows at close range, and around whom the narrative unfolds. We see this tactic in *Le Guide du parc* (*The Park Guide*, 2001) and *Une femme entreprenante* (*An Enterprising Woman*, 2005). In the latter film, there are two protagonists, the storyteller and the subject of the story. In *Spectres*, these two roles are collapsed into one person, the ambiguous Brassinne. Knighted by King Baudouin in 1988, in 2001 he was interviewed by the Lumumba Parliamentary Commission both as a witness and as an expert on the life and death of Lumumba. These are only two of Brassinne's many incarnations. Other roles that he fulfilled include general secretary of the round table preparing the independence of Congo in

16 Gilles Deleuze, *Cinema 2* (1985), London, Continuum, 2005, p. 185.

17 On the question of choreography in Augustijnen's early work, see my 'Neither Fish nor Fowl, But Real Bodies: The Films of Sven Augustijnen', in *Afterall*, no. 31, 2012, pp. 86–93.

1960 and, in 1964, advisor to Moïse Tshombe, the leader of the secessionist region of Katanga, a fierce opponent of Lumumba and one of the movers behind his slaying.[18] Why this Tshombist would subsequently become noticeably dedicated to investigating the death of Lumumba, whom – as is clear from an interview with Augustijnen in the book accompanying the film – he does not hold in great esteem, is a compelling mystery.[19] Yet Brassinne wrote a book on the subject in 1966 before embarking on a campaign of doctoral research that stretched over a period of no less than 30 years, obtaining a dissertation in political science – summa cum laude, the highest distinction – from the Université Libre de Bruxelles.[20]

The film offers no psychological analysis of Brassinne to help answer these questions. There is no voice-over or any revelatory dialogue. By the same token, there is little reflection on the research process, aside from the succinct counterpoint of the on-screen texts. Material evidence is confined to a handful of archive binders and boxes that are opened briefly for the benefit of the camera. Rather, the main text for reading the film is nothing other than the body of Brassinne itself. Walking decisively in ample strides, always aware of the camera and careful to position himself and his interlocutors in its field, the 80-year-old Brassinne restlessly leads us on a tour of

18 The Commission Parlementaire was created by the Belgian government in 1999, shortly before the publication of Ludo de Witte's controversial book *The Assassination of Patrice Lumumba*. It auditioned Brassinne both as historian and witness. The round table conference in preparation of the handover of sovereignty took place in Brussels in January 1960. Brassinne became advisor to the cabinet of Prime Minister Moïse Tshombe in August 1964. Sven Augustijnen (ed.), *Spectres*, Brussels, Asa Publishers, 2011, pp. 172–173.

19 'Every Evening, We Wired News to Brussels', interview with Jacques Brassinne conducted by Sven Augustijnen, 3 February 2011, in Sven Augustijnen, *Spectres*, esp. pp. 104–106.

20 *Lumumba Patrice: Les cinquante derniers jours de sa vie*, (published with Jules Gerard Libois., under the pseudonyms G. Heinz and H. Donnay), Paris, Seuil, 1967.

21 Gilles Deleuze, *Cinema 2* (1985), London, Continuum, 2005, p. 182.

witnesses and places related to Lumumba's ordeal. He takes us through some of the steps of his protracted investigation, relentlessly retelling the story and at times re-enacting it. In doing so, he adopts a performative mode that shows us, as Deleuze phrased it, 'the interior through behaviour'.[21] The film is structured by a succession of scenes that alternate visits to particular sites and to witnesses or their relatives; throughout, Brassinne conducts short interviews. Each of these scenes enables him to reveal his ability to manoeuvre across a wide spectrum of political allegiances as well as to display a rich palette of attitudes: a sycophantic tone to gently coax the daughter of Moïse Tshombe; a mild discomfort in the house of the Lumumba family; a respectful connivance in that of Arnoud d'Aspremont Lynden; and the enthusiasm of a pedagogue with inhabitants of Lubumbashi. There he stood in front of the remains of the Brouwez house, where Lumumba, together with two close allies, Maurice Mpolo and Joseph Okito, were tortured in the hours preceding their murder.

This cinema of bodies is given the complex task of recapitulating Brassinne's investigation in condensed form and of summarising a story that stands at the intersection of post- and neo-colonial politics, justice and history. The linkage of these disciplines surfaced conspicuously in 1999–2001 in the context of the Lumumba Parliamentary Commission, in which experts were asked to review the evidence and propose an authoritative interpretation concerning the responsibility of the Belgian state in the death of Lumumba.[22] Although his dissertation was conducted in a department of political science rather than history, in the film Brassinne adopts the professorial attitude of a historian spelling out dates and places, reviewing the evidence and critiquing the testimonies of the witnesses he interviews. In this sense, the film presents the historian in action.

The first of these scenes is perhaps the most impressive in this respect, for it presents history not only as a discipline, but also as a practice embedded within social and professional networks. It follows Brassinne's arrival at the castle, where he is greeted by Arnoud d'Aspremont Lynden, Harold's son, and his family. After deciding on a suitable spot to stage his interview for the camera, Brassinne fills in the content as well.[23] He begins by instructing d'Aspremont Lynden to reiterate in front of the camera the substance of his response to an accusatory open letter against his father published in 2009 by the collective Mémoire Coloniale in the Belgian daily *Le Soir*.[24] The accusation revolved around the interpretation of a telex sent in October 1960 by Harold d'Aspremont Lynden, as minister of foreign affairs, to the Belgian ambassador in the Congo,

22 Concerning the role of historians as experts in the Commission, see Georgi Verbeeck, 'Coming to Terms with the (Post-) Colonial Past in Belgium: The Inquiry into the Assassination of Patrice Lumumba', in Harriet Jones, Kjell Ostberg, Nico Randeraad (eds.) *Contemporary History on Trial: Europe since 1989 and the Role of the Expert Witness*, Manchester and New York, Manchester University Press, 2007, pp. 46–61. See also Emmanuel Gerard, 'Memories of the Parliamentary Investigation Commission', in Sven Augustijnen, *Spectres*, pp. 128–140.

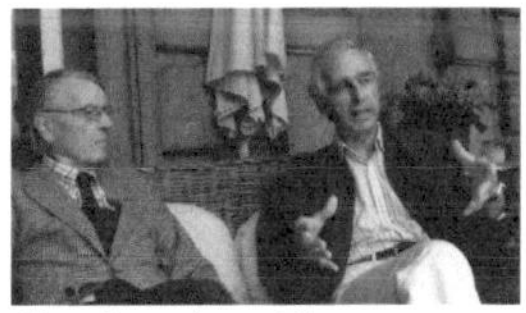

23 Sven Augustijnen, *Spectres*, video still.

24 Pauline Imbach, Collectif Mémoires Coloniales, 'Patrice Lumumba: La Belgique doit reconnaître ses responsabilités historiques', open letter published in *Le Soir*, 28 January 2009. Reprinted in Sven Augustijnen, *Spectres*, pp. 115–120.

Robert Rothschild, in which he expressed the necessity to pursue 'as a main goal' the 'definitive elimination of Lumumba'. For Ludo de Witte, the author of *L'Assassinat de Lumumba* (*The Assassination of Lumumba*, 2000), this telex evidences the government's direct involvement in the assassination. For the Parliamentary Commission it proves at the very least, the moral responsibility of the Belgian government for the death of Lumumba. Prompted by Brassinne, the minister's son repeats his counter-arguments, in support of his conviction that 'the definitive elimination of Lumumba' meant nothing more nefarious than eliminating him from the political game. Arnoud d'Aspremont Lynden begins by reinserting the telex into a series of facts and dates that contradict the more radical interpretation of Ludo de Witte. Soon after, he appeals to his interlocutor's common sense, suggesting that Brassinne was familiar with the arcane of diplomatic and governmental communication but that his accusers were not. Brassinne then improvises a lecture on the complex political situation in the Congo at the end of 1960 and recounts the succession of events that led to what he calls the 'execution' of Lumumba, naming by name Congolese and Katangese politicians whom he held responsible for it. The two men conclude their discussion by agreeing that the assassination was a purely African affair, from which

Belgium should be exonerated of any factual or moral accountability.

Letting his camera linger on the silverware on the table and taking in the plush sofas and gilded stucco of the grand interior as well as the Belgian flag floating on the grounds of the castle, Augustijnen silently evokes the social context in which this discourse is produced, but he does more than that. His camera suggests in addition that this particular framework plays an active role in the discourse Brassinne articulates in the first moments of the film. All of this lends itself as a suitable case for the application of Michel de Certeau's resolutely anti-authoritarian sociological analysis of academia as a power structure indispensable to what he called the 'historiographical operation' conducted in the aftermath of May 1968. In that regard, Brassinne's views come across as 'symptoms' rather than reasoned arguments.[25] One of the strengths of the opening scene of *Spectres* is that the Brassinne presented to us by Augustijnen's film challenges De Certeau's deep mistrust of the historian's independence of judgement while simultaneously comforting it. Indeed, the filmmaker shows Brassinne as a figure who, while breaking open the closed world of academia, embodies another form of authority. Hence, the exchange with D'Aspremont Lynden lapses from a serious questioning of a witness by a

25 Michel de Certeau, *The Writing of History* (1975), New York, Columbia University Press, 1988, p. 65.

researcher into a detached conversation between aristocrats, prolonging itself over drinks and later coffee. Throughout the visit, Brassinne alternates between the posture of the specialist and of the courtier. He claims authority on the subject by mentioning the 2000 pages of his thesis and the 30 years of research he devoted to it. Yet the place from which he speaks is not academia. He does not hesitate to disparage the conceptual narrowness of historians, thereby implying that their knowledge is bounded by the borders of the academic 'place' from which they speak. But whereas Brassinne is willing and apparently able to scrutinise and expose the overblown pretences of the academic field and finger the shortcomings of historians, he is nevertheless unable to adopt a reflexive position as regards his own interpretation.

Moreover, his critical perspective on the discipline of history only leads him to embrace uncritically another power structure. Indeed, the film shows him first and foremost as the author of a history that pays allegiance to Belgian state power. This circumstance casts a particular light on the scene with Arnoud d'Aspremont Lynden. This is made clear in a later scene of the film shot at a ceremony for the anniversary of King Baudouin's death in the church of Laeken. Without recourse to dialogue, but simply by recording the interaction of different groups of people following official protocol, Augustijnen shows the conflation of church, monarchy and political power as well as Brassinne's evident pleasure in being part of these circles. The problematic position of Brassinne and his absence of reflection concerning the historical events he narrates is probably one of the reasons why Ludo de Witte, a sociologist whose research led to a Belgian parliamentary enquiry on Lumumba's death, in his book attempts to systematically re-inscribe Brassinne's whereabouts within the course of the events that they have both investigated.[26]

To this portrayal of an ambiguous scholar who both takes on and rejects the academic label, and who criticises one institution only to enslave himself to another, the artist adds a multifaceted depiction of scholarly practice. De Certeau defined historiography as the process of transforming objects into specific, pre-established formats. Taking his cue from predecessors like Marc Bloch, he argued that a document is not so much found as produced through transcription, photography and copying, in obedience to rules defined within the discipline.[27] In *Spectres*, the artist confronts us with a diverse array of such produced documents. They include diplomatic sources, such as the telex by Harold d'Aspremont Lynden featured in the opening scene of the film, but also statements by witnesses recorded

26 Ludo de Witte, *The Assassination of Lumumba* (2000), London, Verso, 2002.

27 De Certeau, 1975, pp. 71–72.

by Brassinne and reproduced in appendices to his PhD thesis. They also comprise photographic documentation of the site of the killing. All of these documents are discussed, challenged and inserted into Brassinne's account of the last moments of Lumumba's life, but they are never shown on screen. While we seem to be dealing with textbook examples of how documents can be created and then assembled in order to build up a case and construct a historical narrative, their conspicuous absence in the film vitiates the very hypothesis to be proven.

The importance of the telex, the most important document of all, is minimised by Arnoud d'Aspremont Lynden. The witnesses questioned by Brassinne throughout the film and invited to rehearse their statements in front of the camera sometimes appear hesitant – like Jacques Bartelous, Tshombe's chef de cabinet in Katanga in 1960–1961 – or have their statements contradicted, as in the scene where Brassinne talks to Marie Tshombe. Interviewed at the grave of her father in the cemetery of Etterbeek, she is adamant that he was not present at the killing of Lumumba, which in other scenes Brassinne asserts unwaveringly. As for the traces of the killing in the forest, photographed by Brassinne in 1988, they have since then all but vanished. Yet in the penultimate scene we see Brassinne pouring over his notes and scrutinising every bump on the bark of a tree and probing barely visible irregularities on the ground in a laborious attempt to conjure up the evidence.[28]

These moments read as parodies of the historical operation. Their effect might be comic if they did not serve the highly contentious interpretation of facts put forward by Brassinne, an interpretation that has been refuted by numerous other students of the events, including the Lumumba Parliamentary Commission and Ludo de Witte.

As the narrative of the film unfolds we are thus confronted with two contradictory storylines: the first one follows Brassinne as he builds up his case, travelling from one witness to another and visiting particular sites. The second one shows his documentary evidence being challenged, questioned and ultimately disappearing altogether. In other words, the more the film progresses towards building a case, the more Brassinne's hypothesis unravels. The disappearance of the evidence in the forest and the inconsistencies of the witnesses echo the gruesome aftermath of the killing itself, when those responsible for murdering the three men took pains to erase traces of the bodies. The progressive disappearance of evidence works as a counterpoint to Augustijnen's close-range following of Brassinne, which one critic described as the 'quasi-servility' of the camera vis-à-vis the protagonist.[29] This also subverts the

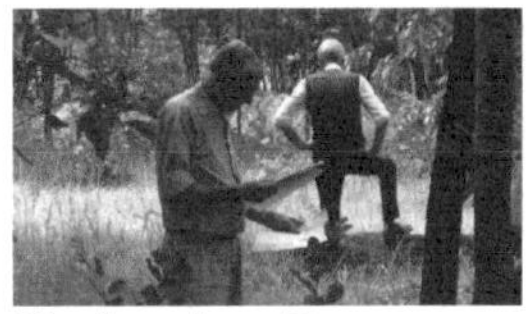

28 Sven Augustijnen, *Spectres*, video still.

29 Jean Pierre Rehm, 'Spectres: Notes sur Spectres de Sven Augustijnen', *Trafic*, issue 86, summer 2013, pp. 65–66.

30 Augustijnen has reiterated this idea in several interviews and public discussions. For example in a discussion with scholars in a research seminar at the Netherlands Institute for Advanced Studies, Wassenaar, 30 October 2012.

31 On the characteristics of testimony and the figure of the witness see Paul Ricoeur, *Memory, History, Forgetting* (2000), Chicago, University of Chicago Press, 2004, especially Part 2, chapter 1, 'The Documentary Phase: Archived Memory'.

idea put forward by the artist on various occasions that the film was entirely 'determined' by its protagonist.[30] Guided, perhaps more than he originally intended by a forceful character, the artist's response is to leave out of the film the material traces produced by Brassinne in his investigation. By collecting and publishing those written documents, photographs, maps and sketches in a book accompanying the film, Augustijnen distances himself from Brassinne's position.

The removal of material evidence from the visual field of the film has another consequence: it brings to the fore the central character of Brassinne and lets us question what kind of witness he might be. For, while he is able to provide and repeat a factual account, we realise how often he was not a direct witness of the events he describes.[31] As we follow him speaking and gesticulating throughout the film, our attention switches from what he says to how he says it: he becomes something of a document to be deciphered, interpreted and challenged at the very same time he is seen performing a historiographical operation.

At the level of verbal expression, Brassinne is a powerful, convincing and authoritative document; he performs his historical narrative as a heroic quest for the truth. The scene in front of the remains of the Brouwez house in Lubumbashi is exemplary in this respect. It shows Brassinne plunging into an impromptu lecture on the last hours of Lumumba's life before an audience of local residents. The jubilant delivery of his talk sits ill with the terrible facts he recounts. His eloquence is such that his wife Martine feels called upon to interrupt him to assure the assembled crowd that it is not Brassinne himself who is responsible for the events he relates with such passion.

The same passionate voice becomes endowed with more tragic overtones in a scene towards the end of the film, when Brassinne returns to the site of the killing that he discovered in 1988. Re-examining the location, he identifies – mimicking their presence – the specific positions taken by the protagonists and describes what he believes was the exact order in which the three prisoners were sentenced to death by the Katangese and Congolese ministers and executed one after the other.

These two sequences show the extent to which Brassinne has internalised the events he describes. The camera, it is important to recall, is filming not the original investigation but a staged rehearsing of that enquiry. This might explain what the viewer would see as a glaring indifference to the missing answers to certain questions. 'Who did it?', for instance, is asked by some of the men assembled around Brassinne and his wife on the remains of the Brouwez house in Lubumbashi, as he describes the

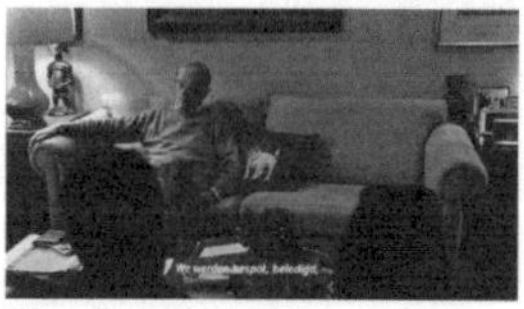

32 Sven Augustijnen, *Spectres*, video still.

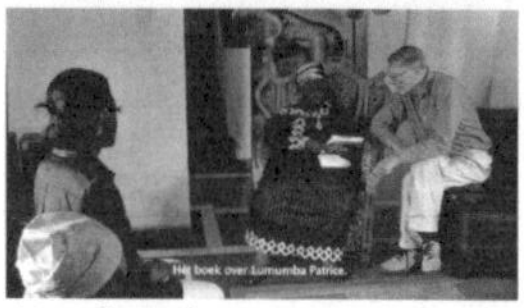

33 Sven Augustijnen, *Spectres*, video still.

treatment to which Lumumba and his acolytes were subjected. This question remains unanswered, as Brassinne, despite evidence to the contrary, rejects the idea that Lumumba, Mpolo and Okito were tortured. Instead, Brassinne moves on to the next scene, to another witness and another site that is to take a predetermined position in the puzzle as he formulates it. Brassinne's control of the situations seems absolute when restricted to verbal expression. Beyond the spoken word, however, his body projects an altogether different kind of evidence.

One of the most striking visions of this body is proffered when, filmed at home, sitting on a sofa, Brassinne is shown listening to recordings of the speeches of King Baudouin and Prime Minister Lumumba on 30 June 1960 in Leopoldville/Kinshasa. Relaxed as he listens to Baudouin, he stiffens when the voice of Lumumba begins to fill the space of his living room. Uncharacteristically deflated, he remains seated on a sofa, as if frozen, until the speech comes to an end and is greeted with a torrent of applause from the Congolese assembled for the handover.[32] At another moment, visiting the Lumumba family and speaking with Lumumba's widow, Pauline Opango and their children, Brassinne never loses his jovial tone, but we do see him becoming increasingly twitchy until at a given moment he takes leave quite abruptly.[33]

In this cinema of bodies, by acquainting us to the point of intimacy with all of Brassinne's gestures and works, Augustijnen turns his 'servile' camera into a microscope. The more familiar Brassinne becomes, the more we are able to read him against the grain of his own words, in spite of himself. The contrast between Brassinne's verbal self-assurance and the uncertainties revealed by his physical motion lay bare the intractable paradox at the heart of this character. Presented at first as a witness of the death of Lumumba, he is then constructed, through the rehash of his investigation into that historical tragedy, as a specialist, a scholar. The film bypasses the simple truth that these two positions are mutually exclusive. To gain authority as a scholar Brassinne must remove himself from history – a tactic that is resisted by Ludo de Witte, who re-situates him emphatically within each stage of Lumumba's final months – while as an adventurer, a politician, a diplomat, he is reluctant to step aside. But *Spectres* is not a podium for Brassinne's views on history. With the camera firmly positioned at close range, it shows us how much he has interiorised those views and yet how easily they can be read by the attentive viewer. Brassinne's body is not that of a witness, but a site of conflict between embodied memory, documented history, ideology and heightened sense of self-interest.

Performing the Archive in Maurits Script

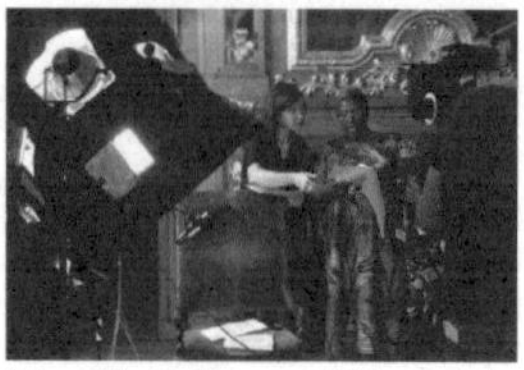

34 Wendelien van Oldenborgh, *Maurits Script*, 2006, two-channel video projection, 67 minutes, video still.

Whereas *Spectres* wrestles with recent historical events that have generated considerable dispute and have polarised positions in Belgium for over 40 years, Wendelien van Oldenborgh's *Maurits Script* (2006), while also dealing with colonial history, investigates a comparatively distant and lesser-known chapter of Dutch and Brazilian history. The film, composed of two parts that are exhibited simultaneously on two screens facing or next to each other, is the result of a day-long performance filmed at the Mauritshuis in The Hague.[34] One of the films shows people scattered across the room reading extracts from archival documents. In the other film, the protagonists of the reading are assembled around a large table looking at and discussing visual documents relating to the Dutch presence in Brazil: reproductions of paintings by Frans Post; illustrations of the fauna and flora of Brazil made by Zacharias Wagener; the well-known life-size paintings by Albert Eckhout portraying different population types in Brazil.

The first film begins with sounds evoking the preparation for a film shoot. We see cameras being set up and people in the care of a makeup artist. We hear chairs scraping on the floor and people calling out to one another. The sound is crisp and the camera movements are smooth, suggesting a controlled and well-rehearsed choreography as one camera gives way to another. The setting is the so-called Gouden Zaal or Golden Room of the Mauritshuis, home today to the Royal Picture Gallery but originally built for Johan Maurits, Count of Nassau-Siegen and governor, from 1637 to 1644, of the short-lived Dutch colony in the northeast of Brazil.

The Gouden Zaal is bathed in a warm, unvarying light. The performance takes place during the museum's regular opening hours and every so often museum visitors are seen popping their heads through the door. One voice rises above the brouhaha and begins to read in Dutch, in an old and formal variant of the language. She is followed by another voice; the camera, identifying the speakers, moves smoothly from one to the other. The participants in the performance each reads extracts of documentary sources on the Dutch colony in Brazil, unearthed from the National Archive in The Hague, the university library in Leiden and the print room or Kupferstich-Kabinett of the Staatliche Kunstsammlungen in Dresden. The film alternates between long close-up shots of monologue reading and images of the other protagonists turning pages of documents, exchanging glances, and seemingly giving one another cues to begin or to continue.[35] The documents recited include minutes of council

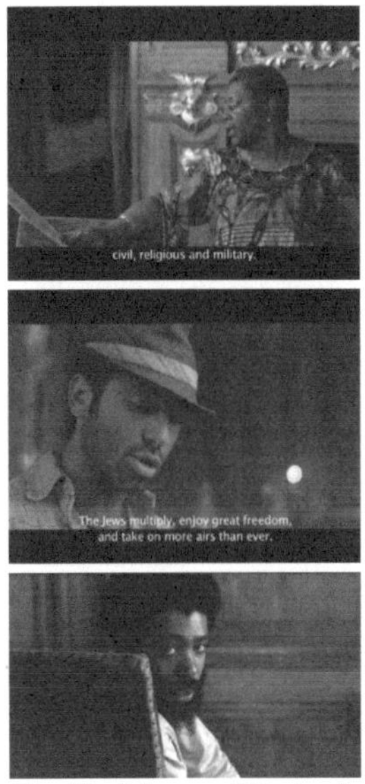

35 Wendelien van Oldenborgh, *Maurits Script*, video stills.

meetings, the diaries of Johan Maurits and other such testimonies of the period as memoirs and accounts published in the Netherlands in the mid-seventeenth century. They describe the interactions between inhabitants from Portugal, the former owner of the colony, and the Netherlands, and discuss the natives of Brazil and the kinds of behaviour attributed to them by the Dutch. Other sources provide details concerning the social and economic relations between different groups in the Dutch colony. What emerges is a fragmented depiction rendered through a multiplicity of voices, of accents, of faces. Delivering their extracts of historical documents, the participants read rather than act. The effect is to emphasise the presentation of documents as raw facts, lacking dogmatic implication and avoiding association between reader and text. The clarity of the voices and the freshness of the accounts, unencumbered by analysis or commentary, recall Arlette Farge's compelling description of the illusion of life that springs from the archive in her book *Le goût de l'archive* (*The Allure of the Archive*, 1989):

> 'This give rise to the naïve but profound feeling of tearing a veil, of crossing through the opaqueness of knowledge and, as if after a long and uncertain voyage, finally gaining access to the

> essence of beings and things. The archive lays things bare, and in a few crowded lines you can find not only the inaccessible, but also the living'.[36]

The fragments selected by the artist and read aloud in the filmed performance do not recount the master narratives of the colonial presence, dates or facts. Instead, they provide contemporaneous, mutually contradictory accounts of the different populations co-existing in the colony. The local Indians, commonly called Tapuyas by the Dutch and the Portuguese; the slaves and former slaves from Africa; the Jews; the Portuguese against whom the Dutch battled for ownership of the land; and the Dutch themselves – each group in turn is described in terms of physical appearance, customs, recommendations on how best to deal with them, legends and anecdotes. These texts form the bulk of the performances. We hear tales of cannibalism from the Tapuyas recited in the same solemn tone of voice as minutes of a meeting of the Heeren XIX, the administrators of the West India Company back in Amsterdam. The contradictory nature of the documents reminds us, as Farge warns the reader, that the vivid sensation of the real as experienced when one reads an archive is nothing but an illusion: 'No matter how much the real seems to be there, visible

36 Arlette Farge, *The Allure of the Archives* (1989), New Haven, Yale University Press, 2013, p. 8.

37 Arlette Farge, *The Allure of the Archives*, p. 11.

38 Ann Laura Stoler and Frederick Cooper, 'Rethinking Metropole and Colony', in Ann Laura Stoler and Frederick Cooper (eds.), *Tensions of Empire: Colonial Cultures in a Bourgeois World*, Berkeley, Los Angeles and London, University of California Press, 1997, p. 21.

and tangible, it reveals nothing more than its physical presence and it is naïve to believe that this is its essence. This can make the "return from the archive" difficult.'[37]

Moreover, the compilation of state archives, personal testimonies and the mix of gossip and official rulings expose the fragmentary nature of the knowledge that can be drawn from the colonial archive. This is a reminder that, as Ann Laura Stoler puts it: 'In taking it as a given that power breeds a certain format of knowledge, we have not questioned the basis of that knowledge or how incomplete it often was. It is only when we focus on the production of the colonial archive and on the sorts of narratives contained within it that we find how much rumour, gossip and fantasy pervades the official field.'[38]

Van Oldenborgh could have followed a conventional documentary mode and allowed one performer to present the documents. Instead, she gives equal weight to various attestations and documents, providing each source with a different incarnation in the person of a different reader. This procedure brings across to the viewer the frailty of the archive as a reliable source.

The second part of the film brings the archive into the present by staging a discussion between the participants of the reading. Gathered around a table covered with books and pictures, and informed by their experience of reading the archival sources, the protagonists examine some of the images that fleetingly appeared in the first part of the film as they turned over the pages of the documents.[39] Many of these images are illustrations of works by Albert Eckhout, one of the painters who accompanied Johan Maurits to Brazil. Eckhout recorded in sketches and oil paintings the 'natural history' of Brazil: his work is considered by one art historian as the single most important legacy of the governorship of the colony.[40] The discussion within the group focuses on Eckhout's painting of an African slave, a painting originally produced as a documentary representation.[41] The protagonists gradually deconstruct it as an ideologically loaded representation, a coded image full of symbols to be decrypted and debated. The exchange leads to a discussion of contemporary issues of nationality, citizenship and ethnic origin. The participants bring their own experiences and knowledge into a dialogue with the historical documents they have just read or that lay before them.

Jay Winter has examined a similar coming together of past and present, history and memory using the performative mode. He defines a virtual 'performance of the past' that comprises 'a set of acts, some embodied in speech, others in movements and gestures, others in art, others still in bodily form.

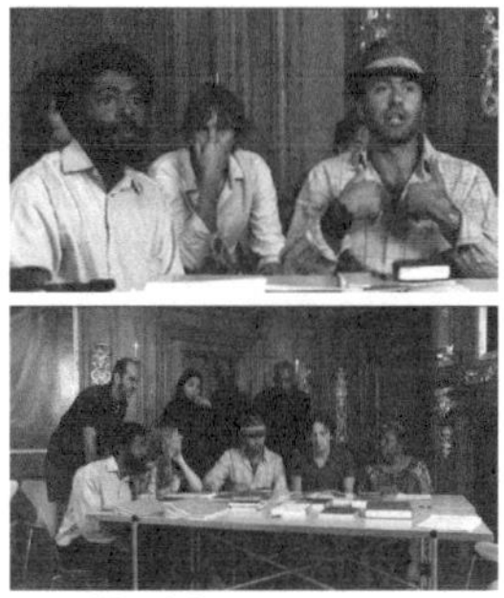

39 Wendelien van Oldenborgh, *Maurits Script*, video stills.

40 On Eckhout's work in Brazil, see Rebecca Parker Brienen, *Visions of Savage Paradise: Albert Eckhout, Court Painter in Colonial Dutch Brazil*, Amsterdam, Amsterdam University Press, 2006.

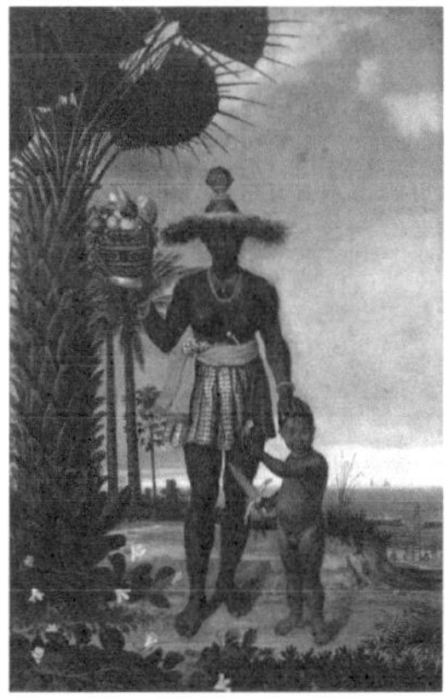

41 Albert Eckhout, *African Woman and Child*, 1641, oil on canvas, 282 × 189 cm, Copenhagen, National Museum of Denmark.

The performative act rehearses and recharges the emotion that gave the initial memory or story imbedded in it its sticking power, its resistance to erasure or oblivion. Hence affect is always inscribed in performative acts in general and the performance of memory in particular.'[42] In such performances – Winter cites the Mothers of the Plaza de Mayo in Buenos Aires; the response to Obama's 2008 election in Grant Park; the site of the violent confrontations between protesters and police at the Democratic party convention of 1968 – emotion plays an important role, as these performances 'galvanize the ties that bind groups together'. By seizing on collective manifestations, in which every participant had motives of their own, Winter avoids having to assign to these 'scripts about the past' a single meaning, a meaning susceptible to subjective distortion. This choice is at variance with the univocal narrative, which tends to freeze the past in the version of the speaker, with the attendant, very real danger of tendentiousness and manipulability.

Other artists take a different tack. In his *Battle of Orgreave,* Jeremy Deller stages a re-enactment of a confrontation between miners and policemen in 1984, underscoring the emotional aspect of events by filming the testimonies of witnesses and the sometimes contentious points of view of experts. In contrast to this approach, affect is kept in check in

42 Winter defines history and memory as follows: 'History is memory seen through and criticised with the aid of documents of many kinds – written, aural, visual. Memory is history seen through affect.' Jay Winter, 'The Performance of the Past: Memory, History, Identity', in K. Tilmans, J. Winter and F. van Vree (eds.), *Performing the Past: Memory, History and Identity in Modern Europe*, Amsterdam, Amsterdam University Press, 2010, p. 13.

Van Oldenborgh's *Maurits Script*, just as it is in Tan's *Facing Forward* and Augustijnen's *Spectres*. *Maurits Script* uses several devices to detach the historical documents from their interpretation. For instance, the make-up artist and the filmmaker occasionally interrupt the participants in their discussion and ask them to move to other parts of the set. Moreover, the participants do not act. They only read, occasionally changing texts. As for *Spectres*, although Brassinne is a creature full of affect, his emotions are systematically undercut by his physical expressions and the reactions of the other characters. All three films thus confront us with a dual script. In *Maurits Script*, the split is made explicit through the juxtaposition of two screens to project the two parts of the film, while in Tan's film, it is the camera operator who reminds us of our own bodily presence as we watch the archival footage.

This disjunction recalls the stratagem employed by Alain Resnais in a scene of *Muriel ou le temps d'un retour* (*Muriel or The Time of Return*, 1963), a film in which the question of the body is central.[43] It is indeed centred on an episode of torture during Algeria's war of independence against France, a story that is both impossible to tell and impossible to forget for Bernard, a young traumatised Frenchman returning from army service in Algeria. Halfway through *Muriel*, the image becomes pale and grainy

43 Alain Resnais, *Muriel ou le temps d'un retour*, 1963, colour film, 116 min.

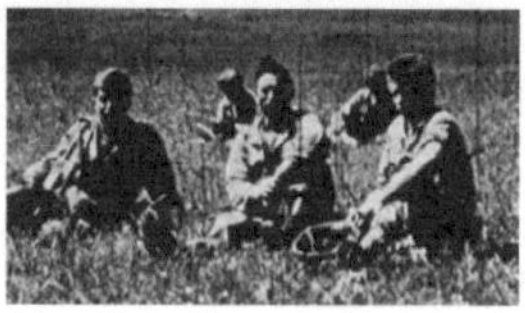

44 Alain Resnais, *Muriel ou le temps d'un retour*, film still.

45 The negotiations that brought the conflict to a halt, known as the Accords d'Évian, were signed in April 1962. The independence of Algeria, following a referendum, was proclaimed on 3 July 1962.

and, without further notice, we are transported from the grey streets of Boulogne-sur-Mer, where the film is set, to the hilltops of the Algerian countryside, and from the 35mm of the fiction film to the shaky 8mm of Bernard's amateur camerawork. As the innocuous footage unfolds, showing French soldiers resting, eating and doing laundry, Bernard begins to narrate his participation in the torture and murder, under the command of a certain 'Robert', of a young woman known as Muriel.[44] Bernard's testimony provides one of the rare moments of continuity in the film amidst a snappy montage of short sequences punctuated by dissonant music and the endless chattering of the other characters. But the homogeneity of this sequence at the heart of the film is challenged by the discrepancy between the story told by Bernard and the seemingly inconsequential images that appear on the screen. Resnais adopts and subverts the techniques of the traditional documentary: archival footage and voiceover are combined, except that here the two elements are completely unconnected. They do not match up, in the same way as the documentary evidence that Bernard painstakingly accumulates fails to implicate 'Robert'. Despite being shot and released in the immediate aftermath of the Algerian war and despite the agitation of its characters, Muriel puts affect at a distance.[45] The discontinuity between Bernard's memory voice and the filmic document keeps the viewer from identifying with any of the characters, from re-enacting the past in a consensual way.

Like Resnais in *Muriel,* artists like Tan, Van Oldenborgh and Augustijnen do not construct a rhetorical opposition between the solidity of material evidence and the flickering of individual memories. Nor do they rely on the force of recognizable emotions and affects to bring history to life. Instead, *Facing Forward, Maurits Script* and *Spectres* show in different ways how material evidence can be revisited and interpreted to accommodate different truths; how history is a discourse constructed by those who read as much as those who write. The work of these artists entails a meditation on the archive as a dispersed collection that is necessarily embodied and enacted, and that needs to be performed and re-enacted – decolonised – in order to prevent it from withering away or stifling into orthodoxy. They represent the archive as a physical corpus of gestural and symptomatic incidents – never finished, nowhere closed, always open to active intervention.

Epilogue

In proposing a genealogy of Jean-Luc Moulène's *Impersonal Diary* that includes surrealist photography and images from *La Nature,* in interpreting the physical gestures of the main protagonist of Sven Augustijnen's *Spectres* as refuting the evidence he verbalises, and in discussing my experience of the peculiar rhythm and distancing procedures at work in Wendelien van Oldenborgh's *Maurits Script,* I have wanted to show how contemporary art can make us more sensitive to the ways in which information is constructed, presented and circulated. Reading these works closely meant turning them into *theoretical objects* – objects that provoke the production of theory. While each chapter focuses on a specific set of works, together the works bring to the surface a number of issues that recur throughout the book and are symptomatic of specific changes in contemporary culture in a broader sense. To round things off, I should like to address briefly four of these issues here.

The first of these could be called the *art work–document*. By this I identify a rather widespread tendency of art to veer towards the document, to become permeated with characteristics, such as fragmentation and instrumentalisation. This phenomenon is broader than what was meant with the so-called 'documentary turn' of the late 1990s and early 2000s, which often involved the wholesale import of documentary film from its habitual festival and television circuits into the black box of contemporary art exhibitions, and the appropriation of traditions of documentary photography into Fine Art. This tendency was supported by a discourse centred on truth, which caused Jacques Rancière to refer to an 'ethical turn' in contemporary art.[1]

The idea of an *art work–document* suggests instead an older logic at work in the field of art, one that includes early twentieth-century traditions of collage and montage, but also conceptual artistic practices and documentary traditions in film and photography. It is about art claiming openly its inability to be complete, to have authority, to have the final word on a topic. The play on authorship that goes on in Jean-Luc Moulène's titles, the deferral in Williams' use of the phrase 'for example'

1 Exhibitions that typify the issues at stake in documentary in art include *Walker Evans & Company* (New York, 2000); *Documenta 11* (Kassel, 2002); *Cruel and Tender* (London, 2003); *[Based upon] True Stories* (Rotterdam, 2003); *Experiments with Truth* (Philadelphia, 2004); *The Need to Document* (Basel and Lüneburg, 2005) and *Making History: Art and Documentary in Britain from 1929 to Now* (Liverpool, 2008). Jacques Rancière discussed the ethical turn in *Malaise dans l'esthétique*, Paris, Galilé, 2004. He returns to this issue notably in Jacques Rancière, 'The Thinking of Dissensus: Politics and Aesthetics', in Paul Bowman and Richard Stamp (eds.), *Reading Rancière*, Continuum, London and New York, 2011, pp. 1–17.

and the system of 'revisions' he has adopted for exhibitions, but also the speculative gaze of Zoe Leonard, and the multi-voiced narrative in Van Oldenborgh's *Maurits Script* – all these elements contribute to a notion of the art work as a self-reflective process and a document of its own making. The idea of *art work–document* affirms the unsolvable dichotomy between the autonomy of art and its entry into discourse and institutional practice: the more it enters sociological, political, and historical discourse, the more it needs to reaffirm its distance from these fields. The *art work–document* is not only present in the visual arts: a novelist who includes Wikipedia entries in his novel is similarly pointing out an impossibility to retain a singular authority, to be conclusive in a culture of open source.[2]

The second issue can be described as the *museum–archive complex*. It is a complex both in the sense of an obsession – as the museum is truly haunted by the archive – and in the sense of a network of relations that the museum and the archive must jointly reinvent. Traditionally the museum display draws up a script that visitors duly follow, while archives, on the contrary, call for individual users and researchers who construct their own script. The museum categorises, establishes hierarchies and obviates utility, whereas an archive is taxonomic rather than pyramidal and derives its value from the

2 See for example, Michel Houellebecq, *The Map and the Territory* (2010), New York, Vintage Books, 2012.

usefulness of the information it contains. The *art work–document* muddles this order. In adopting the formats and protocols belonging to documents in order to make works of art, Fiona Tan's *Facing Forward,* Leonard's *Wax Anatomical Model* and Moulène's *Strike Objects* transform or displace documents from archives to museum spaces. Works such as these turn obscure, invisible sources into covetable, individual objects worthy of lengthy observation. They blur the roles of the archive and the museum and thereby question notions of representation, visibility and knowledge production in exhibition display and historiography.

It is no coincidence that museums and archives are cited in these works: the Louvre, the Josephinum, the National Dutch film archives, the Mauritshuis, the J.F. Kennedy Library and the Getty are questioned, represented, probed and investigated. At times the institutions themselves take the initiative for such probing, revealing a wider process of self-reflection that is at work in the museum world today. The problems are urgent: how do art museums face the pressures of continuous education and the neo-liberal idea of knowledge as a commodity? How do they achieve global reach as markers of cultural identity? Such questions also provoke a re-thinking of the status of the object in the museum: as a unique treasure or an immaterial image destined to be circulated. To give just one example: with its abundance of large glass vitrines that flatten the space of its galleries and turn objects and paintings into two-dimensional images, the renovated Rijksmuseum in Amsterdam has all but become a *walk-in database,* thus epitomising the archive–museum complex.

The third issue is something I experienced in the process of considering the format of this book. The intellectual legitimacy of projects such as Augustijnen's *Spectres* and Moulène's *Strike Objects,* to name only two of the works discussed here, make it impossible not to question, in turn, formats of scientific research emanating from scholars in the academic field. Recent publications such as Ivan Jablonka's *Histoire des grands-parents que je n'ai pas eus* or, in a different way, Roman Bertrand's *L'Histoire à part égales,* show how historians are trying to re-invent academic discourse by the introduction of family histories and shifts of viewpoint; they highlight the ways in which evidence is constructed in historical discourse.[3] What I call *the shape of thinking* is an invitation to drop the pseudo-objectivity of scholarly research and to develop forms of academic writing that acknowledge the vagaries and undecided self-positioning of the author.

My final point is the issue of *amnesic recording,* an expression I use to identify the major paradox of

3 Ivan Jablonka, *Histoire des grands-parents que je n'ai pas eus: Une enquête,* Paris, Seuil, 2012. Roman Bertrand, *L'Histoire à part égales: Récits d'une rencontre Orient-Occident (XVIe–XVIIe siècle),* Paris, Seuil, 2011.

the digital age: while all information and communication is preserved and recorded on servers and hard drives, at the same time, by its transformation into data, everything somehow seems to vanish: Williams' analogue pictures showing defects that digital alterations would remove and Leonard's photographs of a disappearing New York made using a medium that is itself disappearing both provide clues about this apparent paradox that accompanies the move into a digital world. The evanescent images of the *Snapchat* mobile telephone application (introduced in 2011) are typical of *amnesic recording*. The fragility of evidence that the artists discussed in this book highlight, redefining the distinction between analogue and digital forms of registration and representation, exposes some of the dilemmas we face in the digital era.

The practices of these artists are located at the intersection of the four issues I have identified: the *art work–document*, the *museum–archive complex, the shape of thinking* and *amnesic recording*. Taken together, they comprise a pressing transformation in the field of culture, knowledge production and art. They spell out dialectical changes at work in art production, shifting back and forth between a disappearance of contemporary art as a whole and its reinvention in other sectors of culture and knowledge production. This is something of a give and take in which all parties are required to self-analyse and re-think their motivations, aims and forms. By inviting us to pay attention to the shape of evidence, the works discussed in this book invite us to pursue this reinvention.

Bibliography of Sources Cited and Consulted

Abbott, Berenice. *Changing New York* (1939), New York, The New Press, 1997.

Ades, Dawn. *Dada and Surrealism Reviewed*, London, Hayward Gallery, South Bank Centre, 1978.

Ades, Dawn and Baker, Simon. *Undercover Surrealism: Georges Bataille and Documents*, London, Hayward Gallery, 2006.

Adorno, Theodor. 'Valéry Proust Museum' (1953), *Prisms*, Cambridge, MA. and London, MIT Press, 1981.

Agee, James, and Evans, Walker. *Let Us Now Praise Famous Men*, Boston, Houghton Mifflin, 1941.

Allali, Jean-Pierre; Goldmann, Annie; Sebag, Paul; Sitbon, Claude; Taieb, Jacques; Tapia, Claude and Valensi, Lucette (eds.). *Les Juifs de Tunisie: Textes et Images*. Paris, Editions du Scribe, 1989.

Alter, Nora M. *Chris Marker*, Urbana, Chicago, University of Illinois Press, 2006, p. 60.

Appadurai, Arjun. 'Number in the Colonial Imagination', *Modernity at Large: Cultural Dimensions of Globalization*. Minneapolis and London, University of Minnesota Press, 1996.

Arago, Francois. 'Report, 3 July 1839', in Alan Trachtenberg (ed.), *Classic Essays on Photography*, New Haven, Leete's Island Books, 1980.

Aragon, Louis. *Paris Peasant* (1926), London, Jonathan Cape, 1971.

Aron, Raymond. *Dix-Huit leçons sur la Société Industrielle*, Paris, Seuil, 1963.

Augustijnen, Sven (ed.), *Spectres*, Brussels, Asa Publishers, 2011.

Augustijnen, Sven. 'Every Evening, We Wired News to Brussels', interview with Jacques Brassinne conducted by Sven Augustijnen, 3 February 2011, in Sven Augustijnen (ed.), *Spectres*, Brussels, Asa Publishers, 2011.

Bajac, Quentin and Chéroux, Clément (eds.), *La Subversion des images: surréalisme, photographie, film*, Paris, Musée National d'art moderne, Centre Pompidou, 2009.

Baker, George. 'The Relational Field of Photography', *Still Searching: An Online Discourse about Photography*, Fotomuseum Winterthur, 31 May 2013, ‹blog.fotomuseum.ch/2013/05/i-the-relational-field-of-photography/›, retrieved 20 August 22, 2013.

Baronian, Marie-Aude. *Mémoire et image. Regards sur la Catastrophe arménienne*, Lausanne, l'Age d'Homme, 2013.

Barthes, Roland. *Camera Lucida*, New York, Farrar, Strauss and Giroux, 1981.

Bass, Jacquelyn. 'Reconsidering Walter Benjamin's "The Age of Mechanical Reproduction" in Retrospect', in Gabriel P. Weisberg, Laurinda S. Dixon (eds.), *The Documented Image: Visions in Art History*, Syracuse, NY, Syracuse University Press, 1987.

Bataille, Georges. 'Le Gros orteil', *Documents* no. 6, November 1929, Reprinted in *Documents,* re-edition, Paris, Jean-Michel Place, 1991.

Bate, David. *Photography and Surrealism: Sexuality, Colonialism and Social Dissent,* London, I.B. Tauris, 2004.

Baticle, Yveline. *Le Professeur à l'écran,* Paris, Cerf, 1971.

Baudelaire, Charles. *The Flowers of Evil* (1861), Fresno, CA, Academy Library Guild, 1954.

Belcove, Julie L. 'Working Practice: Christopher Williams', *Introspective Magazine,* January 2011, non pag.

Bellos, David. *Georges Perec: A Life in Words,* Boston, David R. Godine, 1993.

Benjamin, Walter. 'The Work of Art in the Age of Mechanical Reproduction', in Hannah Arendt (ed.), *Illuminations,* New York, Schocken, 1969.

Benjamin, Walter. *One-Way Street and Other Writings,* London, Verso, 1979.

Benjamin, Walter. 'A Small History of Photography', in *One-Way Street and Other Writings,* London, Verso, 1979.

Benjamin, Walter. 'The Author as Producer' (1934), in Victor Burgin (ed.), *Thinking Photography,* London, Macmillan, 1982.

Benjamin, Walter. *Walter Benjamin: Selected Writings,* Michael W. Jennings (ed.), Cambridge and London, Belknap Press, 1999.

Berrebi, Sophie. 'Paris Circus New York Junk: Jean Dubuffet and Claes Oldenburg, 1959–1962', *Art History,* 29, no. 1, 2006, pp. 79–107.

Berrebi, Sophie. 'Neither Fish nor Fowl, But Real Bodies: The Films of Sven Augustijnen', *Afterall,* no. 31, 2012, pp. 86–93.

Bertrand, Roman. *L'Histoire à part égales: Récits d'une rencontre Orient-Occident (XVIe–XVIIe siècle)*, Paris, Seuil, 2011.

Bloch, Marc. *The Historian's Craft*, London, Vintage Books, 1964.

Bloch, Susi. 'Marcel Duchamp's *Green Box*', *Art Journal*, no. 34, (1), 1974. pp. 25–29.

Blume, Anna. 'Interview with Zoe Leonard', *Zoe Leonard* (exhib. cat.), Vienna, Wiener Secession, 1997.

Bois, Yve-Alain; Hollier, Denis; Krauss, Rosalind and Damisch, Hubert. 'A Conversation with Hubert Damisch', *October*, vol. 85, summer 1998, pp. 3–17.

Breton, André. *Manifestoes of Surrealism*, Ann Arbor, University of Michigan Press, 1969.

Breton, André. *Manifestes du surréalisme*, Paris, Gallimard, Folio, 1989.

Buchloh, Benjamin H. D. 'Gerhard Richter's "Atlas": The Anomic Archive', *October*, vol. 88, spring, 1999, pp. 117–145.

Buck-Morss, Susan. 'The Flâneur, the Sandwichman and the Whore: The Politics of Loitering', *New German Critique*, Second Special Issue on Walter Benjamin, no. 39, 1986, 99–140.

Buck-Morss, Susan. *The Dialectics of Seeing: Walter Benjamin and the Arcades Project*, Cambridge, MA. and London, MIT Press, 1991.

Carbonell, Charles-Olivier. 'L'histoire dite « positiviste » en France', *Romantisme*, 1978, no. 21–22. 'Les Positivismes', pp. 173–185.

Certeau, Michel de. *The Writing of History* (1975), New York, Columbia University Press, 1988.

Chevrier, Jean-Francois and Roussin, Philippe (eds.), *Communications*, 'Le parti pris du document:

Littérature, photographie, cinema et architecture au XXeme siècle' no. 71, 2001.

Chevrier, Jean-François. 'The Adventures of the Picture Form in the History of Photography' (1989), in Fogle, Douglas (ed.). *The Last Picture Show: Artists Using Photography 1960–1982,* Minneapolis, Walker Art Center, 2003, pp. 113–128

Chevrier, Jean-Francois and Roussin, Philippe (eds.), *Communications,* 'Des Faits et des gestes', no. 79, 2006.

Costanzo, Alexandre and Costanzo, Daniel. 'La puissance de l'anonyme', *L'Intraitable,* no.0, Marseille, Editions la Compagnie, 2006. Non paginated.

Cottingham, Laura. Zoe Leonard interviewed by Laura Cottingham, 'Zoe Leonard', *Journal of Contemporary Art,* vol. 6, no. 1, summer 1993, pp. 64–77.

Cramerotti, Alfredo. *Aesthetic Journalism: How to Inform Without Informing,* Bristol, Intellect, 2010.

Crary, Jonathan. *Techniques of the Observer: On Vision and Modernity in the Nineteenth Century,* Cambridge, MA. and London, MIT Press, 1990.

Crimp, Douglas. 'The Archive's New/ The Museum's Old Subject', Richard Bolton (ed.), *The Contest of Meaning: Critical Histories of Photography,* Cambridge, MA., MIT Press, 1989, pp. 3–14.

Crimp, Douglas. 'The Photographic Activity of Postmodernism', *October,* vol. 15, 1980, pp. 91–101.

Crow, Thomas. 'Unwritten Histories of Conceptual Art', *Modern Art in the Common Culture,* New Haven, Yale University Press, 1998, pp. 216–217.

Daston, Lorraine and Galison, Peter. *Objectivity.* New York, Zone Books, 2007.

David, Catherine. *Poetics/Politics, Documenta X* (exhib. cat.), Kassel, 1997.

Degner, David and Wilson-Bareau, Juliet. *Manet and the American Civil War: The Battle of USS Kearsarge and CSS Alabama,* New York, Metropolitan Museum of Art, 2003.

Deleuze, Gilles. *Cinema 2* (1985), London, Continuum, 2005.

Diamonstein, Barbara. 'An Interview with Garry Winogrand', *Visions and Images: American Photographers on Photography, Interviews with Photographers, New York,* Rizzoli, 1981.

Didi-Huberman, Georges. *La ressemblance informe,* Paris, Macula, 2006.

Diserens, Corinne. 'Entretien avec Jean-Luc Moulène', *Le Monde, Le Louvre,* Paris, 30 November 2005.

Dosse, Francois. *L'Histoire en Miettes: Des Annales à la nouvelle histoire,* Paris, La Découverte, 1987.

Duve, Thierry de, *Voici, 10 ans d'art contemporain* (exhib. cat.), Brussels, Musée Royal des Beaux-Arts and Ludion, 2000.

Elderfield, John. *Manet and the Execution of Maximilian,* New York, The Museum of Modern Art, 2006.

Elias, Norbert. *Engagement et distanciation: contributions à la sociologie de la connaissance,* Paris, Fayard, 1993.

Enwezor, Okwui. *Documenta 11* (exhib. cat.), Kassel, 2002.

Farge, Arlette. *Le goût de l'archive,* Paris, Seuil, 1989.

Fer, Briony. 'Each Any: Interview with Jean-Luc-Moulène, Paris, October 2008', in Jean-Pierre Criqui (ed.), *Jean-Luc Moulène* (exhib. cat.), Nîmes and Cologne, Éditions du Carré d'Art and Verlag der Buchhandlung Walther König, 2009, pp. 134–148.

Fer, Briony. *Zoe Leonard File Note.* London, Camden Arts Centre, 2012.

Ferro, Marc. 'Film, A Counter-analysis of Society?' (1971), in *Cinema and History,* Detroit, Wayne State University Press, 1986.

Fisher, Philip. *Making and Effacing Art: Modern American Art in a Culture of Museums,* Oxford and New York, Oxford University Press, 1991.

Flusser, Vilém. *Towards a Philosophy of Photography,* London, Reaktion books, 2000.

Flusser, Vilém. 'First Lecture, 23 February 1984: "Photo Production"', École de la Photographie, Arles, in *Flusser Studies,* no. 10, November 2010, double issue, online journal, ‹www.flusserstudies.net/pag/archive10.htm›, retrieved 19 January 2012.

Flusser, Vilém. 'Second Lecture, March 15 1984: "Photo Distribution"', École de la Photographie, Arles, in *Flusser Studies, no.* 10, November 2010, double issue, online journal, ‹www.flusserstudies.net/pag/archive10.htm›, retrieved 19 January 2012.

Fogle, Douglas (ed.). *The Last Picture Show: Artists Using Photography 1960–1982,* Minneapolis, Walker Art Center, 2003.

Fontcuberta, Joan. 'Evidence of What?', *The Harvard Photography Journal,* vol. 9, 'Fantastic', ‹www.hcs.harvard.edu/~hpj/evidence.htm›, retrieved online 27 January 2012.

Foote, Nancy. 'The Anti-photographers', *Artforum,* no. 15, 1976, pp. 46–54.

Foster, Hal. 'The Artist as Ethnographer', *The Return of the Real,* Cambridge Mass. and London, MIT Press, 1996.

Foster, Hal. *Design and Crime (and Other Diatribes),* London, Verso, 2002.

Foster, Hal. 'An Archival Impulse', *October,* vol. 110, fall 2004, pp. 3–22.

Foucault, Michel. *Moi, Pierre Rivière, ayant égorgé ma mère, ma sœur et mon frère,* Paris, Gallimard, 1973.

Foucault, Michel. *The Archaeology of Knowledge* (1969), New York, Vintage Books, 2010.

Fraser, Andrea. 'From the Critique of Institutions to an Institution of Critique', in John Welchman (ed.), *Institutional Critique and After,* Zurich, JRP Ringier, 2006, pp. 123–135.

Gans, Eric. 'Balzac's Unknowable Masterpiece and the Limits of the Classical Esthetic', *MLN*, vol. 90, no. 4, 1975, pp. 504–516.

Gerard, Emmanuel. 'Memories of the Parliamentary Investigation Commission', in Sven Augustijnen, *Spectres,* Brussels, Asa Publishers, 2011.

Giard, Luce (ed.). *Michel Foucault: Lire l'oeuvre,* Grenoble, Jérôme Millon, 1992.

Gierstberg, Frits; van den Heuvel, Maartje; Scholten, Hans and Verhoeven, Martijn (eds.), *Documentary Now: Contemporary Strategies in Photography, Film and the Visual Arts,* Rotterdam, NAi Publishers, 2005.

Glaser, Bruce. 'Oldenburg, Liechtenstein, Warhol: A Discussion', *Artforum,* 4, no. 6, February 1966, pp. 20–24.

Godfrey, Mark. 'Christopher Williams in Conversation with Mark Godfrey', *Afterall, no.* 16, 2007, pp. 63–70.

Godfrey, Mark. 'Pop? Progresso Fotografico? Radio Daniele? Christopher Williams? Kodak Color? Kapitalistischer Realismus?', *Christopher Williams,* (Program), Baden Baden, Verlag der Buchhandlung Walther König, 2010.

Goldberg, Vicky (ed.). *Photography in Print,* Albuquerque, University of New Mexico Press, 1981.

Grenier, Catherine. *La Fin des Musées?,* Paris, Éditions du Regard, 2013.

Haffner, Jeanne. *The View from Above: The Science of Social Space*, London and Cambridge, MA., MIT Press, 2013.

Vít Havránek, Sabine Schaschl-Cooper, Bettina Steinbrügge (eds.), *The Need to Document* (exhib. cat.), Zürich, JRP Ringier, 2005.

Hamilton, George Heard. *Manet and his Critics*, New York, W.W. Norton & Co, 1969.

Hollier, Denis. 'La Valeur d'usage de l'impossible', in *Documents*, Paris: Jean-Michel Place, 1991, pp. vii-xxxiii.

Homberger, Eric. 'The Model's Unwashed Feet: French Photography in the 1850s', in Peter Collier and Robert Lethbridge (eds.), *Artistic Relations: Literature and the Visual Arts in Nineteenth-century France*, New Haven and London, Yale University Press, 1994, 130–143.

Imbach, Pauline, Collectif Mémoires Coloniales. 'Patrice Lumumba: La Belgique doit reconnaitre ses responsabilités historiques', open letter published in *Le Soir*, 28 January 2009. Reprinted in Sven Augustijnen (ed.), *Spectres*, Brussels, Asa Publishers, 2011.

Iversen, Margaret. 'Analogue: On Zoe Leonard and Tacita Dean', *Critical Inquiry*, vol. 38, no. 4, summer 2012, pp. 796–818.

Jablonka, Ivan. *Histoire des grands-parents que je n'ai pas eus: Une enquête*, Paris, Seuil, 2012.

La Nature, 1873–1962, ‹cnum.cnam.fr/fSER/4KY28.html›, Retrieved 16 March 16, 2012.

Labaume, Vincent (ed.), *Michel Journiac* (exhib. cat.), Paris and Strasbourg, École nationale supérieure des beaux-arts, Les musées de Strasbourg, 2004.

Lange, Christy. Untitled review of *The Need to document*, *Frieze*, issue 94, October 2005. Consulted online, ‹www.frieze.com/issue/review/the_need_to_document/›. Retrieved 1 September 2014.

Le Goff, Jacques and Nora, Pierre. *Faire de l'histoire: Nouveaux problèmes, nouvelles approches, nouveaux objets,* Paris, Gallimard, 1974.

Le Goff, Jacques and Toubert, Pierre.'Une histoire totale du Moyen Age est-elle possible?', *Actes du 100e congrès national des sociétés savantes, Paris 1975, section de philologie et d'histoire jusqu'à 1610, tendances, perspectives et méthodes de l'histoire médiévale,* Paris, Bibliothèque nationale, 1977.

Le Goff, Jacques. 'Foucault et la "nouvelle histoire"', in Dominique Franche, Sabine Prokhoris, Yves Roussel (eds.) *Au risque de Foucault,* Paris, Centre Georges Pompidou and Centre Michel Foucault, 1997, pp. 132–137.

Lebovici, Elisabeth. 'The Politics of Contemplation', in Zoe Leonard & Elisabeth Lebovici, *The Politics of Contemplation: From There to Back Again,* New York, Murray Guy, 2012.

LeWitt, Sol. 'Paragraphs on Conceptual Art', *Artforum,* summer 1967, pp. 79–83.

Leyris, Jean-Charles 'Objets de grève, un patrimoine militant', *In situ,* issue 8, 2003, ‹www.insitu.culture.fr/article.xsp?numero=8&id_article=leyris-0/›, retrieved 1 May 2012.

Littré, Paul-Emile. *Dictionnaire de la langue française: tome 2,* Paris, Le club français du livre, 1957.

Lugon, Olivier. *Le Style documentaire d'August Sander à Walker Evans 1920–1945*, Paris, Macula, 2001.

Malraux, André. *Psychologie de l'art: le musée imaginaire,* Geneva, Skira, 1947.

Malraux, André and Mossuz-Lavau, Janine (eds.), *La Politique, la culture (discours, articles, entretiens, 1925–1975)*, Paris, Gallimard, 1996.
Mandel, Mike and Sultan, Larry. *Evidence* (1977), New York, DAP, 2003.
Marker, Chris. *Commentaires*, Paris, Seuil, 1961.
Martin, Timothy. 'Undressing the Institutional Wound', in Christopher Williams (ed.), *For Example: Die Welt ist Schön (Final Draft.)*, Rotterdam and Basel, Museum Boijmans Van Beuningen and Kunsthalle Basel, 1997, pp. 14–87.
McCauley, Elizabeth Ann. *Industrial Madness: Commercial Photography in Paris, 1848–71*, Yale, Yale University Press, 1994.
Mehring, Christine. *Wols Photographs*, Cambridge, Busch-Reisinger Museum, Harvard University Art Museums, 1999.
Moulène, Jean-Luc. 'Histoire de l'image de Darek: témoignage de Jean-Luc Moulène', in Vincent Labaume (ed.), *Michel Journiac* (exhib. cat.), Paris and Strasbourg, École nationale supérieure des beaux-arts, Les Musées de Strasbourg, 2004.
Moulène, Jean-Luc. *Opus 1995–2007 / Documents 1999–2007* (exhib. cat), Lisbon, Culturgest, 2007.
Nash, Mark. *Experiments with Truth* (2005) Philadelphia, The Fabric Workshop and Museum, 2008.
Nesbit, Molly. 'Photography and History: Eugène Atget', Michel Frizot (ed.), *A New History of Photography*, New York, Könemann, 1999, pp. 399–409.
Nesbit, Molly. *Atget's Seven Albums*, New Haven and London, Yale University Press, 1992.
Niney, François. *Le documentaire et ses faux-semblants*, Paris, Klincksieck, 2009.

Parker Brienen, Rebecca. *Visions of Savage Paradise: Albert Eckhout, Court Painter in Colonial Dutch Brazil*, Amsterdam, Amsterdam University Press, 2006.

Philips, Christopher. 'The Judgement Seat of Photography', *October*, vol. 22, autumn 1982, pp. 27–63.

Prochasson, Christophe. 'L'histoire et Foucault', *Vingtième Siècle. Revue d'histoire*, no. 50, April-June 1996, pp. 123–124.

Rancière, Jacques. *Malaise dans l'esthétique*, Paris, Galilé, 2004.

Rancière, Jacques. 'The Thinking of Dissensus: Politics and Aesthetics', in Paul Bowman and Richard Stamp (eds.), *Reading Rancière*, Continuum, London and New York, 2011, pp. 1–17.

Reff, Theodore. 'Manet's Portrait of Zola', *The Burlington Magazine*, issue 862, 1975, pp. 34–44.

Rehm, Jean Pierre. 'Spectres: Notes sur Spectres de Sven Augustijnen', *Trafic*, issue 86, summer 2013, pp. 65–69.

Revel, Jacques. 'Le Moment historiographique', in Luce Giard (ed.), *Michel Foucault, Lire l'oeuvre*, Grenoble, Jérôme Millon, 1992, pp. 83–97.

Richards, Thomas. *The Imperial Archive: Knowledge and the Fantasy of Empire*, London, Verso, 1993.

Ricoeur, Paul. *Memory, History, Forgetting* (2000), Chicago, University of Chicago Press, 2004.

Rochlitz, Rainer. *Le Désenchantement de l'art: La Philosophie de Walter Benjamin*, Paris, Gallimard, 1992.

Rosler, Martha. 'An Exemplary Modern Photographer, Lee Friedlander', *Decoys and Disruptions: Selected Writings 1975–2001*, Cambridge, MA. and London, MIT Press, 2001, pp. 113–32.

Rosler, Martha. 'In, Around, and Afterthoughts (On Documentary Photography)', *Decoys and*

Disruptions: Selected Writings 1975–2001, Cambridge MA. and London, MIT Press, 2004, pp. 151–206.

Rouch, Jean. 'Le Vrai et le faux', *Traverses*, no. 47, Paris, 1989, reprinted in Jean-Paul Colleyn (ed.) *Jean Rouch, Cinéma et anthropologie*, Paris, Cahiers du cinéma (essais), INA, 2009, pp. 111–121.

Salles, Georges. *Au Louvre, scènes de la vie du musée*, Paris, Domat, 1950.

Scott, Clive. *Street Photography: From Atget to Cartier-Bresson*, London and New York, I.B. Tauris, 2007.

Seelig, Thomas and Stahel, Urs (eds.), *The Ecstasy of Things: From the Functional Object to the Fetish in 20th century Photographs*, Göttingen, Steidl, 2004.

Sekula, Allan. 'The Body and The Archive', *October*, vol. 39, winter 1986, pp. 3–64.

Sekula, Allan. 'Reading an Archive' (1983), Jessica Evans, Stuart Hall, *Visual Culture: The Reader*, London, Sage Publications, 1999, pp. 181–192.

Smithson, Robert. 'A Tour of the Monuments of Passaic, New Jersey', in Jack Flam (ed.), *Robert Smithson: The Collected Writings*, Los Angeles, University of California Press, 1996.

Sontag, Susan. 'Film Review: *Muriel, ou le temps d'un retour*', *Film Quarterly*, no. 17:2, winter 1963–1964, pp. 23–27.

Soutter, Lucy. 'The Photographic Idea: Reconsidering Conceptual Photography', *Afterimage*, vol. 26, 1999, pp. 8–10.

Stallabrass, Julian. 'Museum Photography and Museum Prose', *New Left Review*, no. 65, September-October 2010, pp. 93–125.

Steyerl, Hito. 'Documentary Uncertainty', *A Prior Magazine*, 2007, pp. 303–308.

Stoler, Ann Laura and Cooper, Frederick. 'Rethinking Metropole and Colony: Rethinking a Research Agenda', in Stoler and Cooper (eds.), *Tensions of Empire: Colonial Cultures in a Bourgeois World*, Berkeley, Los Angeles and London, University of California Press, 1997, pp. 1–40.

Stoler, Ann Laura. 'Colonial Archives and the Arts of Governance', *Archival Science* no. 2, 2002, pp. 87–109.

Stoler, Ann Laura. *Along the Archival Grain: Epistemic Anxieties and Colonial Common Sense*, Princeton, Princeton University Press, 2009.

Tagg, John. *The Burden of Representation: Essays on Photographies and Histories*, London, Macmillan, 1988.

Tagg, John. 'The Archiving Machine; or, The Camera and the Filing Cabinet', *Grey Room*, no. 47, spring 2012, pp. 24–37.

Texte zur Kunst, no. 76, December 2009, theme issue 'Geschichte'.

Trachtenberg, Allan (ed.). *Classic Essays on Photography*, New Haven, CT., Leete's Island Books, 1980.

Valéry, Paul. 'Le problème des musées' (1923), English translation 'The Problem of Museums', in Jackson Mathews (ed.), *The Collected Works of Paul Valery*, vol. 12, New York, Pantheon Books, 1960.

Verbeeck, Georgi. 'Coming to Terms with the (Post-) Colonial Past in Belgium: The Inquiry into the Assassination of Patrice Lumumba', in Harriet Jones, Kjell Ostberg, Nico Randeraad (eds.) *Contemporary History on Trial: Europe since 1989 and the Role of the Expert Witness*, Manchester and New York, Manchester University Press, 2007.

Vogel, Susan. 'Always True to the Object', in Ivan Karp and Steven D. Lavine (eds.), *Exhibiting Cultures: The*

Poetics and Politics of Museum Display(, Washington and London, Smithsonian Institution Press, 1991, pp. 191–204.

Walker, Ian. *City Gorged with Dreams: Surrealism and Documentary Photography in Interwar Paris*, Manchester, Manchester University Press, 2002.

Wall, Jeff. 'Marks of Indifference: Aspects of Photography as or in Conceptual Art', in Anne Rorimer and Ann Goldstein (eds.), *Reconsidering the Object of Art*, Los Angeles, Museum of Contemporary Art, 1995, pp. 247–267.

Webb, Virginia-Lee. 'Perfect Documents', in *Perfect Documents: Walker Evans and African Art, 1935* (exhib. cat.), New York, The Metropolitan Museum of Art, 2000.

Wieviorka, Annette. *The Era of the Witness* (1998), Ithaca, NY, Cornell University Press, 2006.

Wilson-Bareau, Juliet. *Manet: The Execution of Maximilian*, London, National Gallery Publications, 1992.

Winter, Jay. 'The Performance of the Past: Memory, History, Identity', in Karin Tilmans, Jay Winter and Frank van Vree (eds.), *Performing the Past: Memory, History and Identity in Modern Europe*, Amsterdam, Amsterdam University Press, 2010.

Witte, Ludo de. *The Assassination of Lumumba*, London, Verso, 2002.

Index

Abbott, Berenice 120, 121, 124, 125
Ades, Dawn 67, 68
Agee, James 84
Alaska US 106
Alfred Cadart Print Gallery, Paris FR 29
Algiers DZ 111
Antin, Eleanor 145
Appadurai, Arjun 184
Arago, François 50, 51, 101
Aragon, Louis 114–116, 120
Archives nationales du monde du travail, Roubaix FR 72, 74
Aron, Raymond 133
Asher, Michael 144
Aspremont Lynden, Arnoud d' 190–194, 196
Aspremont Lynden, Harold d' 187, 191, 195
Atget, Eugène 17, 18, 120, 121, 124, 125, 128, 157
Aubert, François 31–33
Augustijnen, Sven 14, 179, 186–189, 191, 193, 195, 197, 198, 200, 201, 209, 211, 213, 217, 252

Avant-garde 22, 163
Axel Gnad, Fotostudio, Düsseldorf DE 160

Bach, Johann Sebastian 187
Baker, George 98, 102
Baker, Simon 68
Baldesssari, John 137, 138, 144
Baldwin, James 121
Balzac, Honoré de 35
Barcelona ES 111
Barneville FR 65
Baroque 64
Bartelous, Jacques 196
Barthes, Roland 9–11, 62
Bataille, Georges 1, 19, 66, 67, 69, 70, 140
Baticle, Yveline 9, 11
Baudelaire, Charles 60, 61
Baudouin, King (Albert Charles Léopold Axel Marie Gustave of Belgium) 187, 188, 194, 200
Becher, Bernd and Hilla 113, 126
Benjamin, Walter 18, 20–23, 26, 27, 61, 91, 107, 116, 131, 161–164, 168, 170, 171
Berlin DE 19, 49, 111, 160, 168
Bernini, Gianlorenzo 80, 81
Bertillon, Alphonse 51
Bertrand, Roman 217
Bloch, Marc 39, 40, 195
Blossfeldt, Karl 162, 163
Blume, Anna 106
Body art 57
Boiffard, Jacques-André 1, 66, 69, 70
Botanical Museum, New Haven US 152
Boulogne-sur-Mer FR 210

Braque, Georges 114
Brassine, Jacques 187–201, 209
Brecht, Bertolt 116, 161–164
Breton, André 114, 115
British Museum, London UK 89
Bronzino (Agnolo di Cosimo) 64
Brooklyn NY 118
Buck-Morss, Susan 107
Budapest HU 118
Buenos Aires AR 111, 208

California Institute of the Arts, Valencia US 142
Calvino, Italo 180
Camden Arts Centre, London UK 96, 97, 102, 103
Cannes FR 88
Cappadocia TR 108
Cassavetes, John 188
Centre Georges Pompidou, Paris FR 72, 76, 90
Centre National de la Cinématographie, Paris FR 88
Certeau, Michel de 40, 41, 193, 195
Césaire, Aimé 121
Cherbourg FR 29
Chevrier, Jean-François 159
Colette, Sidonie-Gabrielle 137
Cologne DE 63, 168
Conceptual art 19, 135, 142–145, 148, 149, 151, 157, 160, 214
Conceptual history 90
Conceptualism 35, 47, 131, 135, 136, 145, 148
Conféderation Générale du Travail 71, 76
Contemporary Art Gallery, Vancouver CAN 134, 140
Costanzo, Alexandre 54
Costanzo, Daniel 55

Cottingham, Laura 17, 99
Courbet, Gustave 140
Crary, Jonathan 98
Crow, Thomas 148, 149
Culturgest, Lisbon PT 56

Dada 22, 114
Daguerre, Louis 50
Damisch, Hubert 44
Daston, Lorraine 95, 100–102, 108, 128
David, Catherine 20
Davis, Natalie Zemon 183
Deleuze, Gilles 188, 190
Deller, Jeremy 208
Derrida, Jacques 6
Dia Art Foundation, New York and Beacon US 97, 122, 128, 129
Dibbets, Jan 145
Dirk Schaper Studio, Berlin DE 1, 160, 161
Documenta, Kassel DE 20, 112, 214
Dubuffet, Jean 64, 65
Duchamp, Marcel 34, 35, 41
Duve, Thierry de 75, 76

Eckhout, Albert 179, 202, 207
École Pratique des Hautes Études, Paris FR 9, 11
Elderfield, John 32
Enwezor, Okwui 20
Evans, Walker 17–19, 70, 82–89, 120, 124, 125
EYE Film Institute, Amsterdam NL 180

Fachhochschule Aachen DE 172
Farge, Arlette 204, 205

Febvre, Lucien 39
Fer, Briony 58, 102
Ferro, Marc 184, 185
Fisher, Philip 90
Flusser, Vilém 173–176
Fontcuberta, Joan 155
Force Ouvrière 71
Foucault, Michel 37, 38, 41, 42, 47, 52, 73
France, Anatole 116
French Chamber of Deputies 50, 101
Freund, Gisele 121
Friedlander, Lee 107
Fromentin, Eugène 125
Fustel de Coulanges, Numa Denis 40

Galerie Gisela Capitain, Cologne DE 96, 168
Galison, Peter 95, 100–102, 108, 128
Galleria Borghese, Rome IT 80
Gans, Eric 35
General Atomics, San Diego US 154
Getty Center, Los Angeles US 151, 153, 216
Ginzburg, Carlo 183
Godard, Jean-Luc 169
Godfrey, Mark 133, 168, 169, 172, 174
Grande Dixence CH 165
Grenier, Catherine 90
Grierson, John 125
Gursky, Andreas 158

Haffner, Jeanne 109, 110
Hamilton, George Heard 24
Heartfield, John 163
Hilliard, John 145, 147, 148

Hong Kong CN 118
Huebler, Douglas 144–146

Istanbul TR 108

Jablonka, Ivan 217
John F. Kennedy Library, Boston US 151
Joseph II, Emperor (Joseph Benedikt Anton Michael Adam) 104
Josephinum Museum, Vienna AT 104, 216
Journiac, Michel 57, 58

Kampala UG 118
Kassel DE 112, 127, 214
Katanga CD 187, 189, 196
Kelly, Mary 19
Kennedy, John Fitzgerald 144, 146, 148, 153, 156
Kerstein, Lincoln 83
Kertész, André 65
Kinshasa CD 187, 200
Kodak 115, 140, 150
Krull, Germaine 162–164
Kuniaki II, Utagawa 25
Kunsthaus Glarus, CH 100
Kupferstich-Kabinett, Dresden DE 203

Laeken BE 194
Land art 35
Le Corbusier (Charles-Éduouard Jeanneret-Gris) 110
Le Goff, Jacques 38, 42
Lebovici, Elisabeth 98, 102
Leonard, Zoe 1, 13, 17, 95–100, 102–126, 128, 129, 136, 215, 216, 218

Leroi-Gourhan, André 109
Lévi-Strauss, Claude 109
LeWitt, Sol 144
Leyris, Jean-Charles 74
Liberty US 13
London UK 96, 97, 99, 103, 111, 158
Los Angeles US 13, 118, 151
Los Angeles County Museum of Art, US 138
Lotar, Eli 66, 67, 70
Lumumba, Patrice 186–192, 195–197, 199–201

Madrid ES 127
Malraux, André 28
Mandel, Mike 154, 158
Manet, Édouard 17, 23–34, 36, 76, 140
Mannerism 64
Mannheim DE 32, 33
Marin, Louis 44
Marker, Chris 86–89
Marville, Charles 121
Mauritshuis Museum, The Hague NL 60, 186, 202, 203, 216
Maximilian I, Emperor (Ferdinand Maximilian Joseph) 30, 31, 33
McCauley, Ann 141
Mechelen BE 14
Meessen, Vincent 10
Mehring, Christine 65
Metropolitan Museum of Art, New York US 82, 83
Mexico MX 30, 31
Mexico City MX 48, 118
Miller, Jennifer 100
Modernism 20, 82

Monet, Claude 8, 64
Monroe, Marilyn 100
Moulène, Jean-Luc 13, 43, 47–49, 53–59, 61–81, 85, 86, 88–90, 92, 213, 214, 216, 217
Mpolo, Maurice 190, 200
Murray Guy Gallery, New York 96
Musée d'Orsay, Paris FR 8, 17, 23, 25, 33, 158
Musée de l'Armée, Paris FR 31
Musée de l'Homme, Paris FR 82, 87, 109
Musée du Louvre, Paris FR 77–80, 85, 89, 91, 216
Museum of Modern Art, New York US 32, 82, 85
Museum Schloss Morsbroich, Leverkusen DE 134

Nadar, Félix 110
Naipaul, V.S. 121
Napoleon III (Louis-Napoléon Bonaparte) 30, 40
Nassau-Siegen, Count Johan Maurits van 186, 203
National Archive, The Hague NL 203
National Gallery, London UK 33
National Museum of Denmark, Copenhagen DK 179, 207
Nesbit, Molly 17, 19
Netherlands Institute for Advanced Studies, Wassenaar NL 198
Neue Sachlichkeit 162
New York City US 13, 32, 82, 111, 112, 115, 119, 120, 124, 158, 218
New York Public Library, New York US 158
Newton, Helmut 138
Niagara Falls US, CAN 97, 103, 108, 122, 128
Niepce, Nicéphore 50, 51
Niney, François 87
Nouvelle histoire 40

Obama, Barack 208
Okito, Joseph 190, 200
Oldenborgh, Wendelien van 14, 179, 186, 202, 203, 206, 207, 209, 211, 213, 215
Oldenburg, Claes 64, 65
Opango, Pauline 200

Paris FR 8, 11, 29, 49, 53, 55, 64, 66, 70, 86, 87, 108–111, 115, 116, 120, 124, 141, 158
Passaic US 36, 37, 41
Peabody Museum, Cambridge MA, US 82
Pekan Baru ID 14
Perec, Georges 121–123
Performance art 58, 100
Picabia, Francis 139
Picasso, Pablo 21, 114
Pierre Matisse Gallery, New York US 85
Platel, Alain 188
Poiret, Paul 164
Polke, Sigmar 169
Positivism 39, 46, 52, 69, 115, 116
Post, Frans 202
Présence Africaine, Paris FR 86
Prix Jean Vigo 88
Proust, Marcel 121

Quantitative history 38

Rancière, Jacques 214
Ray, Man 120
Reff, Theodore 25
Reims FR 13
Renger-Patzsch, Albert 161–164, 166, 168, 171

Resnais, Alain 86–89, 209–211
Richards, Thomas 184
Richter, Gerhard 169
Rijksmuseum, Amsterdam NL 217
Ritter Sport Manufacturer, Berlin DE 160, 167, 168
Rochlitz, Rainer 21, 22
Rosler, Martha 54, 107
Rothschild, Robert 192
Rotterdam NL 14, 118
Rouen FR 64
Royal Museum for Central Africa, Tervuren BE 87
Ruscha, Ed 145, 149

San Jose Police Department, US 154
Sander, August 70, 162
São Paulo, BR 111
Sartre, Jean-Paul 10
Scott, Clive 107
Sekula, Allan 47, 51–53, 118, 119, 152, 154
Sholem, Gershom 21
Sloane Collection, London UK 89
Smithson, Robert 36, 37, 41, 42
Smyrna (Izmir) TR 80, 81
Städtische Kunsthalle, Mannheim DE 32
Stedelijk Museum, Amsterdam NL 180
Steyerl, Hito 18
Stoler, Ann Laura 179, 183, 184, 206
Stone, Sasha 163
Struth, Thomas 158
Sultan, Larry 154, 158
Surrealism 22, 23, 65–70, 114–116

Tagg, John 12, 47, 51–53, 55, 56
Tan, Fiona 14, 179–183, 185, 209, 211, 216
Tapia, Viviane de 73
Tate Britain, London UK 34
Tati, Jacques 169
Titian (Tiziano Vecelli) 34
Toubert, Pierre 42
Touitou, Marc 67
Tropenmuseum, Amsterdam NL 90
Tshombe, Marie 196
Tshombe, Moïse 189, 190, 196
Tunis TN 8, 10, 11

United States Department of the Interior, Washington D.C. US 154
Université Libre de Bruxelles, Brussels BE 189

Van Abbemuseum, Eindhoven NL 90
Varda, Agnès 118
Vatican, Rome IT 89
Velázquez, Diego 25
Vermeer, Johannes 60–62
Victoria and Albert Museum, London UK 82, 158
Vogel, Susan 84

Wagener, Zacharias 202
Wall, Jeff 149, 150, 157–159
Warsaw PL 118
Washington D.C. US 108
Webb, Virginia-Lee 83–85
Weston, Edward 99
Wexner Center for the Arts, Columbus US 112
Whistler, James Abbott McNeill 139, 140

Wieviorka, Annette 179
Williams, Christopher 1, 13, 43, 131–136, 138–144, 146–152, 155–161, 164–173, 176, 214, 218
Wilp, Charles 169
Wilson-Bareau, Juliet 31
Winckelmann, Johann 90
Winogrand, Garry 59, 107
Winter, Jay 207, 208
Witte, Ludo de 189, 192, 195, 197, 201
Wols (Alfred Otto Wolfgang Schulze) 65, 70
Woolf, Virginia 121

Zola, Émile 17, 23–26

Acknowledgements

First and foremost, my thanks go to the artists Sven Augustijnen, Zoe Leonard, Wendelien van Oldenborgh, Fiona Tan, Christopher Williams and in particular Jean-Luc Moulène, who were generous with their time, patiently answered my questions and challenged my assumptions. I extend my gratitude to their galleries.

This book has grown out of several exhibitions, talks, essays and seminars, and I am very grateful to those who invited me to curate those exhibitions, who hosted those talks and published those essays, thus encouraging me to start organising my ideas on the subject of the document in contemporary art: Saskia Janssen, Frederique and Philippe Valentin (Galerie Valentin, Paris), Gustave Beumer (Het Nieuwe Instituut, Rotterdam), Dieter Roelstraete (MCA Chicago), Julia Kelly, Melissa Gronlund (Afterall, London), Domeniek Ruyters (*Metropolis M*, Utrecht), Cecilia Grönberg and Jonas (J) Magnusson (OEI, Stockholm), Catherine Sousslof (University of British Columbia, Vancouver), Jon Kear (University of Canterbury, Kent), Mick Finch (Central Saint Martins, University of the Arts,

London), Margriet Schavemaker (Stedelijk Museum Amsterdam) Susanne Kriemann (Air Berlin Alexanderplatz), Urs Stahel and Thomas Seeling (Fotomuseum Winterthur, Ellen de Bruijne (Ellen de Bruijne Projects, Amsterdam) and the students who followed my seminars on contemporary art at the University of Amsterdam.

Chapter 4 and the introduction were written during a fellowship at the Netherlands Institute for Advanced Study in the Humanities and Social Sciences (NIAS), and I thank particularly Aafke Hulk and Petry Kievit, and also Gary Schwartz for his editing of some sections of the manuscript.

I am indebted to a number of friends and colleagues who have provided, over the years, stimulating discussions, inspiration and companionship or a quiet place to write (or all of the above): Hubert and Teri Damisch, Carrie Pilto, Vivian Rehberg, Deborah Cherry, Vincent Meessen, Jennifer Allen, Baptiste Brun, Aglaia Konrad, Willem Oorebeek, Manon de Boer, Etienne Wynants, Agnès Rein, Carlo Galizzi, Saskia Janssen, Sven Augustijnen, Wouter Davidts, Gustave Beumer, Marc Touitou, Berend Strik, Philippine Hoegen, Lieve Joris, Ellen de Bruijne, Snejanka Mihaylova, Arnisa Zeqo, Alexandra Leykauf, Rik Tuithof, Franklin and Noëlle Berrebi, Alexander van Slobbe, Claudia Cristovão and Lisette Smits. Two of them, my closest friends Marie-Aude Baronian and Frederique Valentin, know how important they have been.

Thank you Astrid Vorstermans for your encouragement, and, with the team at Valiz, with Sam de Groot and Wendy van Os-Thompson, for turning this manuscript into a book.

Finally, my deepest gratitude to Camiel van Winkel, relentless critic, supporter, and great love.

About the Author

Sophie Berrebi (1973) is a writer, art historian and curator born in Paris and based in Amsterdam. She has published widely on contemporary art, notably in journals such as *frieze, Afterall, Metropolis M,* and *Art and Research*. She received her PhD from the Courtauld Institute of Art, University of London in 2003, and is based since 2003 at the University of Amsterdam where she teaches art history and theory, mainly in the areas of photography and contemporary art. Her research at the university is based at ASCA, the Amsterdam School for Cultural Analysis. One of her forthcoming publications will be *Jean Dubuffet, un dossier,* an edited volume of writings by Hubert Damisch and Jean Dubuffet.

Sven Augustijnen: courtesy of the artist and Galerie Jan Mot, Brussels

Zoe Leonard: courtesy of the artist and Galerie Gisela Capitain, Cologne

Jean-Luc Moulène: courtesy of the artist and Galerie Chantal Crousel, Paris

Wendelien van Oldenborgh: courtesy of the artist and Wilfried Lentz, Rotterdam

Fiona Tan: courtesy of the artist and Frith Street Gallery, London

Christopher Williams: courtesy of the artist and Galerie Gisela Capitain, Cologne and David Zwirner, New York

Author: Sophie Berrebi
Editing: Gary Schwartz
Copy-editing: Wendy van Os-Thompson
Index and proof check: Elke Stevens
Design: Sam de Groot
Typefaces: Eldorado (William Addison Dwiggins, 1953),
Computer Modern (Donald Knuth, 1984),
SKI DATA (Tariq Heijboer, 2014)
Printing and binding: Ten Brink, Meppel
Publisher: Valiz, Amsterdam, ‹www.valiz.nl›

ISBN 978-90-78088-98-1
NUR 640, 651
Printed and bound in the Netherlands, 2014
POD 2024

PRINS BERNHARD CULTUURFONDS
This publication was made possible through the generous support of the Prins Bernhard Cultuurfonds

Valiz is an independent international publisher on contemporary art, theory, critique, design, typography and urban affairs. Our books offer critical reflection, interdisciplinary inspiration, and often establish a connection between cultural disciplines and socio-economic questions. We publish these books out of our commitment to their content, to artistic or social issues and to the artists, designers and authors.

Our programme consists of two components:

— theory and texts on art and culture;
— books that are conceived and elaborated in close collaboration with artists, designers and art institutes.

Apart from publishing Valiz organizes cultural projects in which certain topics in contemporary art are investigated.

Distribution

USA/CA/*Latin America:* DAP, ‹www.artbook.com›
GB/IE: Anagram Books, ‹www.anagrambooks.com›
NL/BE/LU: Coen Sligting, ‹www.coensligtingbookimport.nl›
Europe/Asia/Australia: Idea Books, ‹www.ideabooks.nl›
Individual orders: ‹www.valiz.nl›